International
Modern Glass

International
Modern Glass

Geoffrey Beard

CHARLES SCRIBNER'S SONS · NEW YORK

Library of Congress Cataloging in Publication Data

Beard, Geoffrey W
   International modern glass.

   Bibliography: p.
   Includes index.
   1. Glassware—History—20th century. I. Title.
NK5110.B39 1978   748.2'904   78-56432
ISBN 0-684-15934-1

1 3 5 7 9 11 13 15 17 19 I/C 20 18 16 14 12 10 8 6 4 2

Printed in Great Britain

'A man that looks on glass,
On it may stay his eye;
Or if he pleaseth, through it pass,
And then the heaven espy'

George Herbert, (1593–1633)

Contents

List of plates   *page*

Acknowledgments   9

Historical introduction   13

1   Late 19th century achievement   17

2   Search for form   23

3   L'esprit Nouveau   27

4   For better living   33

5   Produced to sell   43

A select list of glass manufacturers   209

A select list of designers   217

Bibliography   255

Glossary   257

Index   259

Illustrations

The illustrations are divided into subject groups:
Plates

1–79   Historical glass 1870–1940   49

          1940 onwards

80–95   Cut glass   81

96–159   Table suites, vases, bowls   87

160–184   Various forms of engraving   117

185–213   Commemorative glass, especially
                engraved by diamond or
                steel-point   127

214–245   Shapes: optical forms   137

246–266   Colour: splashes, fusings, enamels   151

267–279   Moulded and pressed   159

280–288   Abraded: sandblast and acid   165

289–325   Sculptures and 'fun' glass   169

326–344   Screens and 'architectural' glass   195

List of plates

Colour

1 'Peacock Feather' Vase, L. C. Tiffany, 1896–8 *opposite page* 80
2 Lustre glass in tulip form, Karl Koepping, 1896–8 80
3 Vase, Daum Frères, 1900–5   80
4 Bottle and stopper, Maurice Marinot, 1930   81
5 Fun sculpture, 'Bubble Tree', Ann and Göran Warff, 1968   96
6 Bowl, Kaj Franck, 1968   97
7 Sculpture, Oiva Toikka, 1969   176
8 Three glasses, 'Polaris' suite, Tapio Wirkkala   177
9 Sundae glass, Richard Latham and Bjørn Wiinblad 177
10 Blown shapes, Pauline Solven, 1974   192
11 Sculpture, 'Emergence XV', Dominick Labino, 1973 193
12 Sculpture, 'Butterfly Wing', Harvey K. Littleton, 1969   193
13 Glass 'landscape', Bertil Vallien, 1974   193

Monochrome

1 Bowl and two glasses, Philip Webb, 1859   *page* 49
2 Elgin Vase, John Northwood, 1873   50
3 Elgin Claret Jug, F. E. Kny, 1878   50
4 A group of Stourbridge glass, 1879–94   51
5 Vase, Emile Gallé, c.1889   51
6 Press-moulded plate, 1887   52
7 Goblet, Joseph Brocard, c.1880   53
8 Vase, Emile Léveillé, 1889   53
9 Vase, Eugène Rousseau, c.1884   53
10 Vase, Emile Léveillé, 1889   53
11 Two vases, Clutha glass   54
12 Vase and bowl, Tiffany   54
13 Vase and bowl, George Walton, c.1896   55
14 Vase, goblet and bowl, c.1892–1920   55
15 Two vases, E. Lorenz, c.1900   56
16 Vase, J. L. Witwe, c.1898   57
17 Vase, J. L. Witwe, c.1902   57
18 Vase, F. Zitzmann, c.1902   57
19 Vase, Daum, c.1900   58

20 Vase, Emile Gallé, 1900   *page* 58
21 'Silveria Glass' vase, c.1900   58
22 Vase, E. Michel, c.1900   59
23 Two vases and jug, Emile Gallé, 1885–1900   59
24 Vase and dish, Emile Gallé, c.1880   60
25 Vase, Emile Gallé, c.1900   60
26 Vase, Emile Gallé, c.1900   61
27 Vase, Emile Gallé, c.1890   61
28 Vase, Emile Gallé, c.1900   61
29 Bas-relief, Henri Cros, c.1900   62
30 Bowl, G. G. Wennerberg, c.1900   63
31(a) Bowl, Albert Dammouse, c.1898   63
31(b) Vase, A. L. Dammouse, c.1900   64
32 Glass made for William Morris & Co., c.1903   64
33(a) Drawing by George Woodall, c.1900   64
33(b) 'Cleopatra' cameo plaque, George Woodall, c.1900 65
34 Communion cruet, 1900   66
35 Vase, J. Powell & Sons, c.1895   66
36 Vase, glass, with bronze stand, c.1900   66
37 Three wine flasks, Salviati, 1902   66
38 Table glass, exhibited 1904   67
39 Vase, J. Powell & Sons, c.1902   67
40 Two beakers, George Walton, c.1902   67
41 Vase, Durand Glass Co., 1912–25   68
42 Vase, F-E. Décorchemont, 1912   68
43 Vase, René Lalique, 1913   68
44 Vase, A. Johnsson, 1920   69
45 Bowl, E. Ollers, c.1918   69
46 Bowl, M. Goupy, c.1920   69
47 Detail of vase, J. Horejc, 1922   70
48 Vase, J. Horejc, 1922   70
49 Bowl, E. Dahlskog, c.1920   70
50 Vase, René Lalique, c.1925   71
51 Detail of vase, René Lalique, c.1925   71
52 Glass fountain, René Lalique, 1925   71
53 Vase, René Lalique, c. 1920   71
54 Cup and cover, L. Přenosil, 1926   72
55 Vase, George Woodall, 1925   72
56 Vase, Iittala, 1929   72
57 Vase, Maurice Marinot, c.1919   73
58 Flask, Maurice Marinot, 1925   73
59 Flask, Maurice Marinot, 1932   73
60 Vase, Maurice Marinot, 1934   73
61 Vase, Edward Hald, c.1930   74

62 Standing cup, Simon Gate, 1923   *page* 74
63 Plate, Simon Gate, 1928   74
64 Ice-bucket and plate, Edward Hald, 1919   74
65 Vase, E. Öhrström   75
66 Vase, Vicke Lindstrand, 1930   75
67 Vase, Elis Bergh, 1925   75
68 Vase, S. E. Skawonius, 1934   75
69 Bowl and vase, Keith Murray, 1932   76
70 Punch Bowl, A. Douglas Nash, c.1933   76
71 Vase, Baccarat, c.1930–5   77
72 Bowl, Steuben Glass, 1935   77
73 Vase, Gunnel Nyman, 1937   77
74 Bowl, A. D. Copier, 1939   78
75 Bowl, Göran Hongell, 1939   78
76 Vase, Elis Bergh, 1939   79
77 Vase, Flavio Poli, 1950   79
78 Vase and bowl, S. E. Skawonius, 1945   79
79 Vase, Paolo Venini, 1940   80
80 Crystal rods, M. Morales-Schildt, 1966   81
81 Cutting glass at Orrefors, Sweden   81
82 Vase, V. Plátek   82
83 Two vases, ashtray, A. Drobnik   82
84 Bowl, M. Morales-Schildt   82
85 Vase, V. Žahour   82
86 Glass block, L. Metelak   83
87 Paperweights, M. Morales-Schildt   83
88 Vases, V. Žahour   84
89 Vase, S. Kasnirova, 1967   84
90 Vases, David Hammond   84
91 Crystal sphere, Floris Meydam, 1969   85
92 Glass crown, Nanny Still McKinney   85
93 Glass column, Floris Meydam   85
94 Bowl, K. Habermeier   86
95 Bowl, John Luxton   86
96 Wineglass making, Orrefors, Sweden   87
97 'Cracking-off' wine-glasses   87
98 Four goblets, M. V. Németh, 1969   88
99 Four goblets, M. Lecjaks, 1966   88
100 Drinking-glasses, Per Lütken   89
101 Wine-glasses, Nils Landberg   89
102 Wine-service, Vicke Lindstrand   89
103 Wine-service, Frank Thrower   90
104 Wine-glasses, Severin Brorby   90
105 Wine-service, Isabel Giampietro   91
106 Two goblets, J. K. Sipos, 1970   91

107 Rose-bowls, C. J. Riedel   *page* 91
108 Saki-glass, M. Awashima, 1959   91
109 Drink containers, Marvin Lipofsky, 1970   92
110 Wine-glasses, goblets, giant glasses   92
111 Wine and fruit-glasses, Timo Sarpaneva, 1969   93
112 Carafe and glasses, M. Backström, 1969   94
113 Schnapps glasses and decanter, R. Sinnemark, 1970   94
114 Decanter, ice-bucket, glasses, C. Holmgren, 1970   95
115 Beer and whisky glasses, Erik Höglund   96
116 Wine-service, David Hammond   96
117 Decanter and glasses, Tom Hill   97
118 Flasks, Lars Hellsten   97
119 Bottle, Nanny Still McKinney, 1968   98
120 Cup and cover, Nils Landberg   99
121 Decanter and glasses, Ingeborg Lundin, 1969   99
122 Orrefors Glass, Sweden, guest houses and studios   99
123 Decanter, Jane Webster, c.1959   100
124 Decanter and glasses, Gunnar Cyrén, 1969   100
125 Decanter and glasses, H. Löffelhardt, 1965   100
126 Vases, Venini, Italy   100
127 Bottle, Dino Martens, 1959   101
128 Bottle, Paolo Venini, 1959   101
129 Decanter, A. D. Copier, 1964   102
130 Paperweights, doorstops, R. Stennett-Wilson, 1969   103
131 Candlesticks and tiered-tray, Erik Höglund   103
132 Vase, Bertil Vallien, 1969   104
133 Vase, Tamara Aladin, 1971   104
134 Punch bowl and glasses, E. Siiroinen, 1972   104
135 Mould-blown 'abstract forms', B. & T. Sarasin   104
136 Three vases, Luciano Gaspari   105
137 Candle-lanterns, Nanny Still McKinney, 1973   106
138 Candle-holders, R. Stennett-Wilson, 1969   106
139 Candle-holder, M. Backström   106
140 Vase, Sergio Asti, 1962   107
141 Vase, with metallic oxide decoration   107
142 Vase, M. Awashima, 1969   107
143 Vase, K. Habermeier   108
144 Three bowls, Inkeri Toikka, 1974   108
145 Vase and plate, Timo Sarpaneva, 1966   108

146 Plate, Erik Höglund   *page* 109
147 Bowl, Tapio Wirkkala, 1969   109
148 Bowl, Marc Lalique   110
149 Bowl, Ingeborg Lundin, 1969   *111*
150 Bowl, Anne and Göran Warff, 1968   111
151 Dish, Anne and Göran Warff, 1968   112
152 Glass jars, Kerttu Nurminen, 1974   112
153 Vase, Marc Lalique   113
154 Ovenproof dish, H. Löffelhardt   114
155 Bowl, Joseph Stadler, 1959   114
156 Vase, P. Venini and G. Cappellin, c.1921–4   115
157 Tiered standing vase, Bjørn Wiinblad, 1965   115
158 Wine-glass and dinner service, Bjørn Wiinblad 116
159 Bowl, Lord Queensberry, 1965   116
160 A copper-wheel engraver at work   117
161 A Swedish engraver at work, 1968   117
162 Detail of engraving, Tapio Wirkkala, 1951   118
163 Bowl, Erik Höglund   118
164 Bowl, Sven Palmqvist   118
165 Vase, John Selbing, 1969   119
166 Crystal forms, Donald Pollard, 1963   119
167 Plaque, Rama Maharana   119
168 Crystal bulb, James Houston   120
169 Lager glass, Simon Whistler   121
170 Goblet, Peter Dreiser   121
171 Glass plate, Simon Whistler, 1965   121
172 Glass jug, David Peace   122
173 Presentation cup, 1960   122
174 'Pye Comedy Script Award', Jane Webster, 1974 122
175 'Victor Ludorum' Ronson Trophy, Jane Webster, 1969   123
176 Bottle, Peter Dreiser, 1968   123
177 Glass slab, David Peace, 1968   123
178 Vase, Pavel Hlava, 1958   124
179 Engraved form, optical glass, Jane Webster, 1973 124
180 Goblet, Helen Monro Turner, 1959   124
181 Glass font, David Peace, 1962   125
182 Jardiniere, Adolf Matura, 1964   125
183 Bowl, Ingeborg Lundin, 1969   125
184 Flask, Nora Ortlieb   126
185 Diamond-point engraving, 1953   127
186 Decanter, Sheila Elmhirst   127

187 Rose bowl, W. J. Wilson, 1954   *page* 127
188 Goblet, diamond-point stipple, Laurence Whistler, 1972   128
189 Dish, Phyllis Boissier   128
190 Plate, Sheila Elmhirst   128
191 Vase, Phyllis Boissier   128
192 Bowl, Sheila Elmhirst   129
193 Book-ends, Helen Monro Turner, 1959   129
194 Bowl, Laurence Whistler, 1973   129
195 Bowl, Laurence Whistler, 1974   130
196 Goblet, Simon Whistler, 1973   131
197 Goblet, Simon Whistler, 1972   131
198 Window-pane, Laurence Whistler, 1972   131
199 Goblet, Laurence Whistler, 1972   131
200 Bowl, Laurence Whistler, 1973   132
201 Crucifix, Sheila Elmhirst   133
202 Bowl, David Peace   133
203 Altar Cross, David Peace, 1958   133
204 Glass Door, Bryant Fedden, 1967   134
205 Plate, Bryant Fedden, 1970   134
206 Bell, David Peace   134
207 Goblet, Honoria D. Marsh, 1968   135
208 Reverse of goblet, Honoria D. Marsh, 1968   135
209 Liqueur glass, D. Maude-Roxby Montalto, 1970 135
210 Rummer, D. Maude-Roxby Montalto, 1969   136
211 Goblet, William Meadows   136
212 Chalice, C. Cejnar & V. Hubert   136
213 Goblet, David Smith   136
214 Cullet block, Vicke Lindstrand, 1959   137
215 An engraver of optical blocks at work   138
216 Crystal block, J. Tockstein & L. Jezèk   138
217 Optical glass plaque, Jane Webster, 1972   139
218 Optical glass block, D. Pollard & T. Haass   140
219 Paperweights, M. Morales-Schildt   140
220 Glass stones, Willem Heesen, 1959   140
221 Glass shape, Tapio Wirkkala, 1952   140
222 'Glass Apple', Ingeborg Lundin, 1965   141
223 Faceted block, Hanns Model, 1959   142
224 Solid 'Torque', Paul Schulze   142
225 Crystal form, Michel Daum   142
226 Crystal block, Aimo Okkolin, 1967   143
227 Two vases, Ernest Gordon, 1959   143
228 Cut obelisks, Max Ingrand, c.1964   143
229 Vase, Rene Roubiček, c.1968   144

230   Two bottles, John H. Cook, 1970   *page* 144
231   Vase, Pavel Hlava, 1968   145
232   Crystalline sculpture, Edvin Öhrström, 1960   145
233   Glass bubble, Ulrica Hydman-Vallien, 1974   145
234   Glass globe, Michael Boylen, 1970   146
235   Blown form, Marvin B. Lipofsky, 1970   146
236   Free form, William H. Boysen, 1966   146
237   Vases, Colin Walker, 1970   147
238   Group of glass, Dominick Labino, 1966–9   147
239   Bottles, Bertil Vallien, 1969   148
240   Sculpture, Samuel Herman, 1969   148
241   Sculpture, Samuel Herman, 1970   148
242   Blown form, Jiri Suhájek, 1970   149
243   Two bowls, John Cook, 1974   149
244   Blown 'people shapes', Wayne Filan, 1970   149
245   Bottles, Bertil Vallien, 1969   150
246   Plate, Maurice Heaton, 1959   151
247   Bowl, Toshichi Iwata Glass, *c.*1954   151
248   Vase, Paolo Venini, 1950   151
249   Vase, M. Morales-Schildt   152
250   Bottle, A. D. Copier, 1960   152
251   Lampshade, Paolo Venini, 1959   152
252   Vase, Sybren Valkema, 1967   152
253   Dish, Floris Meydam, 1959   153
254   Vase, René Roubiček, 1959   153
255   Bottle, Roland Jahn, 1969   154
256   Pitcher, Ercole Barovier, 1951   154
257   Vase, Erwin Eisch, 1967   155
258   Vase, Dominick Labino, 1967   155
259   Vase, Harvey K. Littleton, 1966   155
260   Vase, Per Lütken, 1970   156
261   Laminated form, Heather Cowburn, 1968   156
262   Bowl, A. D. Copier, 1968   157
263   Bowls, Bertil Vallien, 1966   157
264   Vase, Pavel Hlava   158
265   Bowl, Kaj Franck, 1969   158
266   Vertical lamination, Edris Eckhardt, 1968   158
267   Vase, V. Žahour, 1967   159
268   Vase, Rudolf Jurnikl, 1969   159
269   Plate, Adolf Matura, 1968   160
270   Plate, F. Pečný, 1968   161
271   Ashtray, Timo Sarpaneva, 1966   161
272   Bottle, Willem Heesen, 1969   162
273   Paperweights, Erik Höglund   162
274   Vases, Helena Tynell, 1967   162

275   Glass-wagon, Bertil Vallien, 1966   *page* 163
276   Bowls and glasses, Oiva Toikka   164
277   Two vases, Geoffrey Baxter, 1966   164
278   Vase, Ladislav Oliva, 1967   164
279   Decanter and glasses, Nanny Still McKinney, 1973   164
280   Glass screen, John Hutton, 1952–61   165
281   John Hutton at work   166
282   Detail of panel, John Hutton, 1972   166
283   Three sandblasted panels, Eric Hilton, 1967   166
284   'King Lear' panel, John Hutton   166
285   Vase, Ladislav Oliva, 1969   167
286   Vase, Julia Báthory, 1969   167
287   Bottle, Bertil Vallien, 1967   167
288   Glass door, William Meadows   168
289   Glass Mask, Max Ernst   169
290   Sculpture, Vicke Lindstrand, 1968   170
291   Mobile, Alexander Calder   171
292   Sculptures, René Roubiček   171
293   Glass figure, Jean Arp   172
294   Sculpture, Angelo Barovier   172
295   Sculpture, Helena Tynell, 1967   172
296   Sculptures, Edris Eckhardt, 1967   173
297   Sculpture, Miroslav Klinger   174
298   Plates, Rolf Sinnemark, 1969   174
299   Sculptures, Timo Sarpaneva, 1967   174
300   Sculptures, Lars Hellsten, 1967   175
301   Sculpture, Renato Toso, 1968   176
302   Sculpture, Bretislav Novak, 1969   177
303   Sculpture, Michel Daum   177
304   Figurines, Jaroslav Brychta   177
305   Figurine, Vèra Lišková, 1969   178
306   Sculpture, Oiva Toikka, 1969   179
307   Wine-glass 'sculpture', Erik Höglund, 1969   180
308   Stylised birds, Luciano Gaspari, 1969   180
309   Sculpture, Dominick Labino   181
310   Blown form, Harvey K. Littleton, 1969   182
311   Sculpture, Edvin Öhrström, 1965   183
312   Sculpture, Harry Seager, 1967   183
313   Glass 'flower', Rolf Sinnemark, 1969   184
314   Boro-silicate construction, Alan G. Thomson, 1972   185
315   Sculptures, L. E. Rudge, 1969   186
316   Sculpture, Samuel Herman   187
317   Blown form, Harvey K. Littleton, 1968   187

318   Sculpture, Dominick Labino   *page* 188
319   Coil structure, Willem Heesen, 1965   189
320   Blown form, Marvin B. Lipofsky, 1970   190
321   Blown animal figures, Ulrica Hydman-Vallien, 1974
   190
322   Blown form, Joel P. Myers, 1969   191
323   Blown form, John H. Cook, 1970   192
324   Blown construction, Joel P. Myers, 1969   193
325(a) *and* (b)   Glass sculpture, Harry Seager, 1974
   194
326   Installing panel by Erik Höglund   195
327   Section of glass wall, Edvin Öhrström   196
328   Screen, Renato Toso   197
329   Glass mirrors, Monica Backström, 1969   197
330   Glass panel, Michèle Lanoir, 1959   198
331   Fused silica panel, Stephen J. Edwards, 1968   199
332   Detail of lighting screen by György Z. Gács, 1968
   200

333   Lighting screen, György Z. Gács, 1968   *page* 200
334   Glass 'Curtain', B. & T. Sarasin   201
335   'Stained glass' window, Erik Höglund   202
336   'Stained glass' panel, F. H. Lauten   203
337   Prismatic ceiling, Alberto Rosselli   204
338   Two crystal blocks, Sven Palmqvist   204
339   Crystal block 'wall', Sven Palmqvist   205
340   Cast glass, 'Square', S. Libensky & J. Brychtova,
   1968   206
341   Sculptured column, Edvin Öhrström, 1969
   206
342   Section from glass column, Edvin Öhrström, 1969
   207
343   Silvered glass, John Hutton, 1970   208
344   Window decoration, Oiva Toikka, 1974   208

Acknowledgments

Glass attracts attention by its extraordinary and technical properties. It is usually transparent and may be decorated in a variety of ways, is so hard that a diamond is needed to scratch it, so timid that it can shatter to fragments in over-hot water. Made of simple components it has been, and still is, displayed at countless exhibitions throughout the world, and its long history contains many notable landmarks and achievements. It is the purpose of this book to chart those of more recent times, although the history of a minor art such as glass has had many confusing and inexplicable moments since that recounted picturesquely enough by Pliny — when sand and soda fused together to the amazement and subsequent advantage of the Syrian glass-makers of the first century A.D.

It has become fashionable in recent years for authors to say that they are indebted to so many people that a list of their names would be too long to print. Much of my work has been possible only through the kindness and long-suffering of others, but it will be appreciated that on this occasion I cannot follow my normal rule of thanking everyone who has participated.

Even a careful glance at the list of photographic acknowledgments, and the various details of manufacture and ownership recorded in the captions, provides but a partial story. The 350 or so illustrations were chosen from some 2,000 gathered from all over the world, but I have had to omit much that in an ideal context I should have included.

I have tried to choose photographs which are representative but not well known or well used. In the French sections of the historical photographs one or two have, however, appeared previously, and notably in Dr. Ada Polak's important book on *Modern Glass* (1962), published by Faber & Faber. She also kindly allowed me to illustrate one piece in her own collections.

I have been indebted in my glass studies made over many years to a group of scholars in various centres: Robert Charleston (Victoria & Albert Museum, London); Paul N. Perrot (sometime Director at the Corning Museum of Glass, New York); Dag Widman (Nationalmuseum, Stockholm); Helga Hilschenz (Kunstmuseum, Düsseldorf); Dan Hogan (sometime Curator at the Pilkington Glass Museum, St. Helen's); and H. Jack Haden (Stourbridge). My sense of obligation to them is as considerable as it was when, with the same generosity, they assisted me on my earlier, and necessarily shorter *Modern Glass* of 1968. The Swedish Institute for Cultural Affairs, and the Finnish Embassy in London, kindly arranged for me to visit Sweden and Finland and I have also been able to study the industry under favourable conditions in America, France, Germany and Czechoslovakia. For much practical assistance on these trips I am indebted to Nils-Gustav Hildeman; Ann and Göran Wärff (Kosta); Ingeborg Lundin and Mr. & Mrs. John Selbing (Orrefors); Bertil and Ulrica Vallien (Åfors); Jan Erik Anderbjörk (Växjö Glass Museum); Tom Soderman (Finnish Ministry for Foreign Affairs, Helsinki); Marjatta Pauloff (Arabia, Finland); Professor and Mrs. J. L. Clifford (New York); Dr. and Mrs. J. Douglas Smith (Colonial Williamsburg) and Madame Yolande Amic and Mlle M. N. Petiet at the Museé des Art Décoratifs in Paris. The staff of Glassexport at Liberic in Czechoslovakia have done much to expand my knowledge of their industry. For help, particularly with translations, I am indebted to W. G. Roessingh (Holland); Dr. K. Tasnadi-Marik (Hungary); Janet Pamphilon, Sjoerd Hannema, and Anne Hirsch-Henecka.

For assistance of various kinds I am grateful to Michael Hodson at Barrie & Jenkins; to Audrey Taylor who typed the manuscript, to Judith and Nicholas Goodison, and to my wife and daughter who endured smilingly the inconvenience of so many piles of photographs in too many places. It has given me pleasure to dedicate the book to Laurence Whistler as a slight recognition of what we all owe to one who has engraved glass with skill and compassion for over forty years.

Lancaster, November 1975   Geoffrey Beard

Photographic Acknowledgments

Bassano, London *180, 193*
Birmingham City Art Gallery *2*
Jindřick Brok, Prague *15, 47, 48, 54, 178, 182, 229,*
264, 285
Cameraphoto, Venice *136*
Fotografo Clari, Milan *140*
Jean Collas, Paris *228*
Michael Cornell, Ipswich *201*
A. C. Cooper Ltd., London, *Colour plates 13:* Solven,
14: Marinot
Corning Museum of Glass, New York *89, 108, 127–9,*
155, 214, 220, 223, 224, 227, 236, 238, 246, 247, 249,
251, 253, 254, 258, 261, 266, 267, 283, 296, 330
Feruzzi, Venice *135, 308, 325, 328, 334, 337*
Jane Fitzgibbon *109*
Raymond Fortt, Kingston-upon-Thames *123, 174, 175,*
179, 217
Foto-Gauss, Stuttgart *184*
Giacomelli, Venice *289, 293*
Glass Manufacturers' Federation, London *160, 185, 324*
Margaret Harker, London *191*
Wallace Heaton, London *189*
Lars Hellsten, Orrefors, Sweden *118, 300*
Poul Henriksen, Arhus, Denmark, *275*
Graham Herbert, Weymouth *188, 194, 195, 198, 199, 200*
Henrik Hultgren, Bromma, Sweden *329*
John Hutton *280–4, 343*
Fotohaus Sepp Karg, Austria *107*
Stig Karlsson Växholm, Sweden *110, 112, 131, 139,*
146, 163, 273, 335
S. W. Kenyon, Wellington, Somerset *211, 288*
Walter Klein, Düsseldorf, *Colour plates 1:* Tiffany, *3:* Daum,
2: Koepping
Landesgewerbeamt, Baden-Württemberg Museum,
Stuttgart *141, 336*
Foto Archief, Leerdam, Holland *105, 250, 252, 262, 319*
Edward Leigh, Cambridge *172, 202, 206*
Marvin B. Lipofsky, California *109, 235, 320*
Tue Lütken, Denmark *100*
Nanny Still McKinney *119*
W. Moegle, Stuttgart *125, 154*
Kjell Munch, Norway *104*

Musée des Arts Décoratifs, Paris *7, 9, 10, 12, 19–20, 22,*
25, 27, 29, 31, 42–3, 46, 50–1, 57
Nationalmuseum, Stockholm *66*
Lee Nordness Galleries, New York, *Colour plate 10:* Littleton,
310, 317
Jean Novotný, Prague *88*
Foto Ounamo, Helsinki *145, 162*
Robert Packo, Toledo, U.S.A. *318*
Pilkinton Museum of Glass, St. Helen's *91–3, 147, 183,*
218, 225, 231, 265, 272
Photographis Publicité S.A.R.L., Paris *103, 148, 153*
Sten Robert, Kosta, Sweden *30, 45, 49, 67–8, 80, 87,*
102, 113, 150, 245, 287, 290, 298, 313
Jørgen Rone, Copenhagen *114*
Carl-Johan Rönn, Sweden, *Colour plate 5:* Warff
John Selbing, Orrefors, Sweden *62, 64, 81, 96–7, 101,*
120, 121, 122, 124, 149, 161, 164, 165, 222, 338, 339
Skane-Reportage, Malmö, Sweden *132, 151, 239, 263*
E. A. Sollars, Winchester *207, 208*
Steuben Glass, New York *166–8, 224, 255*
Károly Széleny, Budapest *98–9, 106, 227*
Erkki Vaale, Riihimäki, Finland *133, 137, 226, 274*
Victoria and Albert Museum, London, *Colour plate 4:*
Marinot, *1, 3, 6, 8, 11–12, 21, 58–9, 60, 69, 79, 256*
Terry Waddington, Manchester *17–18, 32, 34–40*
Wahlberg, Stockholm *78*
Rosemary Weller, London *116*
Murray Weiss *255*

1 Late 19th century achievement

'I believe the right question to ask respecting all ornament is simply this: was it done with enjoyment?'

John Ruskin
Seven Lamps of Architecture 1849

One might debate which country had most right in the late nineteenth century to be regarded as the leader in the production of good glass. An examination of America's claim in the 1870s has to take account of the turmoil and disruptive influence of the Civil War. It was not a conducive atmosphere for the production of luxury glass. One can see that all the conditions in France were right. The influence of the great international exhibitions held in Paris, the supremacy of the work done by Emile Gallé and his followers at Nancy, and the evocative nuances of Art Nouveau gave France a significant lead in late nineteenth-century glass. Earlier in the century the French factories had been busy making the elaborate *millefiori* paperweights and delicate opalines, although economic hardships had gradually caused the art to slip into oblivion. The more settled political climate at this time also inspired the great Baccarat and St. Louis factories to produce new and colourful glass. The 1878 Exhibition in Paris attracted both makers and public, and the widespread enthusiasm kindled by the glass was felt in France by a number of individuals who were already active in making and selling. The most significant of these at first was François Eugène Rousseau, 1827–91 (*plate 9*). Rousseau had started by having wine-glass services decorated by good engravers to his own design and he soon went on to having glass blown at the works of his former employers – the Appert brothers of Clichy. At the time of the 1878 Exhibition he had ventured into what was already an important area of experiment in both Bohemia and England – glass composed of several layers of colour. In his work, however, the overlays were only put on the top rims of the glasses and the surplus allowed to run down and settle as irregular trails. He was always keen to experiment as were Emile Gallé and, at a slightly later stage in America, Louis Comfort Tiffany.

Within a few years the disciples of Art Nouveau were admittedly to accomplish daring glass designs with more panache, but few had Rousseau's marketing skill, and the Appert brothers, with whom he collaborated, had great technical skill.

The premier position which Venice had long held in glass manufacture caused many to attempt imitations of the products of its great years, for the most part with little success. America rivalled it in a great variety of coloured wares produced to incredibly complicated specifications. In France Rousseau started to copy the craquelé glass which the Venetians, and glassmakers in Belgium and Holland, had produced long before. The problems were considerable but, aided by the Apperts, Rousseau eventually succeeded in making it. For the most part the various methods available (some of which were patented in England), as well as Apsley Pellat's description in his *Curiosities of Glass Making* of that he had made in about 1845, basically consisted of plunging the red-hot glass into cold water. It was then reheated and refashioned by blowing. Rousseau sent examples of it, together with his Marble and Agate Glass and some imitation gems, to the 1884 Paris Exhibition. Perhaps as a result of seeing it there, two American companies, Hobbs, Brockunier & Co., of West Virginia, and the Boston and Sandwich works, redoubled their efforts and produced more effective examples of 'craquelle' glass.

Rousseau's work, and indeed most of that submitted to the important exhibitions in France, England and America was both innovative and practical.

Rousseau must have realised the competition with his own work in the brilliant displays (including lustre glass) of Bohemian and English glass at the 1878 Exhibition in Paris. However his activity in the six years before the 1884 Exhibition suggests that he was also well aware of the envious trade connections that

he had built up, and after fifty-eight active years in the trade he sold his establishment in 1885 to Ernest Baptiste Léveillé (*plates 8, 10*) who at first altered little in the firm's output. Japanese influences were becoming as strong in Paris as elsewhere, however, and in the busy years before the full impact of Art Nouveau, Léveillé worked in the Japanese decorative style, experimenting with acid etching and wheel engraving. He was thus able to adapt easily to Art Nouveau style.

Also important in the later years of the nineteenth century in France were Fernand Thesmar, who provided enamelled cloisonné bowls with elaborate floral decorations of sun and cornflowers, and Philippe-Joseph Brocard, who decorated goblets and lamps in bright enamels in Islamic interlaced styles (*plate 7*). The activities of both, however, were overshadowed by those of Emile Gallé (1846–1904). Although the subject of much close study Gallé's work still presents problems, particularly in its sequence and exact dating – a problem equally acute in the American work of Tiffany, which sometimes resembles that of the French artists. Gallé not only increased the number of available techniques, he modified certain existing techniques and, a true 'experimenter', often benefited by adroit analysis of apparent mistakes and miscalculations – as an author of an article on Gallé in the 1903 volume of *The Studio* pointed out:

'We know from his own writings what combinations produced specially happy effects, and how much he owes to what might almost be called accident in the mixing of certain colours. For instance, in his crystal glass and in his imitations of quartz, he colours the vitreous matter a rich or dull violet with oxide of manganese; he reproduces the gleaming fissures in certain kinds of quartz by pouring cold water into the molten glass, he achieves his blacks with the aid of a solution of peroxide

of iron. Another material which the glass of M. Gallé sometimes resembles is jade, an effect he obtains with sulphate of potash, very slightly tinged with green by the use of variable proportions of bichromate of potash, oxide of iron and copper; and he gets an effect resembling that of an agate or an onyx by the incorporation of coloured ribbons with the diaphanous mass of molten glass . . .'

Gallé's restless quest for new processes and colours and his interest in natural forms is very evident in the pieces housed in the excellent collection at the Museé de l'École at Nancy and in the glass collections of such museums as that at Düsseldorf. Gallé's influence in France was felt most noticeably by the Daum family, represented by Jean (1825–83) and his two sons, Jean-Louis-Auguste (1854–1909), and Jean-Antonin (1864–1930). Jean Daum had opened his atelier at Nancy in 1875 and by 1900 the efforts put into this venture by his two sons were producing results which were widely acclaimed. They were enthusiastic about Gallé's work but managed to keep their own style, blending it with what they considered the best elements of his. They were good technicians, and their early cameo and glassware has a strong individuality which identifies it long before a search for the angular signature 'Daum' surmounting 'Nancy'. An important collection of these early pieces (*colour plate 3 and plate 19*) has been donated by the present family firm to the Museé des Arts Décoratifs in Paris.

Much of the French work, in styles imitative of Gallé, was highly repetitive and many pieces survive with hardly a variation in surface pattern. At the same time, however, an infinite variety of pieces was produced under studio conditions by a number of talented artists following the lead set by Rousseau, Léveillé and Brocard. Most notable were the creators of panels and reliefs in the soft pâte de verre such as

Albert-Louis Dammouse (*plate 31*), Henry Cros (*plate 29*) and Georges Despret. The technical control which they applied to the difficulties of firing these pieces was matched in few other countries.

Gallé's influence was to spread far beyond France to America, Austria, Germany, Sweden and England, mainly through the younger generations of artists who had gathered round him, or who profited by his example. Tiffany, from America had visited the important Gallé exhibit at the 1889 Exhibition in Paris and J. & L. Lobmeyr, Karl Koepping (*colour plate 2*), the cameo-workers in England at Stourbridge (particularly Joseph Hodgetts) and G.G. Wennerberg (*plate 30*) at the Swedish factory of Kosta all imitated his style.

At the same 1889 Exhibition in Paris at which Gallé's work had been acclaimed, Thomas Webb's, the English lead-crystal firm, showed a large cameo-cut bowl measuring some nineteen inches (47.5 cm) in diameter. It was the work of the talented team of cameo-glass cutters led by George Woodall (1850–1925).

When Thomas Webb died in 1869 the works and business were left to his sons, and one of them, Thomas Wilkes Webb, took particular interest in seeing that the finest craftsmen were trained and maintained. The Woodall brothers, Tom and George, joined him just as Webb's art director, J.M. O'Fallon, was bringing a combination of imaginative thought and excellent craftsmanship to planning of Webb's stand at the 1878 Paris Exhibition; this splendid display of glass, with wonderful air twist and cut chandeliers, won them the Grand Prix. It was also at this time that Wilkes Webb commissioned the elder John Northwood (1836–1902) to execute the 'Dennis Vase' for him. Sometimes known as the 'Pegasus Vase', it was eventually sold to the Tiffany Company and was finally obtained for the collections at the Smithsonian Institution in Washington. Northwood's vase is a superb piece of cameo-cutting, some twenty-one inches (53.5 cm) high, and bears eloquent witness, along with George Woodall's vases and plaques (*plate* 33), to a profound technical skill. The figures and scenes they depicted, however, were often cloying and sentimental, and derived from a variety of classical sources. John Northwood's skills (*plate 2*) were based on a sure knowledge of glass-making and, given the financial resources, he could have been as successful as the younger Tiffany. Working for Webb, and later for Stevens and Williams, Northwood and his son and nephew were given adequate opportunity to work on cameo glass — great individual pieces — as well as the many commercial varieties (most of them made with the collaboration of American patentees) for which Webb's were also becoming well known under Woodall's leadership. In these works a perfect blending of individual studio-work, team-work (a group of at least six worked on Woodall's major pieces) and commercial production was achieved. Some of their major triumphs at exhibitions — from Melbourne to Chicago — were achieved not only by cameo-cut pieces but by superb copper-wheel engraved work by Bohemian artists in their employ such as William Fritsche and Frederick Engelbert Kny (*plate 3*). By the early 1890s this engraving had become almost as important as cutting in the Stourbridge industry.

English taste almost always kept to cut and engraved works and flamboyant decorative effects which virtually ignored basic shape. This was only too evident in Stevens and Williams's Silveria glass (*plate 21*), streaked with silver and green, and the same firm's bowls, moulded with channels to form an air twist beneath a pale ruby outer layer with applied rusticated decoration and satin 'finish'. These pieces

were enormously successful with the buying public whose demands soon pressed the English factories into producing imitations of the popular American 'Burmese' and other luridly coloured wares. In America the famous art glass types included 'Amberina', 'Agate', 'Maize', 'Pomona' and 'Wild Rose' — created by the New England Glass Company — and a dozen more types with such intriguing titles as 'Icicle', 'Fireglow' and 'Peach Blow'. Indeed Thomas Webb's 'Queen's Burmese Ware' was produced under a licence granted to them in 1886 by Frederick Shirley of the Mt. Washington Glass Company in America. Ironically enough, it is the Webb product which is now the more revered, although Shirley's work, in an 1885 version of a rococo style (if the wild nuances he adopted may be so described) was presented by Shirley himself to Queen Victoria. She liked it enough — in its deep pink shadings down to its original colour of a pale yellow — to order 'a tea set of the same ware'.

The American figure who dominated these years however was someone much more important than Frederick Shirley — Louis Comfort Tiffany. He became interested in blown glass after his stained-glass factory had burned down in the early 1880s. After a visit to Europe he set up the 'Tiffany Glass and Decorating Company' and, in 1893, the 'Tiffany Furnaces' at Long Island, New York. Like Gallé he was fascinated by colour and his team of skilled makers, working under his close personal supervision, began building up a collection of coloured and iridescent glass. It was first shown at the Chicago exhibition of 1893, an important show at which George Woodall's equally skilled work in cutting cased or cameo glass was shown on the English stand of Thomas Webb & Sons. Egyptian, Persian and the ever-popular Japanese motifs were used by Tiffany as a basis for his work. Most of the practical problems were under the control of Arthur J. Nash and his sons, A. Douglas and Leslie. They had joined Tiffany at Corona, Long Island, on a shareholding basis. It was Leslie Nash who developed Tiffany's iridescent glass 'Peacock' (*colour plate 1*) and the imitation of ancient glass 'Cypriote'. They pushed ahead in trying to rationalise the output and the finances, but at a critical stage Tiffany withdrew his support and reorganised the firm in 1900 as the 'Tiffany Studios'.

By contrast to these, fashioning superb colours and exotic shapes, there were a few individuals who were already much concerned with form. In England, Dr. Christopher Dresser was an important influence, and so too was George Walton (*plates 11, 13*) who later designed the 'Clutha' glass for James Couper & Sons of Glasgow. Harry Powell at Whitefriars, following on the example of Philip Webb (*plate 1*) who, in the 1860s, was producing remarkably forward-looking designs, was also leading his firm in a restless quest for new shapes (*plate 32*), made both in the traditional lead-crystal and in soda-glass.

Outside England there was only one major designer to show the same kind of concern: Louis Lobmeyr, Viennese glass designer and industrialist. Lobmeyr founded a studio in Bohemia at Kamenický Šenov, and put into it good artist-designers. His bold attempts to rebuild the reputation of Bohemian glass were aided to a great extent by the two trade schools in the same region. As early as 1867 the Lobmeyr exhibit at the Paris Exhibition of that year had greatly impressed George Wallis, then curator of the South Kensington Museum in London. He wrote of their work: 'the crystal glass employed by this firm . . . is fine and the designs to which the material has been adapted are the most perfect of their kind in the Exhibition . . .' Lobmeyr's work, as we shall see, was important to the developments in glass design in the 1904–8 period in Czechoslovakia, and

his own work was carried on after his death by his nephew Stephen Rath.

At the Jubilee Exhibition held in Prague in 1891 Bohemian glass, as might be expected, was the centre of interest. The display of 'Kavalier' glass, on a stand designed by the eminent Czech architect, Josef Fanta, reflected the concern, which Lobmeyr's work had encouraged, for the aesthetic aspects of glass and its display. By the time Fanta came, with other architects, to design and arrange the Czech exhibit at the 1900 Paris Exhibition, the Art Nouveau style was at its peak. Gabriel Mourey, writing in the 1900 volume of *The Studio*, expressed the universal infatuation with the style – for him 'one of the most perfect pieces of combined decorative art-work in the whole exhibition was La Maison de L'Art Nouveau Bing' – the six-apartment exhibit arranged by de Feure, Colonna and Gaillard for Samuel Bing. In America, Tiffany's work excepted, the Art Nouveau style soon gave way to a revival of heavily cut glass and it was this which won for the Libbey Glass Company a Citation of Honour at the 1904 St. Louis Fair. The Czech exhibit, designed by architect Jan Kotera, showed a monumental simplicity. Kotera and his colleagues were so absorbed with glass that, apart from their architectural activities, they concerned themselves with glass design work. This applied especially to the architects of the Artel Group whose designs were realised in simple geometric shapes and cut decorations emphasised by the laws of Cubism to which they adhered. Almost the whole message of that important movement was to reduce to a fundamental geometric form the wild disorders of nature. But the influence of Kotera and the new Artel Group was restricted entirely to Czechoslovakia.

Sweden had still not broken free of the restrictions of heavy cutting and the overlay glass in the Gallé style — as a glance through the extensive Kosta archives shows. Finland's Iittala Glassworks, started in 1881, was established firmly enough by the turn of the century, but its production (*plate 44*) was influenced by the traditional pattern moulds it had purchased from Sweden and Germany. France was still producing its *pâte de verre*, poised on the edge of new styles and achievements which René Lalique, Maurice Marinot and others were to introduce. In England, Powell's were producing great green Rhenish-style glasses and silver-mounting the good pieces (*plates 34, 36*). The Stourbridge glass-makers were committed to what their deep-biting cutting wheels could abrade — facets and prisms. George Woodall inspected his great glass cameo plaques cut by hand tools and copper wheel with the new Röntgen rays. It was all fashioned and coloured with the extraordinary hand-skills made fashionable in England by the labours of William Morris, the Century Guild, and others. But it was not a glass which could challenge the new painterly obsessions with the work of the Fauves and the Cubists, or which belonged to the primary world of the De Stijl group. Within Germany — still turning from its brief, flamboyant, brush with the 'Jugendstil' the work of the international modern architects, Peter Behrens, Walter Gropius and Joseph Olbrich gave no room for the spread of what Walter Crane had dubbed 'a strange decorative disease'. With a long swing of the pendulum a brief haunting interlude had almost gone, perhaps only to be realised again in the different world of the contemporary off-hand blowers (*colour plate 10*, Solven). And so a search for purity was borne along on the still buoyant waves of decoration swirling through from the rich years of the *fin-de-siècle*. Eugène Houtart, writing of the 1900 Paris Exhibition, summarised the position: 'steel and glass are without doubt the two elements which will characterise the twentieth century and will give their name to it'.

2 Search for form

'There is no reason why machinery should not be used in certain cases provided always that no attempt is made to use it as if it had brains'

George Walton (1867–1933)
Speaking to the Scottish Architectural Association, 1898

The great world fairs which became the forum for industrial society – the meeting of intellectuals among objects created from fertile ideas – had long been championed in Sweden. Under the sponsorship of Svenska Slojdforeningen (The Swedish Society for Industrial Design, which celebrated 125 years of existence in 1970) Sweden's glass and art objects (and even on occasion its smörgasbord restaurants) were shown at Antwerp in 1869, St. Petersburg, 1870, Moscow, 1872, Vienna, 1873, Philadelphia, 1876, Paris 1878, and Chicago in 1893. In the 1897 report of Svenska Slojdforeningen we read: *'that a strongly progressive movement is taking place in Scandinavian handicrafts, that this progress is not limited only to the revival of the techniques and forms of national handicrafts, but also shows strong signs of a new and independent flowering starting from a complete mastery of the forms . . .'*

By the turn of the century the new emphasis in Sweden on better design of utility objects was well under way, particularly in the wide ranges of furniture and ceramics. Modern features were also beginning to appear in English houses and particularly those by C.A. Voysey. In France Maurice Marinot (1882–1960) began to express an interest in glass about 1911, and in Holland, soon after the outbreak of World War I, the management of the Leerdam Glassworks decided to employ artists for the designing of their products. K.P.C. de Bazel was the first architect who was asked to co-operate towards this new idea. In 1916 these models came on the market for the first time after a great deal of experimenting. The purpose was to come to mass production, to be designed in such a way that not only the relative beauty arising from the function should be sufficient but that beauty itself should be functional – the mass product as a standard for the cultural level. Some of this aesthetic was being expressed by the Functionalist movement — clearly stated by the practice of the Bauhaus and the influential ideas of the architect Le Corbusier, and some by the work of Maurice Marinot. He stated his own philosophy and Gabriel Mourey repeated it in *The Studio* in 1927 (page 247):

'To be a glassmaker' Marinot wrote 'is to blow transparent matter by the side of a blinding furnace . . . to shape sensitive material into simple lines by a rhythm suited to the very nature of glass, so as to rediscover later in the bright immobility of the ware the life which has breathed it into a fitting decorative form. This decorative form will be worthy of respect, or something more, in proportion as it bodies forth the two significant qualities of glass — transparency and lustre. I think that a good piece of glassware preserves, at its best, a form reflecting the human breath which has shaped it, and that its shape must be a moment in the life of the glass fixed in the instant of cooling . . .'

And of course Marinot superbly realised his statement with striking depths, density, reliefs, rich colours and frosted acid effects in his glass (*colour plate 4* and *plates 57–60*). We shall see that his work became better known by the 1925 Exhibition in Paris.

The thick limpidity which Marinot brought into the pieces he fashioned was rarely equalled in his lifetime. Similar concerns for the 'form reflecting the human breath' were observed in the 1920s by several designers — in Sweden by, in particular, Edvin Ollers, (*plate 45*) and in Marinot's own native France by the Daums, and by René Lalique (1860–1945). The Deutscher Werkbund, however, led by Hermann Muthesius, had been proclaiming the 'machine style', and the new forms of glass and concrete factories set up by Peter Behrens and Walter Gropius had introduced part of Europe at least to the rigours of functionalism, with the inevitable reactions to the sinuous line.

In England the formation in 1915 of the Design Industries Association focussed attention on the successful efforts the Germans had been making to improve the quality of all their work. In March 1915 a committee led by Ambrose — later Sir Ambrose — Heal persuaded the Board of Trade to hold an exhibition in London of Austrian and German articles 'typifying successful design'. But there was still a long road to travel before this message had effect. Even in Sweden clashes arose over the intent and purpose of the goods in the important Home Exhibition of 1917 held in Stockholm.

The idea of the arrangers was to try to promote simple household goods, which through industrial mass production could be bought at a reasonable price. The spread of the theories of the Werkbund — the prototype for both the Svenska Slojdforeningen, and the Design Industries Association in England — had been greatly limited by the First World War. The Swedish adherents desperately believed in workers producing from designs they found acceptable, but the movement became a toy for the upper classes, descendants of a strong aristocratic line. In his contemporary book *Beautiful Everyday Goods*, Gregor Paulsson attacked not only producers and salesmen, but also artist—craftsmen 'who now mostly sit around, making trash for the interested wealthy few'. It was a state which had to be rationalised.

At the same 1917 Exhibition in Stockholm, Edvin Ollers had attracted acclaim for his beautiful thin glass made at Kosta. An examination of his designs in the Kosta archives reveals many of clean uncluttered line, which would shame no Functionalist, to be produced in green, grey and clear glass (*plate 45*). At the neighbouring factory of Orrefors the artistic impetus was provided in 1916 by appointing as designer Simon Gate (1883–1945) and a year later Edward Hald (b. 1883).

Unhampered by convention these young designers, helped by master glass-blower Knut Bergqvist (1873–1953), became fully acquainted with the techniques. Like Ollers at Kosta they had started their careers as painters but now they concentrated on the production of everyday utility glass at the Orrefors daughter factory of Sandvik. This led to seemingly endless experiments and the final appearance of 'Graalglass', which carried coloured decorations within the body of the glass. A development, helped by the presence of Edward Öhrström was 'Ariel' (*plate 65*) which utilised air bubbles to give an added dimension. Swedish glass however needed more than this to give it an international name. Gate started to produce almost art nouveau shapes in near black glass (*plate 62*), and the rich almost Byzantine opulence of the designs he and Hald created, to be engraved by Gustaf Abels, won them many prizes and much acclaim, particularly at the Gothenburg Exhibition of 1923. Axel Romdahl writing in the magazine of Svenska Slojdforeningen said 'that all strangers with an interest in art have taken home from their visit to the exhibition the memory of the Orrefors room and this is not just because of the fact that the objects exhibited are good, but also because of the way in which they were presented, the noble dimensions of the room, its discreet colours and successful lighting . . .' They excelled themselves with the Paris Cup presented by Stockholm to Paris at the time of the 1925 Exhibition. At a height of 34 inches and designed by Simon Gate it took Orrefors 600 man hours to make and engrave it. The creation of these important prestige pieces had not gone unnoticed in Europe and particularly influenced Czech glass designers.

In 1918 Czechoslovakia attained its independence from three hundred years of incorporation in the multi-national Austro-Hungarian Empire. In the excitement of pressing forward with new exhilaration, the aesthetic mood favourable to the creation of glass was helped by the foundation of the Prague School of Industrial Art in 1919 and, in 1920, by the Glassmaking Trade School set up at Železný Brod. This school became a centre where both the professorial staff and the students tried out their new schemes of design and decoration directly by making the glass themselves. In addition the staff of the Glassmaking Institute at Hradec Králové, founded in 1923, concentrated on scientific and technical research and could advise their artistic colleagues of ways of achieving better results. The creation of unique engraved pieces particularly attracted the talents and attention of Czech designers. The small but important group of engraved glass created by Jaroslav Horejc, a professor at the Prague School, in 1922 3 (*plates 47, 48*), made by Stephan Rath's Lobmeyr studio at Kamenický Šenov have enjoyed lasting fame. Other countries however, and notably Holland, were mastering the form rather than worrying with decoration.

The De Stijl group, operating in Holland at this time, were more in sympathy with the Swedish notion of aesthetics and function. From the start the group encouraged active collaboration between painters, sculptors, architects and designers. Catching something of the atmosphere generated by this group, the management of the Leerdam glassworks began to employ designers for their glass products. In 1915 P.M. Cochius, then managing director of Royal Leerdam, commissioned K.P.C. De Bazel and H.P. Berlage to make some glass designs. In 1916 after a great deal of experimenting, the first pieces were completed. The eventual aim again was the mass production of well-designed and aesthetically pleasing objects. Another important Dutch designer in these early years was Andries Dirk Copier (b. 1901) who joined

Royal Leerdam in 1914 and created his first designs
in 1920. He added the new dimension in 1923 of
'Unica' pieces. These have always been to a degree
'experiments of the artist realised by himself or by the
glassmaker working with him into forms and colours'. A
single piece shown by Copier at the 1925 Paris Exhibition
won him a silver medal. It also encouraged his colleague
Chris Lebeau (1878–1945) to make unique pieces.
In 1923, when De Bazel died, Lebeau attended the
funeral and in conversation later with Cochius he
was invited to make designs for Leerdam. He was a
versatile artist who excelled in many fields of art. He
made wonderful woodcuts in unusual dimensions,
posters, settings for the stage, portraits and mural
paintings. In 1925 he made a number of 'Unica'
pieces in collaboration with Copier who taught him
numerous techniques. In 1926 Lebeau left for
Bohemia to have 'Unica' manufactured there.
Copier's success at Paris was typical of the effect the
exhibition had in focussing attention on contemporary
design and providing opportunity for the display of
glass fashioned in many different and exciting ways.
Only the year before van Krimpen, the eminent
typographer, had written in *Telegraaf's* issue of
November 14 that 'A.D. Copier seems to me the best –
he seems to be more involved in technics, thus
coming to more natural, more obvious designs than
his older colleagues'. The same adulation has been
given over the years to much of Copier's work
(*plates 74, 129, 250, 262*) but a quotation of 1928
does much to summarise the original direction of his
design. Writing in the April 1928 issue of *Opgang*,
Dr. Joseph de Gruyter indicated that notwithstanding
Copier's youth he was:
*'in my opinion . . . the best of all these glass designers
since De Bazel's death in 1923. Moreover he is the
one under whose management glassware is still being
made at Leerdam as designed by the deceased De Bazel . . .'*

3 L'esprit Nouveau

'It was an epoch of mechanical progress'

Guillaume Janneau
Modern Glass 1931

Art Deco, and the creations of the German Bauhaus and the Dutch De Stijl disciples took their place at the Paris Exhibition of 1925 alongside Le Corbusier's austere 'Pavillon de l'Esprit Nouveau' and René Lalique's interesting glass fountain (*plate 52*). The fountain may have pointed, in its reticulated upward steps, to the unconscious concern of the time to find its artistic way – the Constructivists, the Surrealists, the Purists all suggesting their version of the true and only route. It was however Le Corbusier's writings, projects and buildings which indicated the more understandable gospel of reducing buildings to the basic geometric shapes. For the most part, however, the glass on view at Paris was fashioned with more concern for an exciting appearance than with any Purist ideals, and Lalique's 'ronde d'enfants en haut-relief' almost flaunted their frosted lines (*plates 50, 51*).

René Lalique (1860–1945) began his career as a jeweller and silversmith in about 1885. His anonymous entry in the 1889 Paris Exhibition had won a prize and attracted many subsequent commissions for his jewelled objects, including one from the great French actress, Sarah Bernhardt. He had started experimenting with glass in about 1902, blending glass drops with his jewels. He worked at first in a small factory but, by 1909 had leased a larger factory at Combs la-Ville. In 1914 he turned exclusively to glass production. Some of the scent flasks he made for Coty, together with glass mascots for the radiators of cars have become desirable collectors' pieces. He was not afraid to come to terms with George Walton's comment on machines – that it was in order to use them provided it was realised they had no brains – and he soon installed a stamping press.

Guillaume Janneau, a friend and author, in 1931, of *Modern Glass*, described this press as being:

'composed of two elements: the actual mould consisting of two jaws, one of which is fixed, and the mandrel, controlled by a large lever. The operator collects a certain quantity of glass in a state of fusion, which he allows to run into the mould. At the proper moment his assistant severs with shears the thick, glowing-red mass, then pulls down the lever as far as it will go. The mandrel is set in motion and pushes the molten glass into the two jaws of the mould, which press it and shape it simultaneously from within and without, imprinting on the soft mass every detail of the decoration . . .'

His output was vast, ranging through statuettes, vases, bowls, electric light fittings and door panels to parts of fountains, and he soon had recourse to a stamping press. Work by his fellow countrymen, Maurice Marinot, Jean Sala, the Daum family, and Jean Luce is listed in the same 1925 exhibition catalogue. In addition, the French factory of Baccarat showed perfume bottles, bowls and vases to designs by Lalique's contemporary George Chevalier: the purity of line in their cut surfaces won even Le Corbusier's approval.

The only other glass in the exhibition to command the attention of the Purists was that shown by the Austrian Stephan Rath. A.S. Levetus drew attention to these pieces in the 1926 *Studio*:

'a wonderful column in crystal designed by O.E. Wagner . . . in this it can be seen to what an extent the cube may be applied successfully to crystal glass, and from this to other objects of applied art'. He also commented on Austrian work made at Ernst Lichtblau's Werkstätte: 'the virtues of simplicity . . . form and contour are here the only aesthetic aids'.

Something of this concern for form and contour was, of course, to be found elsewhere, but it would be incorrect to regard it as more than an adventurous phase among much that was completely evolved by recourse to traditional patterns. The new Italian partnership of Giacomo Cappellin and Paolo Venini, who were hailed as young experimentalists at this time of the 1925 Paris Exhibition, even copied the glass which appeared in paintings by Veronese and Holbein (*plate 156*). The Swedish factory of Kosta had now taken on Elis Bergh and Ewald Dahlskog, and gradually their influence ousted the traditional and brought forth much that was good in both shape and cut line (*plates 49, 67*). In America, A. Douglas Nash and Frederick Carder, working respectively for the Libbey and the Steuben companies, tried to keep ahead of the attempts being made in Europe to produce glass which did not need brilliant cutting to attract attention. France had a stylistic lead in fashioning glass which combined the best of the functionalist concern with basic shape with sparse decoration and exciting colour and bubble effects. Glass artists in other countries attempted copies but the general French influence was marred and distorted by crude acid-etched pieces destined for a popular commercial market.

Finnish manufacturers recognised the danger of indiscriminate copying and, in a search for new and good designs, Riihimäen Lasi Oy held a competition in 1928. Its main purpose was to encourage some new thinking about suites of household glass to be made in the cheaper soda metal without additional cut or engraved decoration. The competition was won by Henry Ericsson (1898–1933), a painter and graphic artist. He was the first major artist to be commissioned to make designs for a Finnish glassworks. While many drawings by him show an interest in the grand intricate presentation piece, such as that which was presented to the city of Barcelona at the time of the important exhibition of 1929 there, Ericsson's influence was on glass beautiful for its shape. He believed that the shape should arise naturally from the material used and be related to the techniques involved with working it. Before his death in an accident, Ericsson set Finnish designers on unswerving paths of allegiance to good design. The two most affected by Ericsson's work were Arttu Brummer (1891–1951), and his pupil at the Central School of Industrial Design, Gunnel Nyman (1909–48). While they carried on Ericsson's interest in the great presentation pieces their work was very versatile. Brummer's flower vases in blister glass of 1936 – which were echoed in work done by the Scottish firm of Moncrieff and by Ercole Barovier in Italy – showed him to be an innovator and creator of original forms. Brummer was also an important member of 'Ornamo' (The Finnish Society of Decorative Artists) and as a capable teacher he was able to put his ideas and achievements before a wider audience. He owned an interior design business and it was this which brought him into contact with Gunnel Nyman who was training as an interior designer. On a freelance basis, Nyman started to follow Brummer's lead in glass design and designed her first pieces for Riihimäki in the early thirties. She turned more and more to glass after winning a competition held for participation in the 1937 Paris World Fair. A factory description of her work in 1933 read: 'to her, the reflection and refraction of every ray of light is of supreme importance, and the thicker the surface refracting light the better'. Just before her death she herself wrote:

the material should be so dominant as to make it inconceivable that the object could be made of anything else. It can then be said to satisfy the demands of beauty and harmony. This is particularly true of glass, a sensitive and unique material – and one with a certain bewitching magic. Whoever has yielded to its power, can never give it up'.

Her work (*plate 73*) was produced simultaneously by all three of Finland's glass factories, Iittala, Nuutajärvi and Riihimäen. Her premature death robbed Finland of one of its most active designers.

The influence of this Finnish activity, which intensified as work was produced for the Milan Triennale exhibitions of 1933 and 1936, was felt most in the neighbouring Scandinavian countries. Jacob E. Bang in Denmark and Vicke Lindstrand in Sweden followed the Finnish lead most assiduously. In Sweden, Gate and Hald produced glass of good clean shape as well as their great engraved presentation pieces. Lindstrand (b. 1904) joined them at Orrefors in 1928 and started to combine the good shapes the factory was producing with effects made by grinding, engraving, colouring and painting. Nils Wollin, in his book *Modern Swedish Decorative Art* of 1931, refers to the vases, bowls and dishes which Orrefors was already producing in thick glass, without decoration, and which afforded endless possibilities for exploiting the reflective qualities of glass. With Lindstrand's new effects of making air bubbles in the thicker pieces of crystal, and acid-frosting and cutting – in addition to the grinding, engraving and colouring we have mentioned – the Orrefors range became important and successful. The talents of its designers were allowed full freedom of expression, as were those of Elis Bergh at Kosta nearby, and won Sweden an important role in the creation of good glass which, for the most part, it still retains. Bergh's swirling cut glass bowls – the cut lines were incised in snake-like patterns – were shown alongside Orrefors' great presentation pieces and simple table-glass at an important exhibition in Stockholm in 1930 and in a Swedish exhibition in London in 1931.

Sweden was already concerned in the erection of buildings which had order, light and cleanliness as a prime consideration. It was an environment encouraging to all good designers and led them to considerations of form and functions, such as stackability. This message of design was stated clearly enough at the 1931 Swedish exhibition in London and was applauded by a young New Zealand architect, Keith Murray (b. 1893), who had settled in London. While Murray had been much impressed by the foreign glass he had seen in Paris and in London, he was highly critical of English glass. All the main lead-crystal factories were committed to heavy traditional cutting – the Stourbridge firm of Thomas Webb's, for example, produced some forty-five table services of which twenty-four were cut and six richly cut. Murray tried to analyse his thoughts in the light of such evidence and published an article on the design of table glass in *Design for Today*, June 1933. He set down the 'elements of glass design' thus:

1 The established purpose of the piece must be satisfied by its form.

2 The form is all important; the profile, the mass, the weight, the colour.

3 Decoration, if used at all, must be organized to express the form of the object, not destroy it.

He concluded with a warning (which is still relevant):
'In the meantime, the important thing that manufacturers have to decide for themselves is whether they will be content to struggle for another generation against the current of changing taste and needs'.

Murray's subsequent work in glass was an important influence on the form of English glass although his pieces were never created in sufficient quantities to effect any radical change. During the time he came to terms with techniques Murray paid several visits to Powell's Whitefriars factory, and the late H.S. Williams-Thomas at Stevens and Williams took up his ideas in earnest. After discussions with Gordon Russell (who, while known as a furniture-maker, had produced some glass designs for Whitefriars and for Stevens and Williams) and Ambrose Heal, he put some of Murray's work into production. In the same

issue of *Design for Today* in which Murray had written, Otto Bauer, Manager of the Deutscher Werkbund, wrote that 'the aim of our efforts must always be improvement and refinement of the general demand'. Murray was almost alone in England in attempting this in glass, with designs superior to many of those produced today.

Most of Murray's glass (*plate 69*) had its form enhanced by very simple and shallow engraving, but in an important series of vases which Stevens and Williams produced in the late thirties he tried his hand at designing pieces to be cut in broad planes some two inches square, with as many as three layers set one above the other from foot to rim. The increasing demands of his architectural and design practice caused him eventually to abandon his work in glass and, for Wedgwood's, in ceramics.

Throughout the whole of world glass production at this time the only people with Murray's concern were those in Scandinavia, and at the newly created Steuben Glass in America.

In 1933 Arthur Amory Houghton Jr, great-grandson of the founder of Corning Glass, took over the Steuben Division. Houghton, an art-scholar with an internationally known library, had one main aim: to produce crystal glass to the highest standards of design, quality and workmanship. Two of his three requirements were already at hand. The research laboratories of Corning Glass Works had developed a formula for an absolutely pure crystal. Second, and of equal importance, the Steuben factory, under the direction of its production manager, Robert J. Leavy, was already staffed with a team of accomplished glassmakers. Houghton gave a young architect, John Monteith Gates, complete responsibility for design. Gates, in turn, called in a sculptor, Sidney Waugh (1904–63) to assist him with the more specialised aspects of the task. These three men, 'all under thirty years of age at the time', as the various published accounts of Steuben Glass proudly state, formulated the plan on which the entire development of Steuben was based. Design dictated the course of the company's work.

Three years later, in 1936, Gates arranged for a formal Steuben design department. In the meantime he and Waugh had worked in close collaboration and from the outset had established a firm precedent for simple designs which would enhance the special brilliance of pure crystal glass. The skill of Steuben engravers was also used to enhance the simple shapes and a reputation was established for presentation pieces – sometimes unique – which has rarely been equalled elsewhere.

The American 'Libbey Glass Company' was, like Steuben, capable of excellent work (*plate 70*) as befitted a company led by A. Douglas Nash of a family long prominent in glassmaking. Arthur J. Nash had joined Louis Comfort Tiffany on a shareholding basis and his two sons Leslie and A. Douglas helped him. Leslie Nash was later given a partnership in 'Tiffany Furnaces' for his development of the 'Peacock' Iridescent Glassware. Libbey's work in the thirties was completely different from its earlier wares, cut and engraved in floral, Greek Key and geometric patterns. The apogee was the thirty-two inch high table cut by Libbey's master craftsman, J.R.Denman (1877–1956) for the St. Louis World Fair of 1904. This table is now in the Toledo Museum of Art. Its elaborate design was representative of tradition and there were few in the glass factories who could see ahead to days when public indifference could be turned into acclaim of simple designed glass shapes.

The same dilemma arising from traditional work was present in Czechoslovakia. The Železný Brod Trade School had participated in the 1925 Paris Exhibition and had won the Diplôme d'Honneur, proof of the great strides it had taken in the first five years of its existence – proof also of the considerable talent at its disposal. It was organised with a good balance between theory and practice – a situation in contrast to that in the glass industry itself. Despite the efforts of the school and of enlightened individuals, the majority of those in charge of Czech glassworks remained stubbornly uninterested in co-operation with artists. Cases of collaboration were few and far between, taking place only on special occasions, prior to international exhibitions and similar events.

Despite this major drawback the glassmaking school extended its basic instruction in glassmaking to encompass the specialised decorative skills. Acid-etching and sand-blasting were introduced in the 1935–6 school year and methods of forming hand-sculptured figurines (*plate 305*) were introduced into the wound glass branch. The engraving of metal forms was started in the silversmithing department and mosaic art was also set up.

The school's ideal at the outset in 1920 had been 'to create in the spirit of the material', and in its various departments it did much to show manufacturers that a complete and wide-ranging curriculum was available to apprentices. Gradually the schools began to influence both the technical and artistic sides of glass production. Individual manufacturers began to participate in the annual school exhibitions in order to present students with the opportunity of constant confrontation with the quality of work needed by industry. The manufacturers in turn were stimulated to create products of a higher artistic standard.

While Le Corbusier's pavilion at the 1925 Paris Exhibition was perhaps the only building which gave the feeling of a new era the years which followed produced some who were similarly forward-looking. The Swedes were aware by the time of their 1930

Exhibition that by providing well-designed glass they could also explore cheaper production methods. Pressed glass for utilitarian purposes, designed as carefully as the prestige pieces, became a means of making good work available to a wide public. .
The Scandinavian industry had long been at one with dependence on the skill and initiative of its glass designers. The example set by the three Finnish works and by Kosta and Orrefors in particular in Sweden had encouraged many smaller concerns to take on at least one designer. The small factories headed by such imaginative owners as the Strömbergs at Strömbergs-hyttan in southern Sweden established good competitive positions. Edward Strömberg (1872–1946), one of Sweden's leading glass historians, had spent many years in charge of the production lines both at Kosta and at Orrefors. In 1928 he moved to the small nearby village of Eda and with his wife, Gerda, started to design glass of simple undecorated form. They worked Strömbergshyttan into a commanding position among the smaller firms and the same features characterise the factory's present production. In Gerda Strömberg's work of the mid-thirties glass of clean line and thick walled – with the occasional use of facet cutting – appears dominant.
At Karhula-Iittala in Finland splendid glass was also being produced in the mid-thirties to the designs of the architect Alvar Aalto and his wife, Aino Marsio-Aalto. His undulating vases in clear and green glass were highly praised when shown at the 1937 Paris Exhibition. He had set up his firm named Artek in Helsinki in 1935 with the aim of selling bent plywood chairs and undertaking interior decoration of all kinds. One of the commissions was for the Savoy Restaurant in Helsinki for which the glass vases were first designed. They are still in production by Iittala.
A comparison of Aalto's clean-lined glass with an early 1930s catalogue of any of the Stourbridge glass factories shows the English adherence to heavy cutting. Keith Murray's work for Stevens and Williams (*plate 69*) and that prepared by various artists for the 'British Art in Industry' exhibition in 1935 are notable exceptions. For this exhibition, held at the Royal Society of Arts, the Stourbridge glass firm of Stuart's invited designs from distinguished artists. Among them were Paul Nash, Eric Ravilious, Graham Sutherland, Dame Laura Knight and Dod Procter. There was, however, no commercial success to be obtained from their striking designs. The economic troubles of the thirties meant that it was necessary to match experiment by caution and when *The Pottery Gazette* listed 'what buyers will see' at the British Industries Fair at Olympia, 1937, it said of the Stevens and Williams exhibit:
'Although there will be many examples on view which conform entirely to the growing trend for freer and simpler cutting, after the styles being evolved by Mr. Keith Murray, there will be no lack of the brilliant, prismatic designs which may be said to be traditional of the English taste in cut glass wares . . .'
Meanwhile, by the same year of 1937 Andries Copier at Royal Leerdam in Holland had completed several hundred 'Unica' pieces with no recourse to cutting at all, and in Italy Paolo Venini seemed years ahead of his time with exciting designs which owed their impact to vibrant colour and acid-frosted effects. Only James Powell's Whitefriars glassworks near London came to almost equal terms. Some of the green glass vases designed for them by Tom Hill and Barnaby Powell in the late thirties had the purity of the European glass or of that produced by Gerda Strömberg in Sweden or Goran Hongell in Finland. Some of it got as far as the 1939 World Fair in New York, months before the outbreak of the Second World War.

4 For better living

'The choice of goods is the choice of a style of living'

Nils and Gregor Paulsson
The Use and Pattern of Objects, 1956

In 1940 as Europe plunged itself into war Ake Stavenow wrote in *Form*, the Swedish design magazine:

'The 1940s must not tear down everything the 1930s created of worth, social progress, cultural development, violent expansion both in Sweden and abroad. Everyone, both high and low, must keep going to do everything possible to maintain production in working for a happier future'.

It was not, however, until the 1950s that the great breakthrough for designers in Europe came. As Arthur Hald wrote: 'after forty years the motto about artists in industry had finally taken root. Design began to be profitable . . . good everyday goods became the symbols of general welfare and the democratic way of life'. The 'decade of objects' had begun, and at the Museum of Modern Art in New York a start was made in 1950 by granting a 'Good Design' certificate to objects judged worthy of the award.

It was at the Milan Triennale of 1951 that significant glass of many countries, and Finland in particular, was put on show. Finnish designers were awarded six Grand Prix, seven gold medals and eight silver medals. For a country which then had seven times as many horses as motor-cars the entry to the modern world was sharp and decisive, and design became an integral part of daily life. The glass designer Tapio Wirkkala had done a great deal to bring this about. He was the architect of the Finnish pavilion at Milan and had worked since 1947 as a freelance glass designer for Iittala. With a wide range of glass designs (as well as in many other materials for many purposes) Wirkkala and the Triennale won international respect for Finnish design. The Society of Decorative Artists, 'Ornamo', placed on record its faith in Finnish designers.

'The Triennales have always played an important role in

the work of Ornamo. On the one hand, they have constantly spurred designers to renewed endeavours to produce their best work and on the other hand they have done more than any other institution to spread the renown of Finnish crafts and design outside the country's borders'.

We have noted that Arttu Brummer's death in 1951 had left a void in Finnish design circles and representation for a time rested with Wirkkala and with the many talented members of Ornamo. Writing in *Design* in 1952 (no.38, p.4) Sir Paul Reilly recorded that Finland had in Wirkkala:

'an outstanding and almost universal designer as creative in print as in display, as in glass, as in timber and plywood, and young as he is, he is already something of a national hero, the winner of several awards at the Triennale, and the first recipient of the rich Lunning Prize presented by the George Jensen Corporation of New York to the best Scandinavian designer of the year'.

The concern with good design for a mass market was already the subject of debate elsewhere. John B. Ward, Director of Design at Corning Glass in America set out his views in 1951 on 'how Corning Glass plans better design for the mass market' (*Design* 1951, no.27):

'During the past fifteen years our company has intermittently employed industrial designers, both known and unknown in the design world. The results of their efforts have, to date, never provided us with a wholly satisfactory product, largely because of a lack of knowledge of glass as a material and the techniques involved in its forming and finishing'.

In Finland, however, despite the successes of 1951 there was little understanding of what was meant by industrial design or by design policy in industry. It might be assumed that the same was true for England, but a careful analysis of magazines of the early 1950s shows some signs of a renaissance which never fully developed itself. In assessing the 'glassware

for the 1951 Stock List' a writer in *Design* (1950, no.14) stated that:

'another factor which must militate strongly against innovations in design is the fact that, after some thousands of years of glassmaking, no intrinsically new form in mouth-blown glassware is likely to be evolved. Shapes of domestic glass are thus limited by method of making, and, in addition, by the purpose for which glassware is used; unless there are drastic changes in one or other of these factors, changes in shape are likely to be subtle rather than sweeping. There is more scope for innovation in decoration than in form'.

If one examines, say, in the Webb catalogue of 1952–3 the brandy glasses designed by Sven Fogelberg and T.F. Pitchford, or the decanter and glass crystal cocktail bottle of 1954 by David Hammond – also by Webb's – the opposite seems to be true: the innovation for this factory was not in the development of its traditional decoration. Indeed, Michael Farr writing on 'English Crystal Glass design' in *Design* in 1953 (no.54) indicated that there were 'distinct signs that manufacturers are relying less and less on conventional shapes and decorations'. At Webb's some of this concern was due to Fogelberg's Swedish origins and his frequent visits there. But the whole design process received a sharp reversal by the need to produce souvenirs for the 1953 Coronation of Queen Elizabeth II. There was need for decoration, whether chastely engraved, or diamond-pointed as in Laurence Whistler's exuberantly decorated firework-circled goblet, or pressed with crown and royal arms as in the plates by the Century Glassworks. Even the boro-silicate heat-resisting dinner-services by Phoenix Glass proudly bore the crown and royal cypher.

At Orrefors Sven Palmqvist, who had joined the Swedish company's engraving school in 1928, developed in the early fifties the 'graal' glass techniques pioneered by Gate, Hald and Lindstrand.

The heavy mosaic-like glass known as 'Ravenna', bright with a myriad of colours, was the result. The reverse side of the coin, and a tribute to Palmqvist's technical brilliance, was the introduction in about 1951 of glass (particularly bowls) produced entirely by the centrifugal action of spinning hot glass in a mould. It rises neatly up the outside of the fast revolving mould, untouched by hand, and the spinning action is then cut off by the use of the electronic 'eye'. 'Fuga' is perhaps one of the few designs of this century owing its shape entirely to observation of a physical law and is akin, in a modest way, to the technical break-through of Pilkington's process for making 'float' glass which again relied on intelligent observation and application of a common physical law.

The whole range of available glass of good design was also being increasingly shown in catalogues. The 1953 issue by Leerdam of Holland in particular was a handsome affair, with good layout, and a tribute to the achievements of the design team, led by Copier. He had also opened at Leerdam a glass school comprising day courses spread over five years. Here pupils were, and are, trained in techniques and in aesthetic appreciation – designers working alongside glass-blowers, polishers alongside painters. The school held its first exhibition at the Stedelijk Museum in Amsterdam in 1947 and has moved on to great and merited success.

The slow-down in the Czechoslovak glass industry during the German occupation from 1939 to 1945 was followed by a period of exciting artistic and commercial success. The industry was nationalised in 1948 and glass-designing became the concern of a new generation of designers who had trained under the great Czechoslovak teachers between the two world wars. Great efforts were made to meet the needs of all classes of people in Czechoslovakia and to compete with foreign glass-makers. The Czech glassworks were reorganised so that each specialised in certain types of products and decorative techniques. Artistic glass asserted itself in 1952 at a special exhibition held at the Museum of Industrial Art in Prague. It was also included in subsequent exhibitions in Prague and Liberec and it was possible to assess the gradual build-up towards the dazzling shows at the XIth Triennale in Milan in 1957 and at Expo 58 in Brussels.

The Czechoslovak Glass Review (1967 No.5), in reviewing exhibition successes over a long period, said of the 1957–8 shows:

'In Milan in 1957 the world public was acquainted with artists the majority of whom still today stand at the forefront of our artistic glass-making production. On behalf of all of them let us mention Stanislav Libenský [plate 338]. Important success was gained at this exhibition also by the Academy of Applied Arts in Prague and especially by the class of Professor Jan Kaplický, for its set of novel painted glass'.

The writer goes on to indicate that in the 1958 show at Brussels:

'even greater stress was laid on colour in glass and mobility of shapes than in 1957 at Milan . . . colour and motion characterised Czechoslovak glass at the end of the fifties . . .'.

The dominance of Finland and Sweden at this time tends to overshadow the efforts being made to produce good glass in Denmark and Norway. The ideas which had been fermenting in Scandinavia since the end of the first World War were put into effect, as we have noted, in the large exhibition of 1930 in Stockholm. They had also been put forward in the Danish avant-garde journal Kritisk Revy, which summed them up on its front page: 'modern town-planning, social architecture, economical technique, genuine industrial art'. According to the pioneers of the new functionalism, who were eager to accept the reality of the present, there seemed little point in clinging to old traditions of craftsmanship. Architects and designers were ready to accept new ideas but Danish moderation kept it within reasonable bounds. In any case, in the 1930s, Denmark had not developed in any marked industrial sense, and the German occupation of 1940–5 delayed this development even further.

As an agricultural nation, Denmark, unlike the other Scandinavian countries, had no mighty forests to provide the necessary quantities of fuel for the setting up of a large glass industry. Denmark originally had only one factory, the Holmegaard Glassworks, founded in 1825 in South Zeeland. This was set up conveniently near to some boglands from which peat could be obtained for fuel. In 1847 another glassworks was started in Kastrup on the island of Amager. In 1965 the two groups were amalgamated, and they are still the only glassworks in Denmark manufacturing drinking glasses and art glassware.

In the late 1920s Jacob E. Bang (1889–1965) was appointed as Holmegaard's art director. Later he moved to Kastrup but in both positions he set in motion new ideas and designs. Bang was succeeded at Holmegaard by Per Lütken (*plates 100, 260*), and since the merger he has been art director of both firms. Some of the colours in Bang's early work – the pale grey of the 'peat smoke' glass for example – blended with optical effects created within the glass. His 'Hogla' pattern of 1928 was described as 'an example of modernistic functionalism', but it was Per Lütken's work in the late 1940s and early fifties which brought about a reconsideration of the whole aesthetic and technical process of glass making and glass design. In some bowls of 1950 Lütken introduced the so-called pin-blowing technique, aiming by means of a wet wooden pin to create an excessive pressure, thus blowing the glass into the desired shape. A glance at the illustrations in the catalogue '*140 years of Danish glass*', first circulated as an exhibition in America 1968–70, shows no shape from 1830 onwards which would do disservice to a contemporary designer. The Danish tradition is 'utility and beauty, simplicity and elegance'.

Glass for everyday use had been made in Denmark since the mid-sixteenth century, but manufacture ceased in the seventeenth century when Norway, then united with Denmark, was given the sole glass production rights owing to the abundance of fuel in its ample forests. Glassmaking in Norway (admirably surveyed by Ada Polak) had a somewhat autocratic beginning. In 1739 King Christian VI of Denmark and Norway established a Company by Royal Charter. He commanded it 'to erect a glasshouse or two yonder in the most distant-lying forests and there make every kind of glass'. His determination founded an industry which could exploit Norway's abundant resources of wood and water. Many other raw materials, including the quartz sand, which compose about 70 per cent of the composition of glass, had to be imported from elsewhere in Europe. Above all it was necessary to import craftsmen, and these came mainly from Bavaria. The early companies set up under the King's charter failed – even the transport of the finished glass to Oslo was fraught with difficulty – and it was not until Hadelands was founded in 1765 by the Tanberg and Berg families that glassmaking in Norway achieved some stability and security.

From the beginning Hadeland tried to create an industry that was truly Norwegian. Local apprentices were indentured to learn the craft from Bavarian settlers and some of Hadelands' present staff are direct descendants of the first Norwegian glass-blowers. The Johannsens are one such family – Willy Johannsen, one of Hadelands' designers, won the Diplôme d'Honneur at the 1954 Milan Triennale, and of recent years the company has produced some exciting glass.

In its air-conditioned factory at Jevanaker, forty miles from Oslo, there is a modern glass-pressing plant capable of turning out several hundred items an hour. At the same time the traditional 'chairs' or teams of craftsmen produce individual items, particularly in textured glass. Bowls with bubbles finer than those in aerated water, exquisite frosted surfaces, colour contrasts, and at the same time they also produce all-pressed breakfast sets in steel grey or colourless textured glass. Johannsen's designs have been carried out along with those of Arne Jon Jutrem (now working free-lance) and Severin Brørby. All of them were represented in the important 1959 exhibition at The Corning Museum of Glass, New York, titled 'Glass 1959'.

The fifties closed with this exhibition, in its own way as important to glass designers as the great Paris exhibitions of 1925 and 1937 and the Milan Triennales had been in sorting out some of the future trends. The exhibition was 'selected from 1814 objects representing 173 manufacturers in twenty-three countries . . . Limited to decorative and table glass made since 1955, every type, from the mass-produced machine-made product to the unique handmade one-of-a-kind piece, was submitted'. A distinguished jury of five each chose 100 objects which were illustrated in a comprehensive catalogue, and each member then selected three objects which represented 'the highest ability evident among the entire collection'. While they found it difficult to establish and state their criteria of judgment a listing of their choice is instructive.

Juror	Designer or Object	Factory and Country
Leslie Cheek, Jr	Erik Höglund	Boda, Sweden
	Paolo Venini	Venini, Murano, Italy
	Frank Burkert	Oberusel, Germany
Edgar Kaufmann, Jr	Claus Joseph Riedel	Tiroler Glashutte — Claus Joseph Riedel K.G. Austria
	Erik Höglund	Boda, Sweden
	Dish, in heat resistant glass	James A. Jobling & Co. Ltd., Sunderland, England
Russell Lynes	Claus Joseph Riedel for 'Exquisit' range of goblets	Tiroler Glashütte — Claus Joseph Riedel K.G., Austria
	Dino Martens	Vetreria A. Toso, Italy
	Bengt Edenfalk	Skrufs, Sweden
George Nakashima	Kaj Franck	Notsjo, Finland
	K. Holosko	United Glassworks, Lednicke Rovne, Czechoslovakia
	Bengt Edenfalk	Skrufs, Sweden
Gio Ponti	Verá Liskova	J. & L. Lobmeyr, Austria
	Lucrecia Moyano de Muniz	free-lance, Argentina
	Covered dish, in heat resistant glass	James A. Jobling & Co. Ltd., Sunderland, England

Sweden, Italy, Austria, Finland, England, Czechoslovakia, Germany and Argentina provided 'winners' for one group of selectors – the whole exhibition symbolised a moment in design history, the significance of which is now better understood as the objects can be seen in the context of the emergence of new shapes and improved ideas: the results from good training and experiment. Glass in its contemporary totality has seldom been given a more important showing, and it is to be hoped the venture will one day be repeated. In the meantime America is still taking the lead by the important work at Toledo and by frequent summer workshop programmes which advance the concept that the designer can also be the craftsman. In the field of ceramics this had been understood and practised since the 1930s. There is a clear division between commercial ceramic production where the workers produce the designs of others, often unknown to them, and the studio potters who both design and execute their own ceramics.

In 1962, sponsored by the Toledo Museum of Art, ceramics craftsmen combined with glass technicians to make 'the first tentative efforts to blow glass from a new formula which could be melted at a temperature low enough to be workable in the average studio or classroom situation'. In the first two seminars of March and June 1962 the group worked under adverse conditions in an open garage on the Museum grounds. Harvey Littleton, who had taught ceramics at the Toledo Museum for several years, Dominick Labino, who had been vice-president for research at the Johns-Manville Fiber Glass Corporation, and Harvey Leafgreen, a retired glassblower from the Libbey Glass Company, all contributed their own special talents and skills to this pioneer class. According to the Museum's Director, Otto Wittman, 'the products were pitifully few and inept, but the spark had been kindled . . .' From this first experiment grew about fifteen courses in glass-craftsmanship. By the time of the Autumn 1966 'Toledo Glass National' it was evident that the endeavours of 1962 had been successful. Glass that could not be produced by the industry was sent to the exhibition from seventeen American states. Littleton, teaching at the University of Wisconsin was able to transmit his ideas about glassmaking to his students including Marvin B. Lipofsky and Samuel J. Herman. The latter successfully taught them in England at the Royal College of Art until his move to Australia in 1974. Blown glass was an exciting form of glass working that provided the greatest interest to contemporary artists. When interviewed at the time of the 1967 Dallas exhibition 'Art, Light, Form: New American Glass' Dominick Labino said:

Research into glass compositions which will produce new, unusual, and exciting colours, techniques in the blowing of glass objects, all this is but a part of the fascinating material which can be used as a medium for art. The thrill of discovering a new colour-composition, and the excitement of using it in varying forms, make the research worth while and stimulate one to further work. Colour and composition, these are the magic words in working with glass, which become an integral part of the design and form'.

In six other statements in the catalogue by some of the craftsmen involved, the play of light, the importance of form, the realisation that in its working glass is more exciting and spontaneous than clay were quoted. James Wayne provided one of the reasons for the undoubted and far-reaching success of the Toledo experiment: 'glass in the molten state is a most responsive material and provides inexhaustible variety of form . . .' In a more luxurious context, American glass, as made by Steuben Glass of New York, was assessed by James S. Plaut in his important critical monograph on Steuben of 1951. He asserted:

'Steuben's popular reputation probably rests not on those pretentious exposition pieces of which its own artists and craftsmen are naturally very proud, but on the simple blown objects, more familiar and widely used, which have been produced in volume greatly exceeding that of the cut and engraved pieces'.

There will always be conflicting schools of thought about this. It is to Steuben's credit that it has never relied on cutting as a sole mode of decoration: the pristine brilliance of the glass, coupled with precise engraving, has usually been enough to ensure ready acceptance.

The concern with blown shapes (*plates 221–265*), is one of the best motives a glass designer can have, and this has been exploited with consummate skill in many parts of the world. Ingeborg Lundin, until her retirement from Orrefors in Sweden, was supreme — the great swell of her design 'Glass apple' (*plate 222*) has had few equals, and reminds one of the enormous skill shown by Finnish glassmakers before the First World War. In the Nuutâjärvi Glassworks Museum one can see cylinders of glass, each some eight feet in height, blown with a blowpipe weighing about fourteen pounds. The cylinder was then cut open and flattened out in much the same way that crown glass was made and prepared for use in the eighteenth century.

New interests in colour and pattern associated with use gave Orrefors designer Gunnar Cyrén the chance to practise his belief that 'the problem of design is to constantly create new and different forms that fit the times'. In his 'pop' type glass Cyrén wrapped as many as eleven bright colours round the wine glass stem, contrasting them sharply against white: in his punch bowl and glasses he used bright greens, blues and orange. The shapes he produced for Orrefors were enhanced by these vibrant colours – some enamelled on the glass – and are of the strident present, rather than a traditional past.

The same pressures have caused some designers to think in fundamental terms of what needs to be added or taken away from design to achieve fluent results acceptable to a wide public. The Finnish designer, Kaj Franck, after a long career as designer and artistic director of Nuutâjärvi-Notsjo Glass has become a revered teacher and 'Professor' Franck since 1973. But in his article 'Anonymity' published in 1966 in Arabia's house magazine *Ceramics and Glass* he stated that 'instead of resting on the designer's name the product must stand on its own merits of which the design is an essential part'. At the time of this article an exhibition of glass by Franck and his colleague, Oiva Toikka, the 1970 Lunning prize-winner, took place in Arabia's Helsinki showrooms. Pressed glass and *objets d'art* were displayed side by side – 'part of the anonymity line'. The individuality which gives a piece of glass its life was emphasised in the glass sculptures and bowls. The pressed-glass production, on the other hand, represented industrial design, with its subordination to discipline and social aims.

Pressed glass is a recent innovation and its development has been slow. In the last few decades designers, with Franck well to the fore, have become increasingly interested in designing for pressed glass. While blowing depends entirely on a handicraft skill, pressing relies on a blend of machine and hand-work skill (*plates 269, 270*). Double moulds, one shaping the glass outside and the other the inside of the glass are brought together by the machine and the process of formation and assembly is swift and repetitive. Pressed glass offers interesting possibilities as far as form is concerned. The mould shapes only the outer surface when glass is blown into it and the inner surface takes a free shape in rough accord with the outside.

In pressing glass it is possible to impress embossed figures upon the outer surface while the inner surface is left smooth. It is also possible to make with considerable ease objects which would be both time-consuming and expensive to blow. By decreasing the number of phases involved in finishing the glass, and by creating variations in a large series it can be made cheaply available to a wide public. This has been the aim of the Scandinavian production of utility glass. The automatic machine-made glass produced in England by Ravenhead Glass of St. Helen's has had a comparable success. Hardie Williamson has added to his successful 'Five Star' range with a series of 'Monarch' glasses which have machine-cut decoration. In England, and in other countries which are successfully producing pressed and machine-made glass, such as America, Czechoslovakia and Scandinavia, a once negative public attitude is gradually becoming more receptive. The young designer, continually conscious of economics is aiding the process. He has been keen to introduce lead crystal with a lower lead content (8 to 20 per cent) which allows good design and cheapness to be combined. This is a characteristic imparted in the design schools. The other main English school, apart from the post-graduate work done at the Royal College of Art under Professor Queensberry and Samuel J. Herman, is at Stourbridge. Here it is led by Irene M. Stevens, a former designer with the Stourbridge lead-crystal firm of Webb Corbett.

In 1968 the Edinburgh, Stourbridge and Birmingham College glass departments exhibited work at The Corning Museum of Glass in New York. On this occasion the Museum's director, Paul N. Perrot discussed the efforts in America and England to encourage designers to work with the glass itself, and went on:

'As is the case in the United States, it is too early to assess what long-term contributions the academically trained designer-artist-craftsmen will make to the glass scene. Nevertheless, it is clear that anyone in the future studying the history of twentieth-century glass will have to take their work into account . . .'

One suspects, however, that students who are taught by such talented designer-craftsmen as Harvey Littleton, Dominick Labino, Stig Lindberg, Sam Herman, René Roubicek and Julia Báthory can hardly fail to produce interesting and even, on occasion, memorable work.

Mention has been made of the important Czecho-slovakian schools at Nový Bor, Kamenický Šenov, and Prague, through which most, if not all, Czech designers have passed in a thorough five-year programme. Comparison in syllabus can be made with the comprehensive American university programmes which stemmed in the main from the work of Harvey Littleton and Dominick Labino at Toledo, and with the Stockholm Konstfackskolan led by the distinguished ceramist Stig Lindberg. The best of the commercial schools is that set up by A.D.

Copier in 1940 at Leerdam.

Leerdam already houses Holland's National Glass Museum where the history and modern developments in glass design in Europe and America can be traced. The 'Glasvormcentrum' there was officially opened on September 27, 1968. The centre is Leerdam's answer to the need to gather 'artist, works engineer, designer, craftsman, marketing specialist and research worker in one compact operation unit'. All the talents present can be put to work in the best way to benefit both artist and craftsman and, ultimately, the customer.

As part of its programme the 'Glasvormcentrum' invites artists of other nationalities to work there for limited periods. Marvin B. Lipofsky, then from the University of California at Berkeley, was there in the autumn of 1970. His 'Colour Series 1970' (*plate 235*) was described by Leerdam's chief designer, Willem Heesen, as being for them all a 'new experience'. Normally Lipofsky, in the usual American approach to off-hand glass, works his own designs. At Leerdam he worked with the master glass-blower L. van der Linden. In other circumstances this type of collaboration might have entailed some compromise. However, in his attempt to integrate forms into a sculptural image, using specific qualities of glass, colour and transparency, no compromise is evident. The close collaboration between Lipofsky and the skilled craftsman has been an important development 'because here professional craft and technical skill do not stand in between the artist and his work, but are as one'. Hitherto the Swedish designers have come nearest to this ideal, standing near to the craftsmen in repeated attempts to achieve with advice and skill a desired result.

If we can regard the foregoing accounts (of experimentation in America, the development of 'pop' glass, the provision of utility glass to bring better concepts of design within some homes, and the better education of young designers) as having a quality, we must also consider the missed opportunities.

In commercial production it is usual practice to pay the maker and the decorator according to the number of pieces they produce. They in turn naturally resist the introduction of unfamiliar designs which slow the process. In consequence, a designer often compromises between too much and too little decoration. John Ruskin's condemnation of cutting glass – 'death by a thousand cuts' – was obviously aimed at the traditional lead-crystal industry in England. Since cutters accounted for such a large proportion of those engaged in the industry it would even today cause distress in certain areas if the traditions of cutting were abandoned.

Attempts have been made in Czechoslovakia to introduce new methods of cutting glass (*plates 278, 285*) but it may still be regarded as a decorative addition, which, under certain conditions and encouraged by tradition, full order-books and continuing demand for cut glass, allied to conservative training, inhibits the whole design process. Markets should continue to demand designs for cut glass which bring out the sheen and brilliance of the glass without obscuring what may basically be a shape of great aesthetic appeal. Manufacturers should seek to establish good contemporary design standards and they should try to do this without needing to reorganise drastically. The design and manipulative talents are available and all glass concerns should be able to utilise these.

It is still far from common practice for industry to allow designers and apprentices to create unique pieces. The nineteenth-century employers, noted for their concern with decoration above shape, understood well enough the international prestige which could be won by the unique statement – Osler's of Birmingham glass fountain at the 1851 Exhibition for example. There is a great need for wider adoption of the American system of competitive exhibitions with good prizes and for more travel scholarships such as those annually awarded by Jensen of New York to two of the best Scandinavian designers.

One of the leading organisations to realise this is the German Rosenthal group. The Rosenthal factory was started by Philip Rosenthal in 1879 by the establishment of a porcelain painting works at Eckerareuth. This was the beginning of an internationally respected complex which now consists of eight ceramic factories, two glassworks, a technical plant and a cutlery factory. When Philip Rosenthal died in 1936, his son, another Philip, took charge. Design in Germany immediately after the war still lacked understanding of the need to break with old forms and decorations. Competition from Scandinavia was on the increase and it was necessary to set new standards of excellence. Solutions to such a situation, however, are both difficult and expensive. Philip Rosenthal Jr, decided to form a team of designers of leading talent who would devote some of their time to creating a broad range of table objects in ceramic, glass and steel, many of which were complementary to each other. A committee of critics drawn from England, Sweden and Germany was to judge the work of this design group and the final selection might then reflect the standard of quality aimed at. Finally the products would be offered for sale in studio departments in other shops, and also in specially created Studio Houses.

Apart from Philip Rosenthal's keen but sensitive direction of the 'Rosenthal Studio Line', a policy that could have gone wrong, but didn't, the designers are all eminent, successful, and not afraid to follow the motto of the House – 'without mistakes – no discoveries'.

The best known of Rosenthal's free-lance designers is
Tapio Wirkkala of Finland. One of his classic designs
for Rosenthal is his 'Composition' service. The
porcelain and cutlery is by Wirkkala and Claus
Joseph Riedel, and Richard Latham, the American
designer in the field of rocket-ships, designed the glass.
The other internationally known designer in the team
is the versatile Danish artist Bjørn Wiinblad. His
concern to bring colour and well-devised colour-
combinations to the table outweighed any initial
thoughts about function, size or durability. His table
set, 'Lotus', exploits the translucency of the porcelain
body and adapts the motif of the lotus petal to
decorate the glass (*colour plate 9*). His five-foot-high
'Hanging Garden' (*plate 157*) engraved vases have a
folk-art simplicity.

The Rosenthal design team feels it is going the right
way to bring gradual acceptance of good design. In
their studios at Selb in Germany the new shapes are
designed, tested, developed and eventually packaged
ready to be sold. Many design teams the world over
have similar stimulating conditions in which to work.
The efforts of a few enlightened manufacturers and
designers, and the awareness of the need for
stimulating and industrially orientated design
education, will bring more to experiment with similar
policies to stand alongside traditional effort and
pattern.

5 Produced to sell

'This establishment is conducted on the strictest business principles, with the full intention of making it self-supporting, so that everyone may frequent it with a feeling of perfect independence'

Charles Dickens
Rules of 'The Self Supporting Cooking Depot for the
Working Classes' *The Uncommercial Traveller*

Although there are general ideas on the desirable appearance of glass for everyday use, it is difficult to formulate the ideal solution. Each designer tries to choose a technique of manufacture and decoration he is most familiar with in asserting his own individual opinion. It is agreed that drinking sets in particular should be of attractive appearance, and shaped so that they are functional and hide any signs of mass production. Opinions and ideas vary greatly and producers who are keen to sell their glass to the widest possible market must be aware of specific requirements and even adapt their production capacity to meet them. It would be pointless for example to try to make a lemonade set for sale at a cheap rate in supermarkets, multiple stores or petrol station forecourts, in cut lead crystal. A Micawber-like situation of profit and loss immediately intervenes. Interest in recent years in the enormous trade in drinking glasses has split into two divisions — those produced by machine in various soda-lime compositions, often with silk-screen applied decorations, and those in lead crystal. Both can be designed well, and the price of those in lead crystal can be made at least acceptable to more people — as in the Dartington ranges — by reducing the amount of lead oxide to less than a full third of the weight. It has also become more usual for discerning purchasers of lead crystal glass to buy that which is plain and unadorned by later decoration. The stem may be occasionally cut but Scandinavian designers have been setting a double pace: to concentrate on shape in clear terms, or to impart a surface texture (*plate 299*) during manufacture in textured moulds.
There is also consideration in exact design terms about convenience and durability. A ripple or ridge on the side of the glass provides a convenient hold for thumb and forefinger. There is also need to allow for the action of the dishwashing machine. The Institute of

Glass Research at Växjö, Sweden, made tests (No.871) in 1969 on some clear glass tumblers made by the Finnish firm, Iittala. The glasses were washed in four different types of washer which were kept continuously running for 300 washing operations. The glasses were then removed, washed in acid and distilled water and dried. They were studied for any surface dullness resulting from the use of five different types of washing liquid in water at 70°C. In most cases no surface changes noticeable to the naked eye were discerned, but it was concluded that there were, 'as yet, no generally accepted norms for evaluating surface damage in glass caused by washing up'. The resilience of the glass to the test was judged to be 'excellent'.

Finland has tried to take this information to the public by providing labels for its goods which have been approved by the Informative Labelling Association. The object of this state-supported, official and impartial organ is to guide and promote informative labelling in Finland along with uniform standards for the benefit and guidance of consumers. The label provides information on the essential utility features of the product. When different manufacturers use the same formula for similar groups of products, the consumer receives information about the various competing products which helps him make comparisons and decide which of them is the most suitable and the best buy. A similar system operates in England through the consumer magazine 'Which', but the triangular black and white label which denotes acceptance of the product for the Design Centre Index has no further information on it.

Another attempt to provide discriminating customers with practical and aesthetically pleasing articles for table settings was the formation in 1963 of 'Gruppe 21'. This is a group of factories producing china, glass, enamel, cutlery and other household articles.

It has 21 members from 8 countries. Although the member firms are competitive, they all seek to reach the consumer circle desirous of getting the best, artistically and technically, in their purchases. Gruppe 21 thus competes against inferior products. This object is attained through joint exhibitions, marketing policy and joint advertising. In 1967 the group arranged its first exhibition outside its actual area of operation, Western Germany, at the Finnish Design Centre in Helsinki. The critic Kerttu Niilonen, herself the author of an excellent book (1966) on Finnish glass, has written that the exhibition provided:

'an excellent opportunity of getting to know European form at its best, a true selection of elite objects, and it gives an excellent picture of how well these articles by different factories, even from different countries, harmonise and how pleasant and intimate an atmosphere they create in the right combination'.

Some of the ways this harmony is created involve great trust on the part of management. Johan Beyer, the owner and manager of the Swedish factory of Orrefors, interviewed on behalf of the Swedish Design Annual *Kontur* (No.10), said:

'You always have to keep in mind the aesthetic feelings of the artists. If I don't like a new design I'll certainly say so and hope that when the artist thinks it over and maybe even hears some other opinions he may change his mind. But if he remains adamant about the design I tell him to go ahead and let it run its course'.

The sales people are not expected to lead in a production like this. The designers, Beyer feels, 'ought to be ahead of the public and salesmen are here to sell what the artists create'. Regrettably it is not a universal philosophy, even in respect of the basic employment of the designer himself. And yet the aim, which has been proved successful, is easy enough to apply. The handmade art glass should be very elegant and the machine-made glass should be simple and functional. To some there is no in-between stage. The requirements of design are said to require consideration of principles of arrangement, geometrical relationships, strengths, access, cost and appearance. The factors leading to the acceptance of good design have appeared in the last fifty years, largely encouraged by the economic need to sell to a public which has become selective and discriminating.

Czechoslovak industry has tried since 1967 to encourage and clarify thinking about design by its annual competition for 'the year's outstanding product'. A typical year might produce some 700 entries which are reduced to a third in number. The Czech Council of Industrial Design brings these before an eminent and representative jury. The exacting and arduous task of making a final selection takes some time and makes allowance for the design, engineering and performance standards. Each entry has to be compared with goods of a similar character representing the peak of what is produced abroad. Further account is taken of the scope or practical application of the product, its economic contribution, the volume and period of its serial manufacture, and even its packaging design, whenever the latter forms an integral part of the product.

The entries often reflect the fact that in many factories design problems have not yet been sufficiently thought out. In the first exhibition in 1967 eighteen entries won a final award and five of these were for objects in glass. In the range of ornamental and household glassware the highest awards were obtained by hand-moulded glass, which in recent years has shown some outstanding well-designed pieces. The glass designed by Ladislav Oliva at the Bohemia Glassworks at Poděbrady, making maximum use of the optimum properties of lead crystal glass (*plate 278*) was judged a winner at all levels.

The Design Council in London has a similar selection process for its Design Awards and a further prize is awarded for the most elegant design of the year. Den Permanente, the Danish display of well-designed goods in Copenhagen, has an independent jury to select work worthy of sale. In Japan manufacturers and exporters of table-ware register their original designs at a Design Centre. This Centre aims to guard against imitation, whether of Japanese or foreign origin, and to encourage the creation of original designs. It has also been long recognised in Scandinavia that the only way to sell glass which, by reason of high wages and the use of good materials, is expensive to produce, is to produce it to good design and try to keep ahead in that aspect. Indeed Finland's future economic growth has its foundations firmly in industry and the solution to most of its problems presupposes expansion of industrial output.

In days when it seems there is little technology cannot do in the creation of glass, large research studios are becoming more evident. The Murano glass firm of Fratelli Toso, under the energetic direction of the Toso brothers, has formed the 'Sezione di Produzione'. Accumulated knowledge and skill is put at the disposal of architects and designers. One development has been Giusto Toso's clear ribbed glass elements which loop together in loose chains to form curtain screens or chandeliers. The firm's 'Lagunna' range uses the same method of formation. The Japanese firm of Awashima was founded in 1956 as a development of the former Awashima Glass Design Institute.

In Israel it is years of experimentation first, and then the product second. Three years of trial workings went into the development of new glass processing for Lenoy's artistic glass creations in lamp design. Where conventional glass objects are produced by blowing, casting or pressing Lenoy fuses together laminations or sheets of glass. Painted designs or patterns are applied on the surface of the object, generally between layers.

An analysis of three glassmakers' catalogues selected at random and dated 1923, 1969 and 1973 shows something of the variety of shapes and articles on offer. It also shows how some English factories have relied over a long period on traditional cutting as the main decoration. The 1923 catalogue of Thomas Webb & Sons, the famous English lead crystal manufacturer, contained 46 pattern table services, of which 24 were cut, 6 richly cut, 2 engraved, 4 richly engraved, 6 etched and 4 available as plain. In addition there were 19 varieties of cut rose bowl, 12 cut salad bowls and an infinite variety of flower vases, candlesticks and electric lamps, jugs (including 16 cut varieties), toilet bottles, salts, sweet-dishes, etc. While comparisons are difficult in this field the same firm's 1963 list shows the availability of 16 pattern services, a reduction of two thirds in the endeavour to rationalise. All of it was, and is, full lead crystal, for the most part free-blown without much use of moulds.

The 1969 catalogue of Peill lead crystal, made by the German firm of Peill and Putzler of Duren, shows 27 named sets, each available in 3 to 5 different shapes and sizes. It is necessary to remember that the catalogue is concerned with 'gifts' and is therefore filled with illustrations of attractive cases, bowls, candlesticks and ashtrays. There is wide variety of shapes and sizes, but the concentration is on four or five basic articles with decoration among the most attractive of any lead crystal range.

Finally a look at the 1973 Iittala catalogue, the renowned Finnish firm. It divides its hand-blown glass (but with frequent use of the mould) into the two categories of utility and art glass. There are 93 patterns of utility glass, issued in a variety of sizes, and concentrated on the main areas of drinking glasses, decanters, jugs, bowls and candlesticks. The art glass section, from designs by Alvar Aalto, Timo Sarpaneva and Tapio Wirkkala, provides a further twenty-four patterns, many of them formed in wood-textured moulds (*plate 271*). Iittala tests its displays and packaging in the factory's experimental shop, a feature which, with advantage, could be more widely adopted. One needs to know about this in marketing machine-made glass to the general public.

It has been said that machine production results in monotony and uniformity but this is far from true. Experiments show that the variations are limitless and enable many different forms to be produced. The interplay of technology and design in glass was examined in 1968 by the Dutch designer, Andries D. Copier of Leerdam. He wrote:

'What may we expect, then, in the future. To my mind the answer is quite clear. To an increasingly greater extent, the objects that we use every day will be made by automation and their quality will be such as to raise the standard of living. . . . Alongside all this I foresee that there will have to be definite changes in handwork. Whether or not it can continue to exist at all will depend on its remaining substantially different from the products of full automation and this applies to glass as much as to any other type of product. New criteria will have to be established for hand-made glass, which will make possible a definite renewal'.

There is obviously room for further experiment with compromise between full machine production and that done by hand. The Japanese designer Masakichi Awashima has designed good glass (*plate 108*) to be mould-blown, and has taken this a stage further with his Shizuku Glass. This is made of the best quality semi-crystal, and in order to give it the soft, limpid quality of Japanese ceramics, the designer invented the special hand-made clay or stone moulds into which the liquid semi-crystal glass is poured and then blown. The feature of this glassware is that, in addition to the 'homespun' touch of the glass, the specialised skin shows the iridescent gleams of the diffused reflection, which becomes more evident when water is poured into it. Because of the raindrop-like pattern it was titled 'Shizuku' — Japanese for waterdrop.

In whatever is produced to sell, and the illustrations in this book show how wide the range is, the choice therefore reduces to the differences between mass production and hand-made glass. The control of production of millions of glasses, each exactly as the previous one from the machine can be computer-controlled. This will also enable variation of form to be produced from the same amount of material, and control all the necessary requirements of size, thickness, weight and other critical factors.

Handwork will inevitably still incorporate the individuality and chance happenings — the turning of accident to success — and the championing of causes which are dearly held, although difficult to express, in glass alone.

D = Designer M = Manufacturer O = Owner
The combination, 'DM' implies that the artist has both
designed and made the piece: occasionally the
abbreviation 'DE' is used specifying 'Designer and
Engraver'
s. = signed d. = dated h. = height w. = width
dia. = diameter

1 Bowl and two glasses, 1859, presumed to be part of
that shown by Morris & Co., at the 1862 Exhibition
D Philip Webb (England)
M James Powell, Whitefriars
O Victoria & Albert Museum, London,
   Inv. C.79–80, 1939; C.263, 1926

Historical glass 1870–1940

11 Two vases of green bubbled and streaked glass, known as 'Clutha' glass, late 1880s, hs. 5 in. and 3 in.
D   Christopher Dresser (England)
M   James Couper & Sons, Glasgow
O   Victoria & Albert Museum, London, Inv. Circ. 81 – 1952; 167 – 1952.

12 Vase and bowl, blown and cased, c.1895. hs. 3½ in. and 4 in. Made for Samuel Bing's *L'Art Nouveau* shop in Paris
DM Louis Comfort Tiffany, (U.S.A.)
O   Musée des Arts Décoratifs, Paris, Invs. 8202–3

International Modern Glass

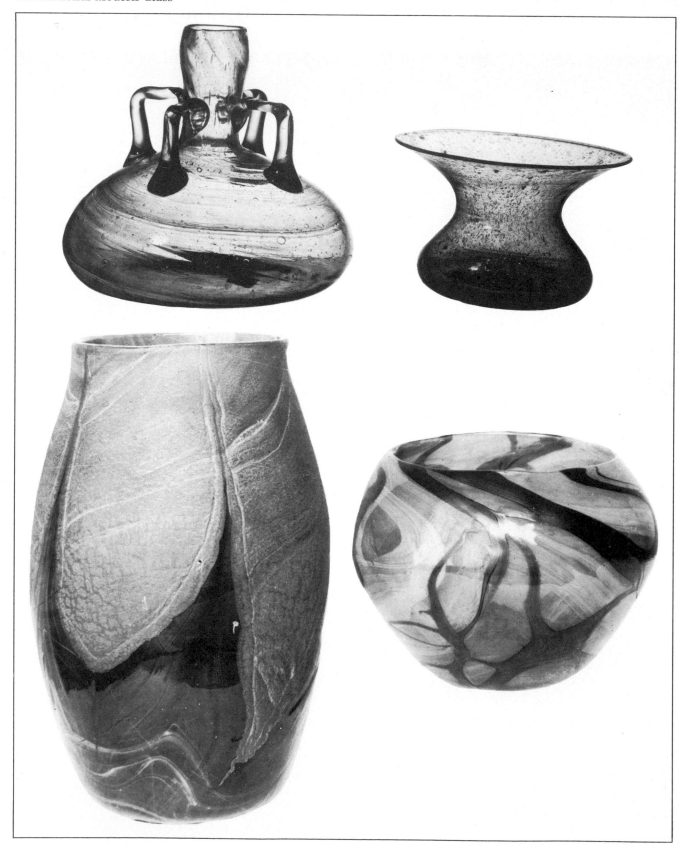

13 Vase and Bowl of green bubbled and streaked glass, the bowl also with aventurine patches; known as 'Clutha' glass, c.1896, hs. 5½ in. and 3 in.
D   George Walton (England)
M   James Couper & Sons, Glasgow
O   Victoria & Albert Museum, London,
    Inv. Circ. 109 – 1953; 227 – 1958

14 Vase, goblet and bowl, c.1892–1920,
left to right: vase, orange and violet cased glass, h. 4⅝ in. 'Favrile' glass; goblet, white, green and pink glass, h. 12 in.; bowl, iridescent 'Favrile' glass, h. 1⅜ in., dia. 4⅝ in.
M   Tiffany Glass Works, (U.S.A.)
O   The Toledo Museum of Art,
    Invs. 62,29; 62,73; 62,30

Historical glass

6   Plate, press-moulded. Design, with head of Queen
Victoria, patented in 1887
M   Sowerby & Co., Gateshead
O   Victoria & Albert Museum, London,
      Inv. Circ. 716 – 1966

International Modern Glass

6   Plate, press-moulded. Design, with head of Queen
Victoria, patented in 1887
M   Sowerby & Co., Gateshead
O   Victoria & Albert Museum, London,
      Inv. Circ. 716 – 1966

7   Goblet, blown, decorated with enamel colours, c.1880
DM Joseph Brocard (France)
O   Musée des Arts Décoratifs, Paris,
    Inv. 365

8   Vase, crackled glass tinted and splashed with colours
and gold, 1889, h. 6½ in.
DM Emile Léveillé (France)
O   Victoria & Albert Museum, London,
    Inv. C.77 – 1890

9   Vase, with 'smoked' pattern cased over, c.1884
DM Eugène Rousseau (France)
O   Musée des Arts Décoratifs, Paris,
    Inv. A.624

10   Vase, blown, crackled, colour-streaked and ribbed,
1889, h. 6 in.
DM Emile Léveillé (France)
O   Musée des Arts Décoratifs, Paris,
    Inv. 5690

Historical glass

53

2 'Elgin' vase, flint glass, blown and engraved, h. 15½ in.
DE John Northwood I, s. and d. 1873 (on base)
M   Stone, Fawdry and Stone, Birmingham;
    (glass-blower, Daniel Hancock)
O   City of Birmingham Art Gallery. Presented in 1878 by
    Sir Benjamin Stone (1845–1921)

3 'Elgin' claret jug, blown, engraved for the Paris
Exhibition, 1878, h. with stopper, 14¼ in.
DE Frederick Engelbert Kny (Bohemian, in England)
M   Thomas Webb & Sons, Stourbridge
O   Victoria & Albert Museum, London,
    Inv. C.32 & A. – 1960

International Modern Glass

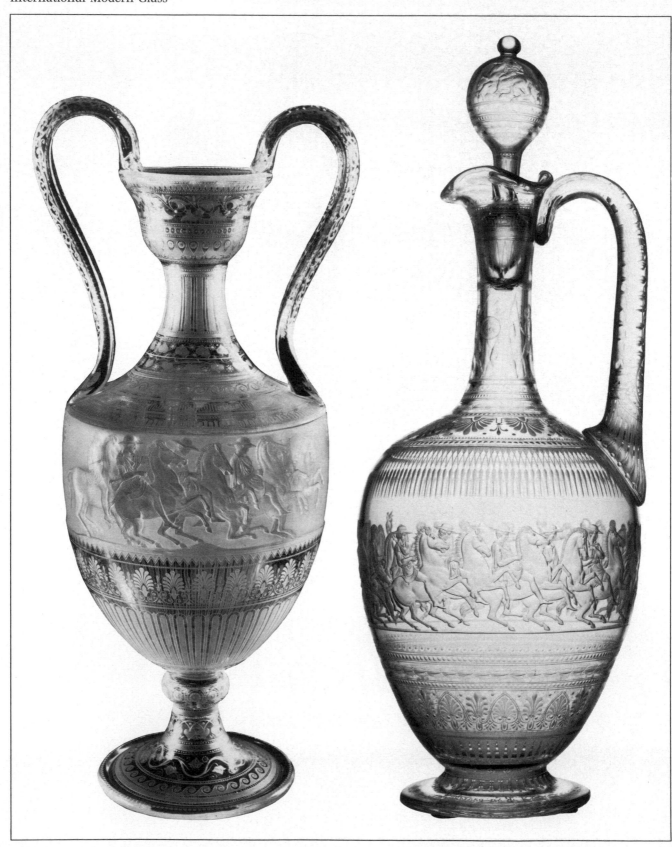

4 A group of Stourbridge glass, blown, cut and engraved, 1879–1894
left to right: bowl, 4½ in. dia., with six panels of 'rock crystal' design (S & W, 1894); decanter and stopper, h. 15 in., engraved by F.E. Kny, 1890; covered jar, engraved by J. Keller (S & W, 1884); cup and saucer, etched-out design in relief (S & W, 1884); vase, h. 9 in., engraved by F.E. Kny, 1880; wine-glass (S & W, 1885); decanter and stopper, rich cut spirals (S & W, 1890); oval basket with cut-out handle (S & W, 1879)

M Stevens and Williams (S & W), Brierley Hill; Kny items at Thomas Webb & Sons, Stourbridge
O Stevens and Williams; F. Kny, Esq.

5 Vase, translucent with Japanese pattern, c.1889, h. 4½ in.
D Emile Gallé (France)
O Dr. Ada Polak

Historical glass

51

15   Two vases, blown and engraved, *c.*1900
DE   Emanuel Lorenz (Czechoslovakia)
M   Kamenický Šenov
O   Museum of Industrial Art, Prague

International Modern Glass

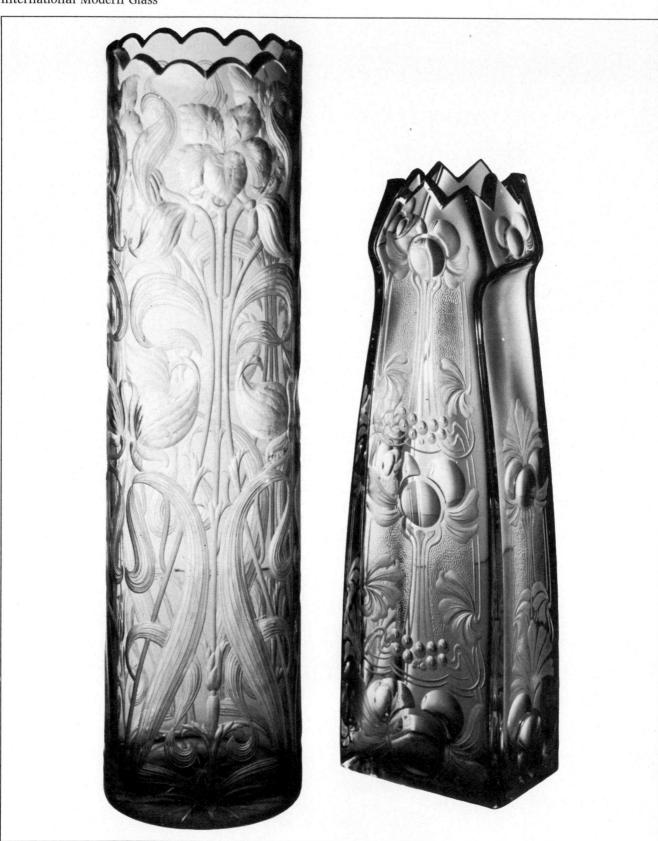

16   Vase, blown, blue-violet iridescence, banded and combed, *c.*1898, h. 11½ in.
DM Joh. Lötz Witwe, Klostermühle, Austria
O   The Toledo Museum of Art, Inv. 66,119

17   Vase, pink mother of pearl with iridescent dark purple base, *c.*1902, h. 7 in.
DM Joh. Lötz Witwe, Klostermühle, Austria
O   Manchester Polytechnic, Faculty of Art,
      Inv. 50/1902, acquired from Liberty & Co., 1902
18   Vase, streaked in simulated mother-of-pearl, *c.*1902, h. 9 in.
DM Freidrich Zitzmann, Wiesbaden, Germany
O   Manchester Polytechnic, Faculty of Art,
      Inv. 53/1902, acquired from Liberty & Co., 1902

Historical glass

29   Bas-relief in pâte de verre, *c*.1900, 12 × 11 in.
DM Henri Cros (France)
O   Musée des Arts Décoratifs, Paris,
      Inv. 34666A

International Modern Glass

30 Bowl, blown, cased, cut and etched, *c.*1900, h. 5 in.
D   Gunnar Gunnarsson Wennerberg (Sweden)
M   Kosta Glass, Sweden
O   Kosta, factory collections.
    Wennerberg made his glass in the same way as Gallé
    and similar to his style, but was somewhat more
    formal in approach than the French artist.

31 (A) Bowl, in pâte de verre, *c.*1898
DM Albert Dammouse (France)
O   Musée des Arts Décoratifs, Paris,
    Inv. 14255

Historical glass

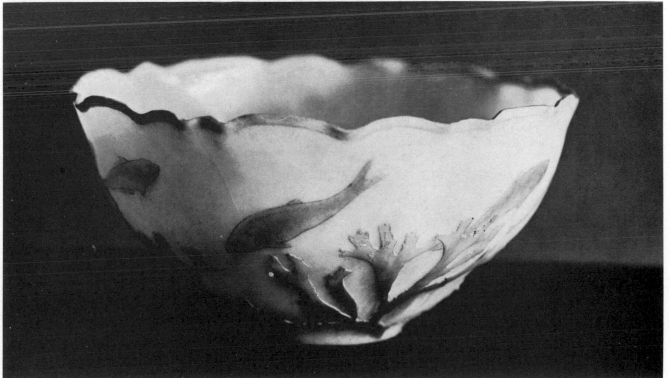

24   Vase and sweetmeat dish, c.1880–1900
above and below: vase, marquetry style, blown, cased and
cut, c.1900; sweetmeat dish, enamelled in the 18th
century style of Preissler, c.1880
DM Emile Gallé (France)
O   Richard Dennis, Esq.

25   Vase, blown and engraved with scenes of *putti* on
snails, c.1900, h. 11 in.
DM Emile Gallé (France)
O   Musée des Arts Décoratifs, Paris
      Inv. 4533

International Modern Glass

26   Vase, marquetry style, mounted in silver, *c.*1900,
h. 9 in.
DM Emile Gallé (France)
O   Richard Dennis, Esq.

27   Vase, colour enamelled, *c.*1890, h. 13 in.
DM Emile Gallé (France)
O   Musée des Arts Décoratifs, Paris,
    Inv. 7649

28   Vase, iridescent amber glass with overlay Iris pattern,
*c.*1900, h. 14½ in.
DM Emile Gallé (France), s. 'Gallé'
O   The Toledo Museum of Art,
    Inv. 51.360

Historical glass

19 Vase, in form of conch-shell with applied polychrome tail, after 1900, h. 12 in.
DM Daum (France) s. 'Daum, Nancy'
O   Musée des Arts Décoratifs, Paris, Inv. 36315

20 Vase, blown, cased, and cameo cut, 1900, h. 11½ in.
DM Emile Gallé (France) for the Paris Exhibition of 1900. The silver mounting was designed by Bonvallet of Cardeilhac, rue Royale, Paris

O   Musée des Arts Décoratifs, Paris, Inv. 27982

21 Vase, silver foil encased between an inner and outer layer of glass and streaked with green to simulate tree forms, c.1900, h. 10½ in. Known as 'Silveria Glass'
M   Stevens & Williams, Brierley Hill, England, (marked on base)
O   Victoria & Albert Museum, London, Inv. Circ. 391 – 1964

International Modern Glass

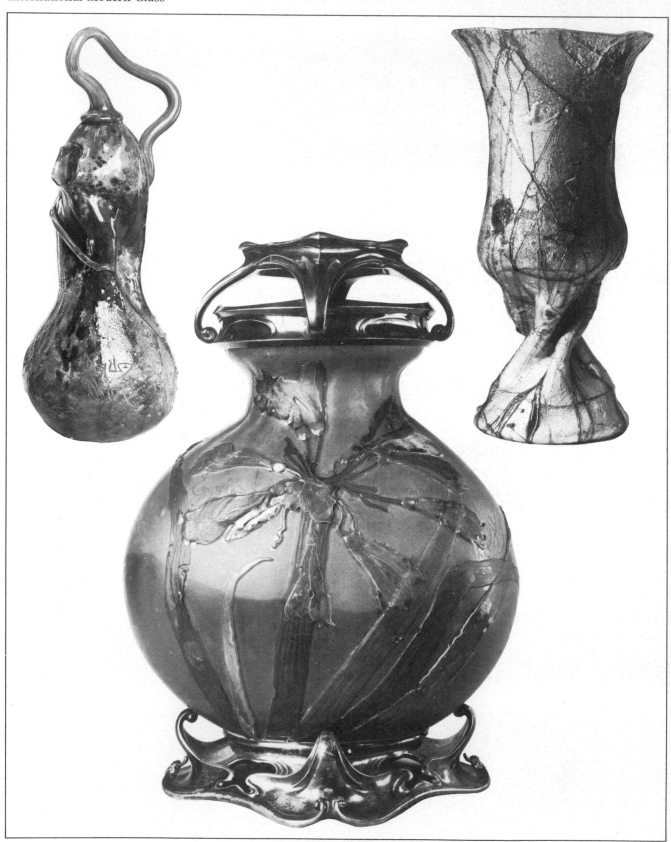

22   Vase, blown in brown and amethyst glass, *c.*1900
h. 8½ in.
DM Eugène Michel (France)
O   Musée des Arts Décoratifs, Paris,
       Inv. 14393

23   Vase, jug and stopper and vase, *c.*1885–1900
left to right: vase, commercial type, acid-engraved, with
inset cabochons, *c.*1900; enamelled jug and stopper,
*c.*1885; enamelled vase, acid-eaten background
DM Emile Gallé (France)
O   Richard Dennis, Esq., London

Historical glass

31 (B) Vase in pâte de verre, *c.*1900, h. 5 in.
DM Albert Louis Dammouse (1848–1926) France
O Musée des Arts Decoratifs, Paris

32 Group of 'German or Netherland style' glass made for William Morris & Co., blown, coiled and prunt decorations in green glass, *c.*1903
M James Powell & Sons, London
O Manchester Polytechnic, Faculty of Art, Inv. 14/1903. Acquired from William Morris & Co., 1903

International Modern Glass

33 (A) & (B)   'Cleopatra', drawing by George Woodall
(1850–1925) for his 18 in. cameo glass plaque made at
Thomas Webb & Sons, Stourbridge, *c.*1900

Historical glass

34 Communion cruet, blown, and silver-mounted, hallmarks of 1900, h. 7½ in.
M   James Powell & Sons, London
O   Manchester Polytechnic, Faculty of Art

35 Vase, blown, c.1895, h. 8¾ in.
M   James Powell & Sons, London
O   Manchester Polytechnic, Faculty of Art. Acquired in 1902

36 Flower vase, streaked blue glass, c.1900, h. 15 in.
M   James Powell & Sons, London. Bronze stand wrought by W.A. Benson of W.A. Benson & Co.
O   Manchester Polytechnic, Faculty of Art, Inv. 1903/3a and b

37 Three wine flasks, blown soda-glass, 1902
M   Salviati, Venice
O   Manchester Polytechnic, Faculty of Art. Acquired from maker in 1902

International Modern Glass

38   Blown Table Glass shown at St. Louis International
Exhibition, 1904
left to right: dented goblet; beaker with glass 'tears';
decanter after a Florentine flask; decanter mounted with
hammered silver; decanter based on drawing of a vase in
a picture in the Uffizi Gallery; two-handled vase with
thread and prunts; goblet with prunts on triangular
twisted stem
M   James Powell & Sons, London

39   Two-handled vase, with thread and prunt
decoration, *c.*1902, h. 6 in.
M   James Powell & Sons, London
O   Manchester Polytechnic, Faculty of Art

40   Two beakers, blown, one with applied trails, and
engraved with flowers, *c.*1902, h. 4½ & 6½ in.
DM George Walton
O   Manchester Polytechnic, Faculty of Art.
      Acquired from G. Walton in 1902

Historical glass

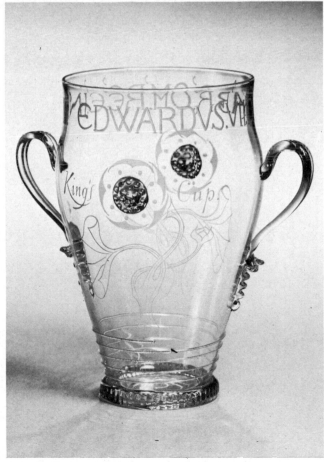

41 Vase, blown lead glass, iridescent gold with applied glass threading, 1912–25, h. 10 in.
M Durand Glass Co., Vineland, New Jersey, U.S.A.
O The Toledo Museum of Art, Inv. 64.139

42 Vase, in pâte de verre, 1912, h. 7 in.
DM François-Emile Décorchemont
O Musée des Arts Décoratifs, Paris, Inv. 18501

43 Vase, with applied representation of vegetable forms, 1913, 7¾ in.
DM René Lalique
O Musée des Arts Décoratifs, Paris, Inv. 19309

International Modern Glass

44   Vase blown with colour threads in body, 1920, h. 17 in.
D   Alex Johnsson (Sweden)
M   Iittala (Finland) for the first Finnish National Fair, 1920
O   Iittala factory collection

45   Bowl (sometimes with cover) in greenish glass, c.1918, h. 9 in.
D   Edvin Ollers (Sweden)

M   Kosta Glass, Sweden
O   Kosta, factory collections.
    A covered example in grey glass may be seen in the Nationalmuseum, Stockholm

46   Bowl, blown, decorated in enamels, c.1920, h. 6 in.
DM Marcel Goupy (France)
O   Musée des Arts Décoratifs, Paris, Inv. 21822

Historical glass

47   Detail of engraving on cut crystal vase 'Vine' shown in Plate 48

48   Vase, blown, cut lines and engraved scenes, entitled 'Vine', 1922, h. 7½ in.
DE   Jaroslav Horejc (Czechoslovakia)
M   Stephan Rath's studio (Lobmeyr), North Bohemia, Kamenický Šenov
O   Museum of Industrial Art, Prague.
      Some replicas were made in 1960 at Borské Sklo

49   Covered bowl, blown and cut, entitled 'Carousel', c.1920, dia. 11½ in.
DC   Ewald Dahlskog (Sweden)
M   Kosta Glass, Sweden
O   Kosta, factory collections

International Modern Glass

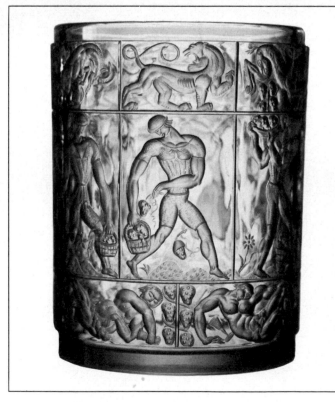

50 Vase, moulded in opaque glass, *c.* 1925, h. 10½ in.
DM René Lalique (France)
O Musée des Arts Décoratifs, Paris,
    Inv. 27667

51 Detail of vase (shown in Plate 50) by René Lalique

52 Glass fountain, illuminated at night, 1925
DM René Lalique (France)
    The fountain was a feature of the 1925

'L'Exposition des Arts Décoratifs' in Paris.
Photographed from *Art et Décoration*, 1925

53 Vase, frosted and clear glass, with four applied and
carved plaques of horses, entitled the 'Camargue Vase',
*c.*1920, h. 11⅜ in.
DM René Lalique
O The Toledo Museum of Art,
    Inv. 47.43

Historical glass

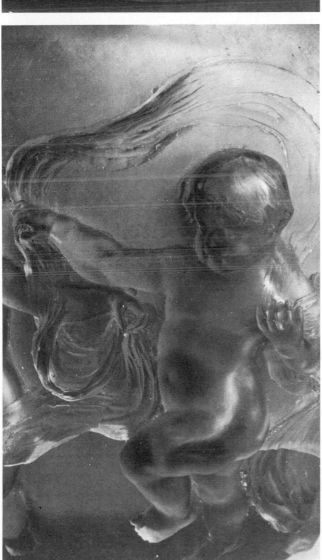

54 Standing cup and cover, blown, cut, and engraved with three allegorical heads, 1926, h. 17½ in.
DE Ladislav Přenosil (Czechoslovakia)
M Železný Brod
O Museum of Industrial Art, Prague

55 Vase, lead glass, blown, cut and engraved, 1925, h. 13½ in.
DE George Woodall (England), s. 'Geo Woodall'
M Thomas Webb & Sons, Stourbridge
O Philip Budrose, Esq., Marblehead, Mass., U.S.A.

56 Vase, blown and cut, 1929, entitled 'Empire Vase' and made for the Barcelona World Fair, 1929
M Iittala Glass, Finland
O Iittala, factory collections

International Modern Glass

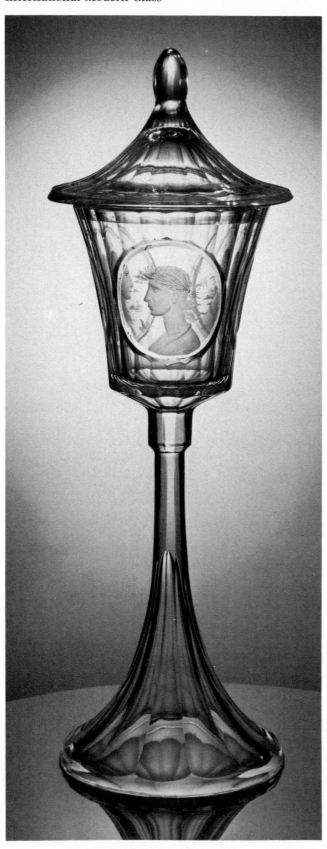

57 Vase with cover, coloured in green, acid-etched, c.1919, h. 16 in.
DM Maurice Marinot (France)
O Musée des Arts Décoratifs, Paris, Inv. 21633

58 Flask and stopper, acid-roughened surface, enamel decoration, 1925, h. 5½ in.
DM Maurice Marinot (France)
O Victoria & Albert Museum, London, Inv. C.2 & A, 1964

59 Flask and stopper, clear glass, enclosed air bubbles, surface acid-etched and wheel cut, 1932, h. 9⅝ in.
DM Maurice Marinot at Bar-sur-Seine, France
O Victoria & Albert Museum, London, Inv. C.17 & A, 1964

60 Vase, clear glass, enclosed air bubbles, wheel cut. The bubbles are worked to depict the form of a face, 1934, h. 7¼ in.
DM Maurice Marinot (France)
O Victoria & Albert Museum, London, Inv. C.12 – 1964

Historical glass

61　Vase, clear glass, with green and black stain, called
'Graal', *c*, 1930, h. 8¼ in.
D　Edward Hald (Sweden)
M　Orrefors Glass, Sweden
O　The Toledo Museum of Art, Inv. 61.37

62　Standing Cup in dark glass 1923, h. 8 in.
D　Simon Gate (Sweden), blown by Knut Bergqvist
M　Orrefors Glass, Sweden
O　Orrefors, factory collections

63　Plate, clear glass, engraved
1928, dia. 10⅝ in.
D　Simon Gate (Sweden), engraved by Gustaf Abels
M　Orrefors Glass, Sweden
O　The Toledo Museum of Art, Inv. 48.30

64　Ice-bucket and plate, blown engraved, 1919, h. 12 in.
D　Edward Hald (Sweden)
M　Orrefors Glass, Sweden
O　Orrefors, factory collections; another in
　　Nationalmuseum, Stockholm

International Modern Glass

65   Vase, clear glass with pattern blown in, titled
'Ariel', c.1925–, h. 6¼ in.
D   Edward Öhrström (Sweden); s. 'Orrefors Sweden
Ariel No. E. Öhrström'
O   The Toledo Museum of Art, Inv. 48.29

66   Vase, blown and engraved, 1930, h. 8 in.
D   Vicke Lindstrand (Sweden)
M   Orrefors Glass, Sweden
O   Nationalmuseum, Stockholm

67   Vase, blown and engraved, 1925, h. 10 in.
D   Elis Bergh (Sweden), s. and d.
M   Kosta Glass, Sweden
O   Kosta, factory collections

68   Vase, blown, cut and acid-roughened, 1934, h. 9 in.
D   Sven Erik Skawonius (Sweden), s. and d., 1934
M   Kosta Glass, Sweden
O   Kosta, factory collections

Historical glass

69   Bowl and vase, blown and engraved, 1932, hs. 2¾ in.
and 5 in.
D   Keith Murray (England)
M   Stevens & Williams, Brierley Hill
O   Victoria & Albert Museum, London

70   Punch Bowl, and 8 of 24 cups, free-blown with
applied prunts and engraving, c.1933, h. 7¾ in. (bowl),
3 in. (cups)
D   A. Douglas Nash (U.S.A.)
M   Libbey Glass Company, Toledo, Ohio, U.S.A.
O   The Toledo Museum of Art,
     Inv. 68.59A, B1–24

International Modern Glass

71 Vase, blown and cut, *c.*1930–35, h. 8⅞ in.
M Baccarat Glass, France
O The Toledo Museum of Art,
    Inv. 48.3

72 Bowl, heavy glass with cut and engraved pattern;
cut base, called 'Gazelle' Bowl, 1935, dia. 6⅜ in.
M Steuben Glass, U.S.A.
O The Toledo Museum of Art,
    Inv. 36.36

73 Vase, blown and sand-blasted, 1937, h. 8 in.
DM Gunnel Nyman (Finland)
O Karhula Glass Museum, Finland.
    This vase was shown at the Paris World Fair in 1937

Historical glass

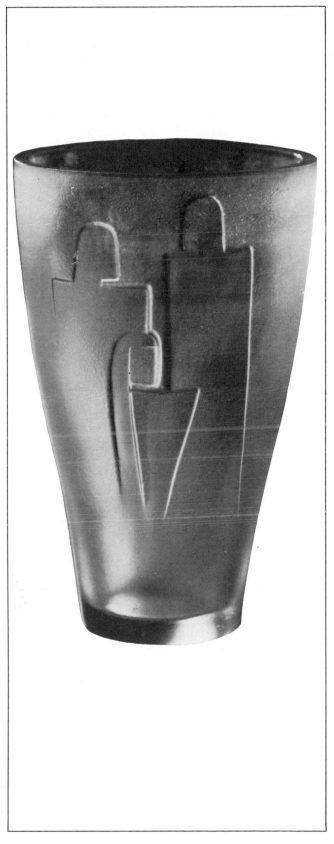

74   Bowl, blown and sand-blasted design of Zodiac signs, 1939, dia. 20¼ in.
D   Andreas Copier (Holland)
M   Royal Leerdam Glass, Holland
O   The Toledo Museum of Art,
     Inv. 40.39.
     This bowl was exhibited at the New York World
     Fair, 1939

75   Bowl, blown and cut to shape, 1939, h. 4 in.
DM Göran Hongell (Finland)
O   Karhula Glass Museum, Finland

International Modern Glass

76 Vase, clear glass with spiral cutting, 1939, h. 12½ in.
D Elis Bergh (Sweden)
M Kosta Glass, Sweden
O The Toledo Museum of Art,
   Inv. 40.42.

77 Vase, rose and opaque grey glass, flecked with gold,
swirling ribbing showing opaque white edge, 1950,
h. 8¼ in., dia. at top 11¾ in.
D Flavio Poli (Italy)

M Seguso Vetri D'Arte
O The Toledo Museum of Art,
   Inv. 54.50. Gift of the Italian Government

78 Vase and bowl, 1945, hs. 12 in. and 4 in. The vase
overlaid and cameo cut with engraved lines, the bowl
with enamel loops trailed inside
D Sven Erik Skawonius (Sweden)
M Kosta Glass, Sweden
O Kosta, factory collections

Historical glass

79   Vase, blown with colour threads, 1940, h. 10 in.
DM Paolo Venini (Italy)
O   Victoria & Albert Museum, London,
     Inv. Circ. 118 – 1958

International Modern Glass

'Peacock Feather' Vase, 1896–8. Ht 13 in.
DM Louis Comfort Tiffany (1848–1933), U.S.A.
Signed 'Louis C. Tiffany O 7260'
O   Kunstmuseum, Düsseldorf (Inv P. 1970–433)

Ornamental glass, lustre, in tulip form, 1896–98. Ht 12½ in.
DM Karl Koepping (1848–1914) Germany.
Signed 'Koepping'
O   Kunstmuseum, Düsseldorf (Inv P. 1970–34)

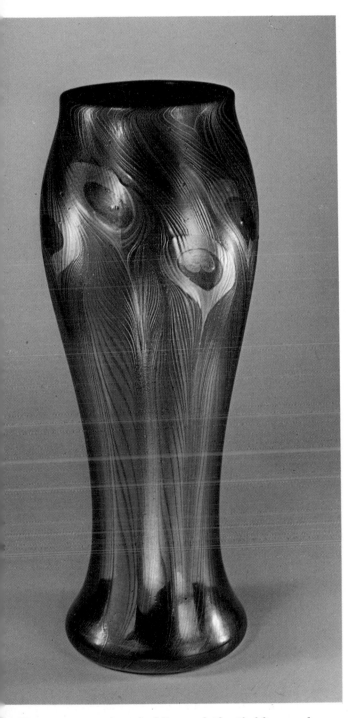

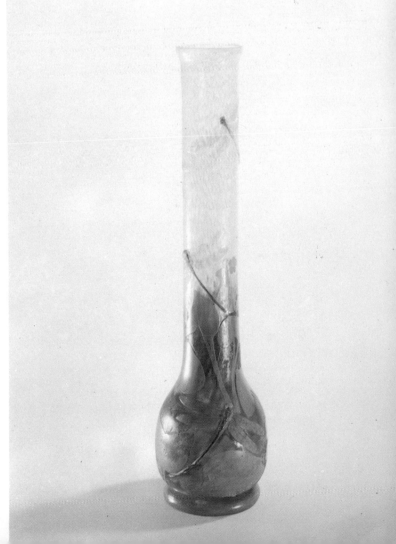

Vase, green, purple and white, overlaid with foliage and
dragon-fly, (1900–05) Ht 23 in.
DM Daum Frères at Nancy, France, Signed 'Daum Nancy'
O   Kunstmuseum, Düsseldorf (Inv P. 1970–117)

4   Bottle and stopper, in purple and opaque-red 1930. Ht with
    stopper 6⅜ in.
    DM Maurice Marinot (1882–1960), France, etched
    signature 'Marinot'
    O   Victoria and Albert Museum, London (Inv C 10 and
    A 1964. Given by Mlle. Florence Marinot in memory of
    Maurice Marinot).

80 Solid rods of glass in full crystal, subsequently cut.
Titled 'Metropolis', 1966
D   Mona Morales-Schildt (Sweden)
M   Kosta Glass, Sweden

81 The cutting of glass is done on a large steel wheel
assisted by a flux containing abrasive powders. Here at
the Orrefors Glassworks, in southern Sweden the cuts are
being smoothed on a large stone wheel with running water
to cool the glass and wheel. At this stage of decoration the
vase is of course fully formed, cold, and annealed.

Cut glass

82 Vase, cut to six sides (current)
D Varoslav Plátek (Czechoslovakia)
M Železný Brod

83 Two vases and an ashtray shaped by cut (current)
D Antonin Drobnik (Czechoslovakia)
M Železný Brod

84 Bowl, lead crystal with blue border and cut ball facets, titled 'Playing the water' (current)
D Mona Morales-Schildt (Sweden)
M Kosta Glass, Sweden

85 Vase, lead crystal with cut facets giving many reflections. First shown at the Expo '67 in Montreal
D Vladimir Žahour
M Bohemia Glass at Poděbrady

International Modern Glass

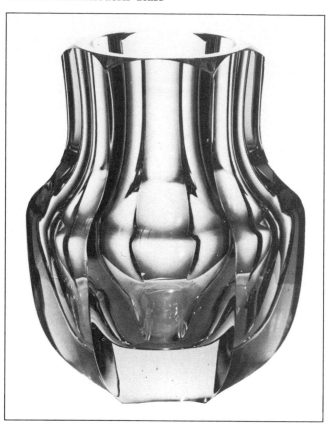

86   Glass block with cut holes and facets, 1970
DM Luboš Metelak (Czechoslovakia)

87   Paperweights, in 'Ventana' technique, lead crystal
with two layers of colour, cut both sides, 1964
D   Mona Morales-Schildt (Sweden)
M   Kosta Glass, Sweden

Cut glass

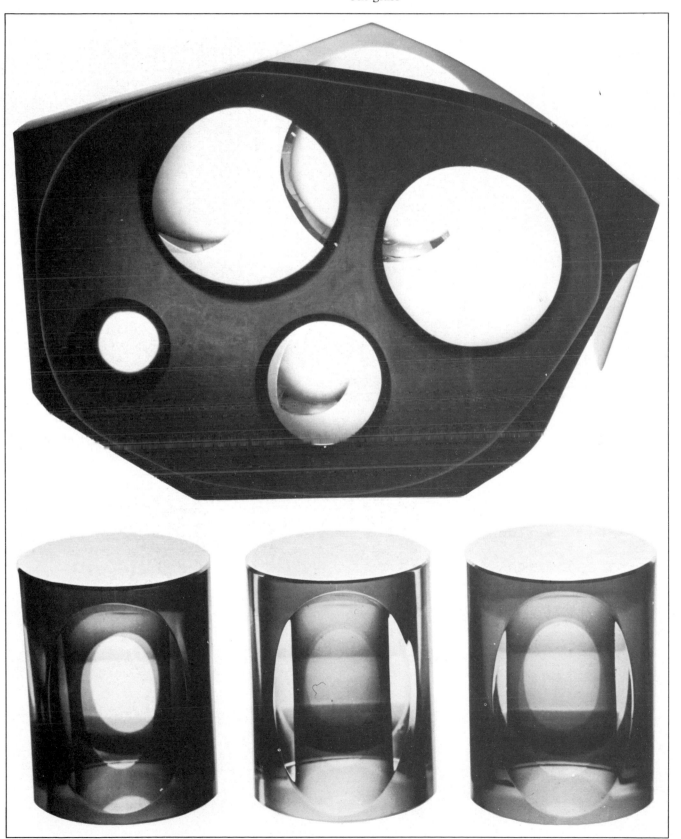

88 Vases, lead crystal, undulating cuts
D   Vladimir Žahour (Czechoslovakia)
M   Bohemia Glass at Podébrady

89 Vase, moulded and cut, 1967
D   S. Kasnirova (Czechoslovakia)
    Exhibited at Expo '67 in Montreal
O   Corning Museum of Glass, New York,
    Inv. 67.3.37

90 Vases, lead crystal, cut, titled 'Bodiam' (current)
D   David Hammond (England)
M   Thomas Webb & Sons, Stourbridge, England

International Modern Glass

91 Sphere of polished lead crystal resting freely on a disc in which has been cut a letter 's', 1969
D Floris Meydam (Holland)
M Royal Leerdam Glass

92 Crown of cut glass, titled 'Tiara', 1969
D Nanny Still McKinney (Finland)
M Riihimäki Lasi Oy

93 Column with deeply incised horizontal cuts, 1970
D Floris Meydam (Holland)
M Royal Leerdam Glass
O Mrs. Arthur Pilkington

Cut glass

94 Bowl, cut lead crystal, dia. 13 in.
D Konrad Habermeier (Germany)
M Staatliche Werkkunstschule, Schwäbisch Gmünd

95 Shallow bowl, lead crystal, polished cutting, dia.
12½ in. Current pattern 29850
D John Luxton (England)
M Stuart & Sons, Stourbridge, England

International Modern Glass

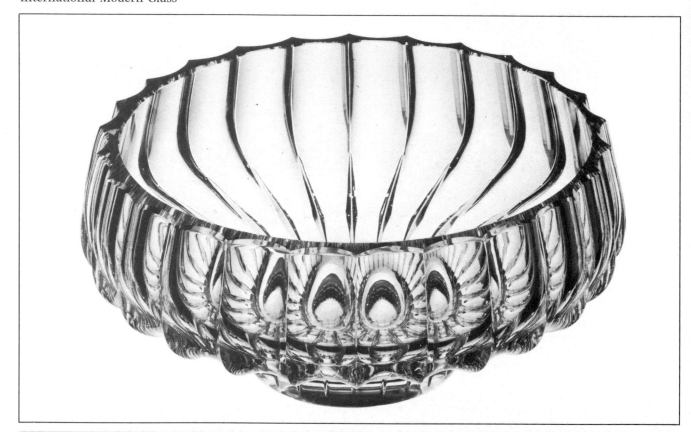

96   The process of 'cracking-off' the surplus glass from the bowls of glasses. The glass revolves against a diamond. A gas-jet plays on the diamond mark on the still revolving glass. It then becomes easy to break off the surplus. The gas-jet reheats the raw edge which melts to smoothness. Photographed at the Orrefors Glassworks in southern Sweden

97   Adding the hot glass to form the stem of a wine-goblet at the Orrefors Glassworks in southern Sweden

Table suites, vases, bowls

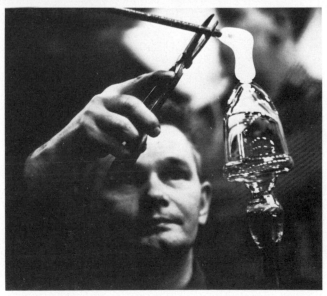

98   Set of four goblets, pale aquamarine, 1969
D   Magda Vadászi Németh (Hungary)
M   Ajkai Üveggyár, Ajka

99   Set of four goblets, to be used both sides, pale grey
and light amber, 1966
D   Mária Lecjaks (Hungary)
M   Parádi Üveggyár, Parádsasvár

International Modern Glass

100   Drinking glasses from the 'Perle' range. Ht. 4 to
6¼ in. (current)
D   Per Lütken (Denmark)
M   Kastrup-Holmegaard Glass, Denmark

101   Wine-glasses, blown, with thin stem and conical
hollow foot (current)
D   Nils Landberg (Sweden)
M   Orrefors Glass, Sweden

102   Wine-service, full lead crystal, titled 'Gracil' (current)
D   Vicke Lindstrand (Sweden)
M   Kosta Glass, Sweden

Table suites, vases, bowls

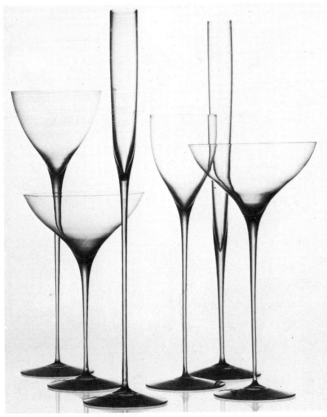

103 Wine service, clear glass (8 per cent lead content),
titled 'Victoria' (current)
D Frank Thrower (England)
M Dartington Glass, Devon

104 Stacking wine-glasses, clear or antique-grey colour,
(current)
D Severin Brorby (Norway)
M Hadelands Glass, Norway

International Modern Glass

105 Wine service, titled 'Narciso'
D   Isabel Giampietro (Italy: working in U.S.A.)
M   Production rights, Royal Leerdam Glass, Holland

106   Set of two goblets, 1970
D   Judit Kékesi Sipos (Hungary)
M   Parádi Üveggyár, Parádsasvár

108   'Saki-glass', mould-blown, 1959, h. 3⅛ in.
D   Masakichi Awashima (Japan)
M   Awashima Glass, Tokyo, Japan

107   Rose bowls, No. 499 (current)
The bowls, half filled with water are decorated with
floating rose-buds
D   Claus J. Riedel (Austria)
M   Tiroler Glashütte, Kufstein, Austria

Table suites, vases, bowls

109 'Drink Containers', set of three, handled, stemmed
and footed, in shades of green and smoke, 1970, hs.
7–8 in.
DM   Marvin B. Lipofsky (U.S.A.)

110   Various wine glasses, goblets and giant glasses, lead
crystal, (current)
D   Erik Höglund (Sweden)
M   Boda Glass, Sweden

International Modern Glass

111 Wine and fruit glasses, mould-blown in textured
moulds (1969). Titled 'Senator'
D Timo Sarpaneva (Finland)
M Iittala Glass, Finland

Table suites, vases, bowls

112 Carafe and glasses, lead crystal, engraved flower
patterns, 1969
D Monica Backström (Sweden)
M Boda Glass, Sweden

113 Schnapps glasses and decanter, cut facets, 1970
D Rolf Sinnemark (Sweden)
M Kosta Glass, Sweden

International Modern Glass

114 Decanter, ice-bucket and drinking glasses, 1970.
Titled 'Ice Pole'
D   Christer Holmgren (Denmark)
M   Kastrup-Holmegaards Glass, Denmark
     The 'ice' effect is achieved with the use of a special
     tool which forms the melted glass before it is blown.

Table suites, vases, bowls

115 Beer and whisky glasses, mould-blown
D   Erik Höglund (Sweden)
M   Boda Glass, Sweden

116 Wine-service, lead crystal, cut, (current). Titled
'Frensham'
D   David Hammond (England)
M   Thomas Webb & Sons, Stourbridge, England

5   Fun sculpture, blown form, unique item, Titled 'Bubble
Tree', 1968. Ht 16 in.
D   Ann and Goran Wärff (Sweden)
M   Kosta Glass, Sweden

International Modern Glass

6   Glass bowl, blown by a 'bubble glass' technique: unique
     item. 1968. Ht 9 in.
     D   Kaj Franck (Finland)
     M   Arabia Glass, Finland

117　Decanter and glasses, lead crystal, cut, (current).
Titled 'Knight'
D　Tom Hill (England)
M　Stevens & Williams, Brierley Hill, England

118　Flasks, lead crystal, mould-blown
D　Lars Hellsten (Sweden)
M　Skrufs Glass, Sweden

Table suites, vases, bowls

119 · Decorative bottle, mould-blown, 1968, titled
'Grapponia' available in clear, amber, blue, yellow
D   Nanny Still McKinney (Finland)
M   Riihimäen Lasi Oy, Finland

International Modern Glass

120 Standing cup and cover, blown lead crystal, cut, knopped stem and finial
D   Nils Landberg (Sweden)
M   Orrefors Glass, Sweden

121 Decanter and glasses, blown lead crystal, cut lines, 1969
D   Ingeborg Lundin (Sweden)
M   Orrefors Glass, Sweden

122 The Orrefors Glass Company guest house and artists' studios set in the forests of southern Sweden

Table suites, vases, bowls

123 Decanter, lead crystal, engraved, *c*.1959. Titled 'Lace Flowers'
DE Jane Webster (England)

124 Decanter and glasses, lead crystal, blown, 1969
D Gunnar Cyrén (Sweden)
M Orrefors Glass, Sweden

125 Decanter and Burgundy glasses, blown, potash crystal, 1965, No. 2027
D H. Löffelhardt (Germany)
M Vereinigte Farbenglaswerke, Zwiesel, Germany

126 Vases, blown, with colour bands, Nos. 4414 (right), 4462
M Venini, Murano, Italy

International Modern Glass

127   Bottle, clear glass, with multicoloured *latticinio*
decoration, 1959, h. 24 in.
D   Dino Martens (Italy)
M   Vetreria A. Toso, Murano

128   Bottle, blue and green stripes, 1959, h. 18⅛ in.
D   Paolo Venini (Italy)
M   Venini, Murano, Italy

Table suites, vases, bowls

129 Decanter, with stopper, 1964, h. 10 in.
D   Andries Copier (Holland)
M   Royal Leerdam Glass, Holland
O   The Corning Museum of Glass,
    Inv. 64.3.119

International Modern Glass

130   Paperweights and doorstops, clear, amethyst or blue,
various sizes, 1969
D   R. Stennett-Willson (England)
M   Wedgwood Glass (formerly King's Lynn Glass)

131   Candlesticks, and 8-layer party tray
D   Erik Höglund (Sweden)
M   Boda Glass, Sweden

Table suites, vases, bowls

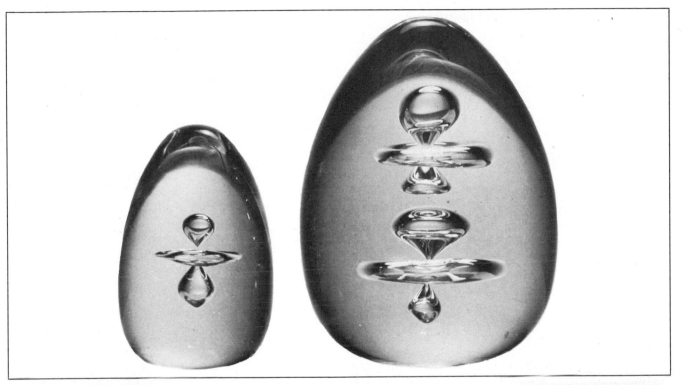

132   Vase, with parts blown in a wire mould, 1969
D   Bertil Vallien (Sweden)
M   Åfors Glass, Sweden

133   Vase, blown lead crystal, 1971. Titled 'Harmonikka'
D   Tamara Aladin (Finland)
M   Riihimäen Lasi Oy, Finland

134   Punch Bowl and glasses, 1972
D   Erkkitapio Siiroinen (Finland)
M   Riihimäen Lasi Oy, Finland

135   Abstract composition of mould-blown forms, cut cylinders, etc.
D   Betha and Teff Sarasin (Switzerland)
M   Salviati & C., Venice, Italy

International Modern Glass

136   Three vases, cased with colour over clear glass,
(current)
D   Luciano Gaspari (Italy)
M   Salviati & C., Venice, Italy

Table suites, vases, bowls

137 Candle lanterns, 1973. Titled 'Lighthouse'
D   Nanny Still McKinney (Finland)
M   Riihimäki Lasi Oy, Finland

138 Candle-holders, in blue, amethyst and clear, 1969
D   R. Stennett-Willson (England)
M   Wedgwood Glass (formerly King's Lynn Glass)

139 Silvered glass candle-holder
D   Monica Backström (Sweden)
M   Boda Glass, Sweden

International Modern Glass

140 Vase, mould-blown, 1962
D Sergio Asti (Italy)
M Salviati & C., Venice, Italy.
  Awarded the 'Golden Compasses Award', 1962
141 Vase, lead crystal with metallic oxide decoration,
h. 13 in.
DM Staatliche Fach und Ingenierschule für Glas, Zwiesel,
  Germany
O Landesgewerbeamt Baden-Württemberg, Stuttgart,
  Germany

142 'Vetmoul' glass vase, in grey, 1969, h. 13 in.
D Masakichi Awashima (Japan)
M Awashima Glass, Tokyo, Japan

Table suites, vases, bowls

143 Vase, oval, cut lead glass, some polished facets, h. 9½ in.
D Konrad Habermeier (Germany)
M Staatliche Werkkunstschule, Schwäbisch Gmünd, Germany

144 Two bowls, blown lead crystal, opaque with red splashes, unique, 1974
D Inkeri Toikka (Finland)
M Arabia Glass, Finland

145 Vase and plate, blown, and pressed in wooden moulds, 1966
M Timo Sarpaneva (Finland)
M Iittala Glass, Finland

International Modern Glass

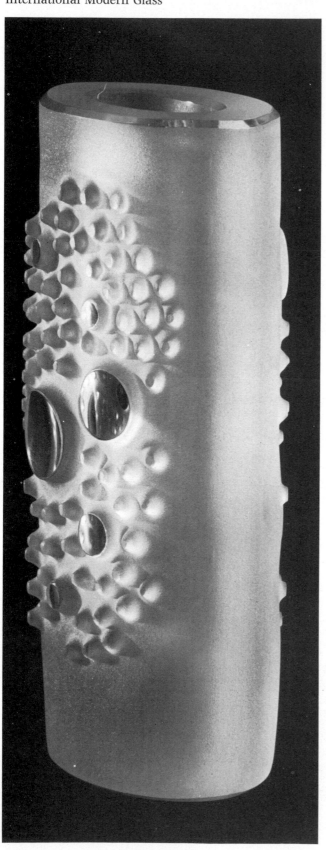

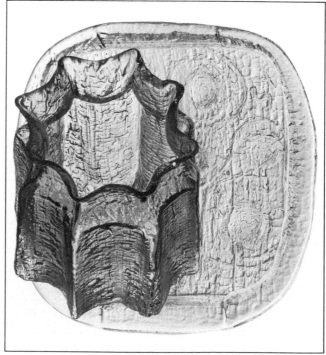

146 Detail of plate rolled in sawdust, combustible gas
'blisters' surface
D   Erik Höglund (Sweden)
M   Boda Glass, Sweden

147 Bowl, blown in a prepared wood mould, 1969
D   Tapio Wirkkala (Finland)
M   Iittala Glass, Finland

Table suites, vases, bowls

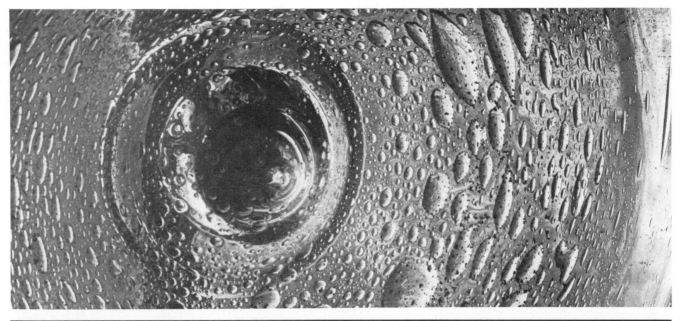

148   Bowl, threaded surface, titled 'Stresa'
D   Marc Lalique (France)
M   Lalique et Cie., Paris, France

International Modern Glass

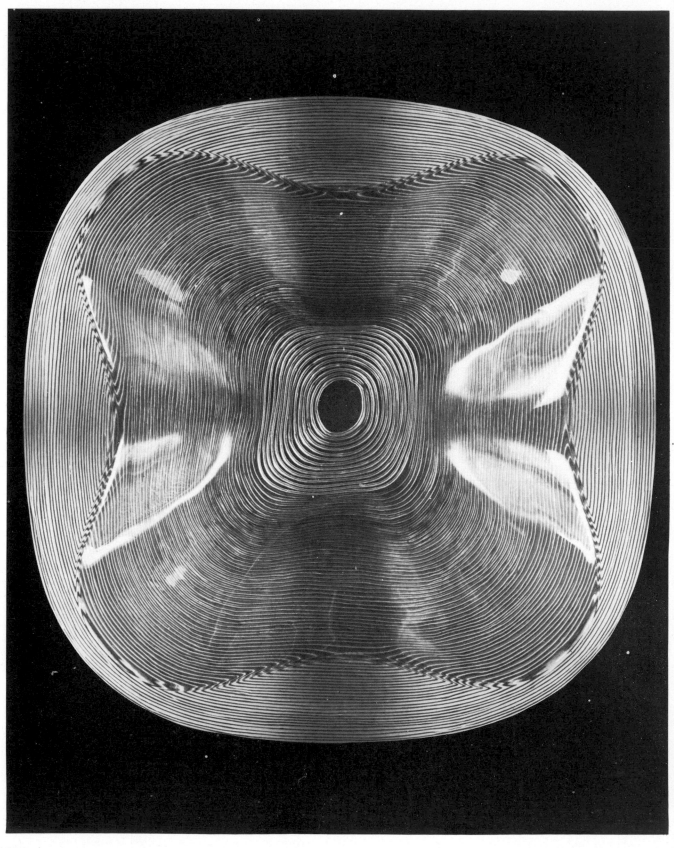

149   Bowl, blown, lead crystal, cut grooves, 1969
D   Ingeborg Lundin (Sweden)
M   Orrefors Glass, Sweden

150   Bowl, etched and engraved, colour layer inside and outside, 1968, dia. 8 in. h. 5½ in.
D   Ann and Göran Wärff (Sweden)
M   Kosta Glass, Sweden

Table suites, vases, bowls

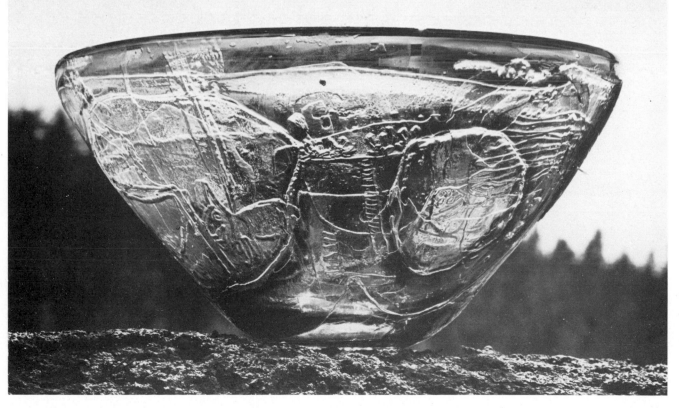

151 Dish, lead crystal, cased into a mould, gathered on the rod, heated and turned so that the edge gets 'life', 1968, dia. 8 in.
D   Ann and Göran Wärff (Sweden)
M   Kosta Glass, Sweden

152 Glass jars, blown lead crystal, in clear red and green, unique, 1974
D   Kerttu Nurminen (Finland)
M   Arabia Glass, Finland

International Modern Glass

153 Vase, lead crystal formed as a flower, titled 'Ingrid',
(current)
D   Marc Lalique (France)
M   Lalique et Cie., Paris, France

Table suites, vases, bowls

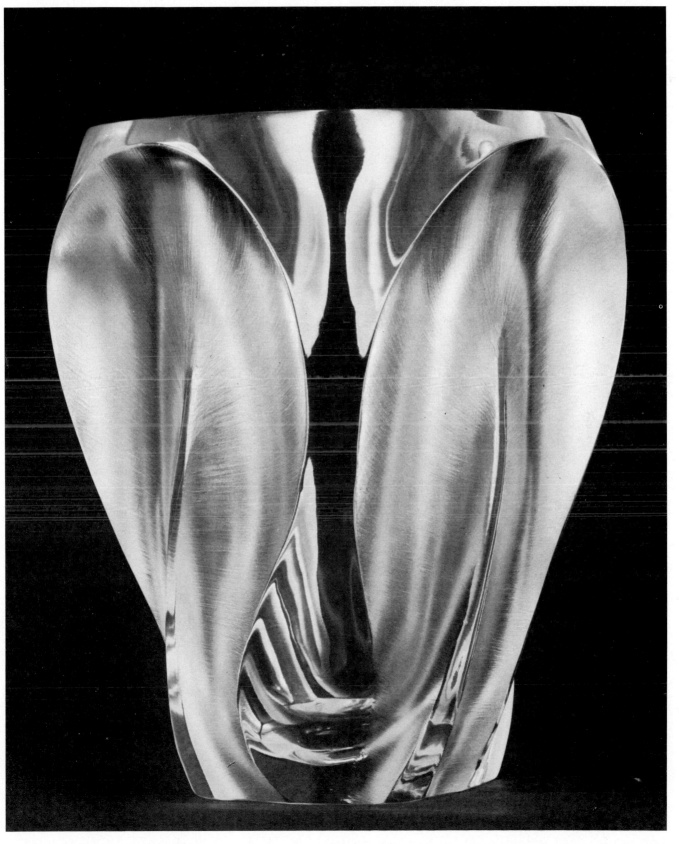

154   Dish, ovenproof glass, (current)
D   H. Löffelhardt (Germany)
M   Jenaer Glass, Mainz, Germany

155   Bowl, pale amber-grey, 1959, dia. 13 in.
D   Josef Stadler (Germany)
M   Gralglashütte GmbH, Dürnau/Göppingen, Germany.
      Exhibited at Corning Museum, New York, 'Glass 1959',
      No. 114

International Modern Glass

156 Vase, in shape derived from glass in pictures by Veronese, c.1921–24 (still produced on occasion)
D Paolo Venini with Giacomo Cappellin (Italy)
M Vetri Soffiati Muranesl Cappellin-Venini & C; (later Venini & C, Murano, Italy)

157 Standing vase, five tiers, blown and engraved, 1965, titled 'Hanging Garden'
D Bjørn Wiinblad (Denmark)
M Rosenthal, Studio Line, Germany

Table suites, vases, bowls

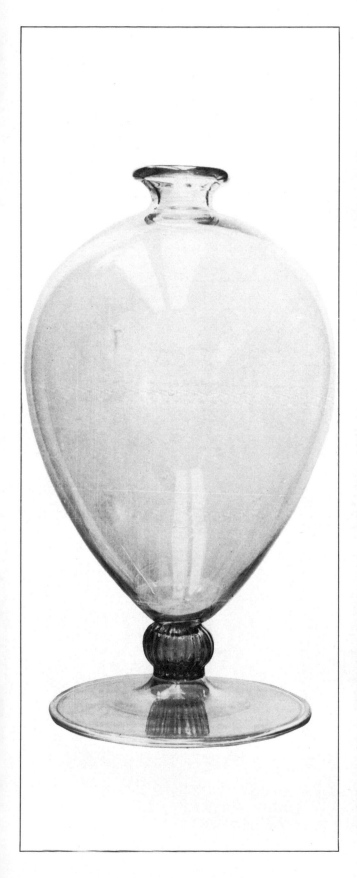

158 Set of glass for spiced wine; part of the dinner-table service in glass porcelain and silver. Titled 'Romanze-Dreiklang'
D   Bjørn Wiinblad (Denmark)
M   Rosenthal, Studio Line, Germany

159 Bowl, lead crystal, cut and polished flutes and facets, 1965, dia. 8 in. Tilted 'Queensway', No. 6514Q
D   Lord Queensberry (England)
M   Webb Corbett, Stourbridge, England

International Modern Glass

160 The copper-wheel engraver uses copper wheels attached to a small lathe. The wheels are moistened with a mixture of fine emery powder and oil

161 A copper-wheel engraver at Orrefors Glass in southern Sweden copying a design by resident designer Sven Palmqvist, 1968

Various forms of engraving

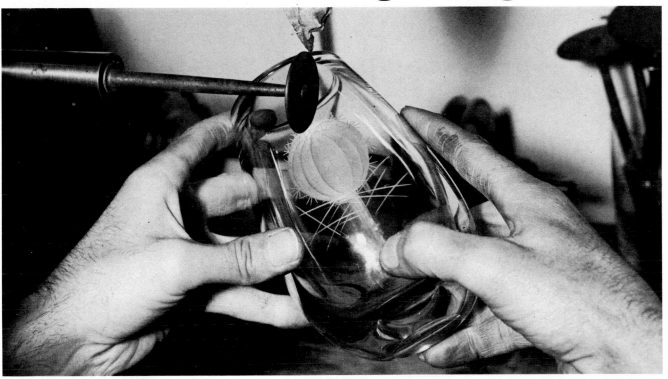

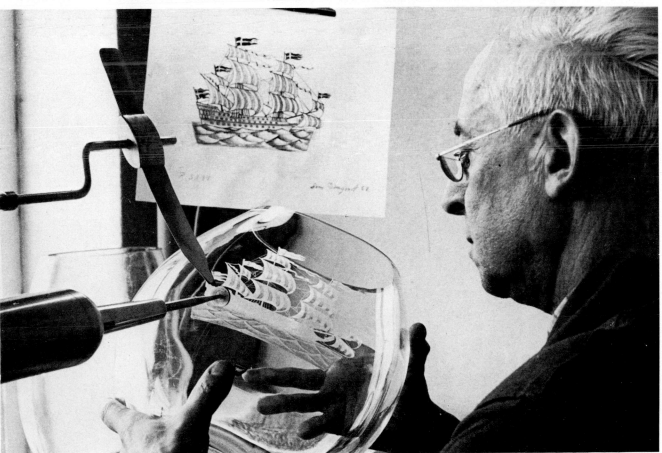

162   Detail of engraving on 'Campanile', a glass sculpture,
1951
D   Tapio Wirkkala (Finland)
M   Iittala Glass, Finland. Exhibited at the Milan Triennale,
1951

163   Bowl, blown, lead crystal, engraved
D   Erik Höglund (Sweden)
M   Boda Glass, Sweden

164   Bowl, blown, lead crystal, engraved
D   Sven Palmqvist (Sweden)
M   Orrefors Glass, Sweden

International Modern Glass

165   Vase, blown, lead crystal as rectangle, engraved birds on front, and etched representation of façade of Strasbourg Cathedral on back, 1969
DE   John Selbing (Sweden)
M   Orrefors Glass, Sweden

166   Two crystal forms, one set on top of the other to form a mirror image at the centre, 1963, Width 8 in. An interpretation of John Holmes's poem 'The Certainty' and commissioned for the collection 'Poetry in Crystal'

D   Donald Pollard (U.S.A.)
E   Dale Joe (U.S.A.)
M   Steuben Glass, New York

167   Ornamental plaque on wooden base, engraved with a traditional representation of the Hindu Spring Festival of Krishna and Radha
D   Rama Maharana (India)
M   Steuben Glass, New York

Engraving

168   Crystal bulb rising to three fern fronds and engraved
with the sleeping figure of Rip Van Winkle, h. 12 in.
D   James Houston (Canada)
M   Steuben Glass, New York

International Modern Glass

169   Lager glass, blown, and engraved with the opening lines of 'The Lark Ascending' by George Meredith arranged by Vaughan Williams for violin and orchestra, 1964 (on a Swedish glass)
DE Simon Whistler (England)

170   Goblet, lead crystal, engraved with initial 'D' and fruiting vine with birds, h. 6½ in.
DE Peter Dreiser (Germany: working in England)

171   Glass plate, engraved with inscription and names commemorating its presentation to Szymon and Maria Goldberg by the Netherlands Chamber Orchestra, 1965.
DE Simon Whistler (England)

Engraving

172 Jug, blown, and engraved with a dedicatory
inscription for Sir Joseph Hutchinson, Professor of
Agriculture at Cambridge
DE David Peace (England), on a Swedish Orrefors jug

173 Presentation cup, blown, lead crystal, engraved.
Presented to the City of Bristol by the Gloucestershire
Regiment, 1960
E   Cyril Kimberley (England)
M   Thomas Webb & Sons, Stourbridge, England

174 Asymmetrically cut plate of ½ inch optical glass
bent to a shallow curve and copper-wheel engraved on
the back with a 'comedy' mask. On a polished dark green
marble base, 1974, h. 11 in. Known as the Pye Comedy
Script Award and presented annually
DE Jane Webster (England)

International Modern Glass

175 Asymmetrically cut plate of ½ inch optical glass bent to a shallow curve, and copper-wheel engraved with a representation of Pegasus flying over the sun. The sun's corona diamond-point engraved. On a rosewood base, 1969, h. 15 in. Known as the 'Victor Ludorum Ronson Trophy' for the Horse of the Year Show.
DE Jane Webster (England)

176 Wine bottle, cut off, green glass, carved in relief by carborundum and diamond, commemorating man's first orbit round the moon, December 24, 1968, h. 4 in.
DE Peter Dreiser (Germany: working in England)

177 Glass Slab designed to be photographed as a Christmas card, 1968, h. 6 in.
DE David Peace (England)

Engraving

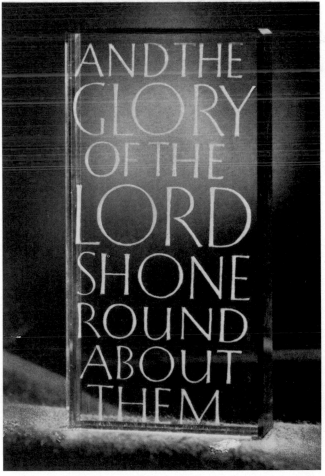

178 Vase, lead crystal, engraved with figures representing 'Cooperation among Nations', 1958, h. 17 in. DE Pavel Hlava (Czechoslovakia)

179   Asymmetrically cut piece of ½ inch optical glass bent to a shallow curve with a polished faceted bevel. Decorated in shallow sandblast, copper-wheel engraved with diamond-point detailing, h. 13½ in. 1973
DE Jane Webster (England)
O   Philip Whatmoor Esq.

180   Goblet, blown and engraved with 'Angel Musician', 1959, h. 6 in.
DE Helen Monro Turner (Scotland)
O   C.C. Manley, Esq.

International Modern Glass

181 Glass font, carborundum engraving on outside of bowl. Letters derived from an 11th century Spanish form: 'Renounce the devil and all his works: believe in God and serve him', 1962, h. 18 in.
DE David Peace (England)

182 Jardiniere, blown and engraved, 1964, h. 4¾ in.
DE Adolf Matura (Czechoslovakia)

183 Bowl, blown lead crystal, engraved with representation of fruit trees growing from splashes of encased white colour, 1969
D Ingeborg Lundin (Sweden)
M Orrefors Glass, Sweden

Engraving

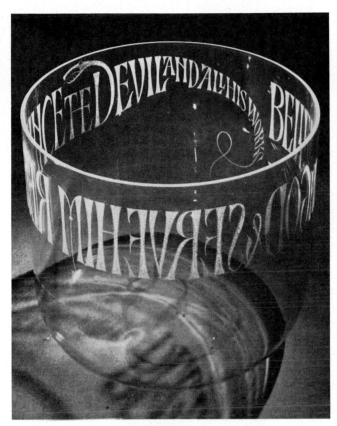

184 Flask with stopper, deep engraved. A 60th birthday
gift from a son to his mother, h. 11 in.
DE   Nora Ortlieb (Germany)

International Modern Glass

185   The technique of diamond-point engraving, 1953
DE   W.J. Wilson (England)
M   Whitefriars Glass, Wealdstone, England

186   Decanter, one of a pair, diamond-point engraved
with a view of Chatsworth House as a presentation for the
21st birthday of the Earl of Hartington, 27 April, 1965
DE   Shiela Elmhirst (England)

187   Rose bowl, blown and diamond-point inscribed
'Presented to the President of the Board of Trade The
Rt. Hon. G.E. Peter Thorneycroft, M.P. by the Glass
Manufacturers' Federation on the Occasion of the Opening
of their Premises, 19 Portland Place, 24th May, 1954'
DE   W.J. Wilson (England)

Commemorative glass

188 Goblet, blown lead crystal, steel-point stipple, 1972. Titled 'The Bow Window'.

The landscape beyond the window shows Spring. The middle pane appears to be broken with pieces of window-glass littering the sill. The enigma of no landscape appearing beyond the hole is not explained by the artist, who acknowledges a slight debt to Magritte.
DE Laurence Whistler (England)
O   Fitzwilliam Museum, Cambridge

189 Dish, diamond-point engraved with representation of ferns
DE Phyllis Boissier (England), on a Leerdam dish.

190 Plate, diamond-point engraved both sides to give third dimensional effect, titled 'St Girolama'
DE Shiela Elmhirst (England)

191 Vase, diamond-point engraving of a squirrel
DE Phyllis Boissier (England)

International Modern Glass

192 Bowl, diamond-point engraving of dragon-fly and raindrops, titled 'Rain' and engraved inside the glass as well as outside
DE Shiela Elmhirst (England)

193 Book-ends, engraved and presented by the British Glass Industries Research Association to the Earl of Halifax, 1959
DE Helen Monro Turner (Scotland)

194 Bowl, blown lead crystal, h. 9 in., dia. 10 in., 1973. Titled 'A Dazzling Darkness'.
A new departure in technique for this artist, chiefly, but not entirely, engraving with a drill on bowls made to his own design (scc also Plates 196–198)
DE Laurence Whistler (England)

Commemorative glass

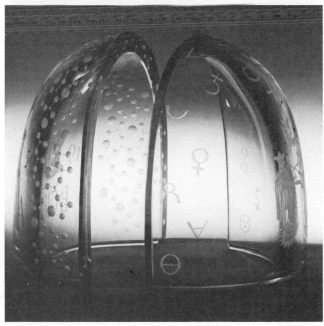

195 Bowl, blown lead crystal, h. 9 in., dia. 10 in., 1974.
Titled 'The Overflowing Landscape'.
    To the left a country bedroom, engraved on the inside
of the glass. The framed landscape hanging on the wall
has overflowed, to join the actual scenery on the right.
This is on the outside of the glass — except that some of
the boughs on the right dip into the room
DE Laurence Whistler (England)

International Modern Glass

196   Goblet, blown lead crystal, steel-point engraved, 1973. Titled 'House in Co. Fermanagh, N. Ireland'
DE   Simon Whistler (England)

197   Goblet, blown lead crystal steel-point engraved, 1972. Titled 'House in the Lake District'
DE   Simon Whistler (England)

198   Window-pane, engraved with a drill, at Leck Hall, Lancashire, dated '5 Nov. 1972'.

A picture of the house on one of its own windowpanes, but set in an imaginary setting
DE   Laurence Whistler (England)
O   The Lord Shuttleworth

199   Goblet, blown lead crystal, steel-point stipple, 1972. Titled 'Corridor of Lights'.
    Through a forest stretching to the horizon two paths finally join and move towards a far-off beacon
DE   Laurence Whistler (England)

Commemorative glass

200   Bowl, blown lead crystal, h. 9 in., dia. 10 in., 1973.
Titled 'Thrae'.
   An illustration to the allegory which introduces Walter
de la Mare's anthology *Come Hither*.
   The house called 'Thrae' is an anagram for 'Earth' and
the scenery depicted follows each detail of de la Mare's
story
DE   Laurence Whistler (England)

International Modern Glass

201   Three layers of glass, bound and mounted in brass
(with lamp in base) diamond-point engraved as a crucifix
for Stradbroke Church, Essex
DE   Shiela Elmhirst (England)

202   Bowl, engraved with initials C S P & G M H:
C S & G M P
DE   David Peace (England)
O   Mr. and Mrs. Christopher Peace

203   Glass altar cross at St. Clement Danes, Strand,
London given by a group of former members of the Royal
Air Force, 1958
DE   David Peace (England)

Commemorative glass

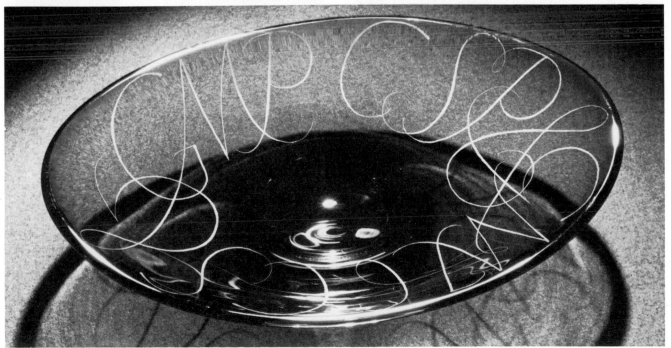

204 Plate Glass Door, engraved, 1967
DE Bryant Fedden (England)

205 Glass plate, engraved with the alphabet, 1970
DE Bryant Fedden (England)
M   Dartington Glass, Devon

206 Glass bell, engraved with lines from George Herbert,
    '. . . An earthly globe on whose
              meridian was engraven
        These seas are tears and
              heaven the haven'
DE David Peace (England)

International Modern Glass

207   Goblet, blown, lead crystal, diamond-point engraved, 1968, h. 12 in.
DE   Honoria D. Marsh (England)
     Commissioned for the centenary of Rothschild ownership of the Château Lafite the work on this glass took over 400 hours to engrave. Engraved on foot: 'Château Lafite Rothschild, 1868–1968'
O   Château Lafite-Rothschild, France

208   Reverse view of the Château Lafite-Rothschild

Centenary goblet, 1968 shown in Plate 207

209   Liqueur Glass, engraved in diamond-point stipple with a portrait of Yehudi Menuhin. Titled 'The Virtuoso', 1970. Ht. 3 in.
Presented to Yehudi Menuhin by The Crafts Council of Great Britain on his opening The Windsor Festival, 1970
DE   David Maude-Roxby Montalto (England)
M   Glass made by Bergdalla Glass, Sweden
O   Yehudi Menuhin, Esq.

Commemorative glass

210 Rummer, one of a pair, made at Waterford, *c*.1800, engraved in diamond-point stipple, 1969. h. 7 in.
DE David Maude-Roxby Montalto (England)
O Paul de Laszlo, Esq., (the gift of his wife for his sixtieth birthday)

211 Goblet, lead crystal, engraved in diamond-point stipple, showing a view of Cothay Manor, Somerset
DE William Meadows (England)
O Mrs. Astley-Rushton

212 Chalice, with engraved portraits of John Wyclif and his Czech disciple, John Hus, the religious reformer
DM C. Cejnar and V. Hubert (Czechoslovakia), at Kamenický Šenov

213 Goblet, cut and engraved, for presentation to King Olaf of Sweden (Colonel in Chief, Green Howards Regiment) by officers of the Regiment
D David Smith (England)
M Webb Corbett, Stourbridge, England

International Modern Glass

214   Cullet block of lead crystal engraved with the head
of 'Medusa', 1959, dia. 14 in.
D   Vicke Lindstrand (Sweden)
M   Kosta Glass, Sweden

Shapes: optical forms

215 Engraver Čestmir Cejnar of the Exbor Glass
Workshops. Czechoslovakia creates engraved blocks from
optical glass, each a unique item

216 Crystal block with engraved motif, titled 'Pilgrim',
dia. 5 in., h. 3 in.
D   Jindřich Tockstein (Czechoslovakia)
E   Ladislav Jezěk, (Czechoslovakia)
M   Železný Brod, Czechoslovakia

International Modern Glass

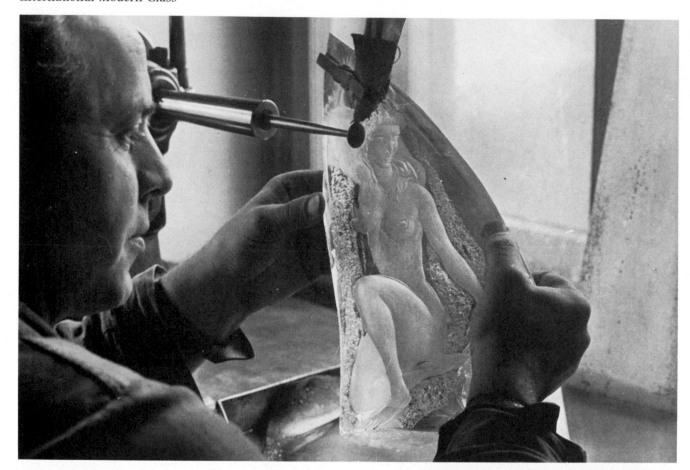

217   Optical glass plaque, ¾ in. bent to a shallow curve, copper-wheel engraved on back, sandblasted on front with formalised sea pattern, diamond-point detailing, h. 11 in., w. 10 in. Titled 'Branwen', (from *The Mabinogion*), 1972
DE   Jane Webster (England)
O   H.R.H. The Princess Anne, Mrs. Mark Phillips. Gift of Pilkington Bros Ltd on the occasion of a visit to their St. Asaph factory

Shapes

139

218 Optical glass block, engraved, titled 'Genesis'.
Duplicate to piece presented to President Kubitschek of
Brazil by President Eisenhower
D   Donald Pollard (U.S.A.)
E   Terry Haass (U.S.A.)
M   Steuben Glass, New York

219 Paperweights in different colours and designs
D   Mona Morales-Schildt (Sweden)
M   Kosta Glass, Sweden

220 Five Glass stones, cut, with a roughened surface,
1959. Average width, $2\frac{1}{4}$ in.
D   Willem Heesen (Holland)
M   Royal Leerdam Glass, Holland

221 Glass shape, blown crystal, 1952, dia. 8 in.
D   Tapio Wirkkala (Finland)
M   Iittala Glass, Finland

International Modern Glass

222   Blown 'Glass Apple', 1965
D   Ingeborg Lundin (Sweden)
M   Orrefors Glass, Sweden

Shapes

222   Blown 'Glass Apple', 1965
D   Ingeborg Lundin (Sweden)
M   Orrefors Glass, Sweden

223 Faceted block, cut and engraved, 1959, h. 4¼ in.
DM Hanns Model, Stuttgart
    Model is a glass designer and cutter with his own
    workshop

224 Solid formed by the revolving-through-space of an
equilateral triangle, titled 'Torque', Depth 7 in.
D   Paul Schulze (U.S.A.)
M   Steuben Glass, New York

225 Shaped crystal form, titled 'Voile' (Sail), current
D   Michel Daum (France)
M   Cristallerie de Nancy: DAUM, France

International Modern Glass

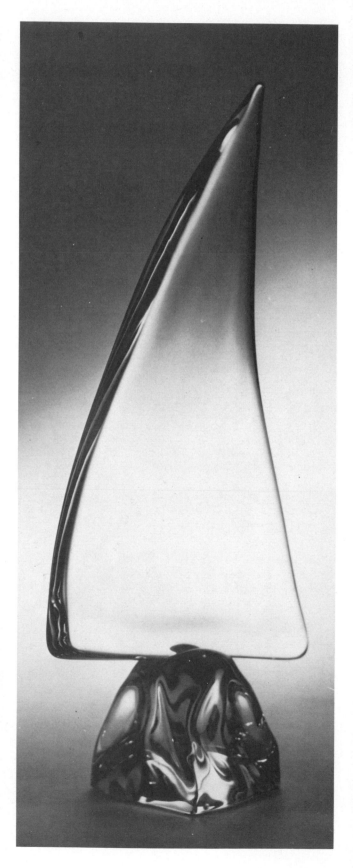

226 Block of crystal cut and polished into irregular facets. Titled 'Pack Ice', 1967, h. 16 in.
D   Aimo Okkolin (Finland)
M   Riihimäen Lasi Oy, Finland

227 Two vases, blown with air tears and of furnace-worked shape, 1959, h. 4⅛ in. and 4⅝ in.
D   Ernest Gordon (England: working in Sweden)
M   Åfors Glass, Sweden

228 Obelisks of cut and roughened glass to form a sculptural 'statement', c.1964
DM Max Ingrand (France)

Shapes

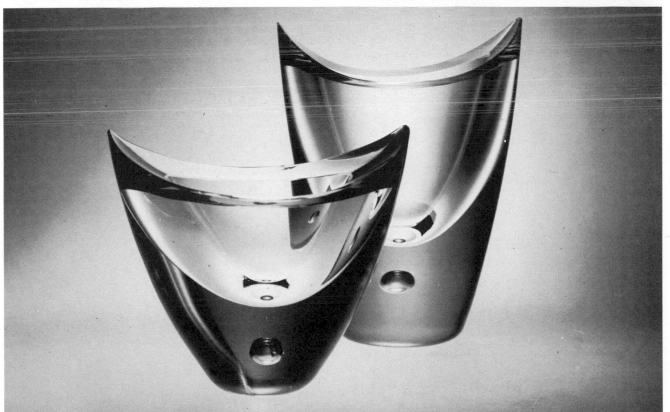

229 Hand-blown vase in green-blue glass, *c.*1968
DM René Roubíček (Czechoslovakia)

230 Two bottles, *left*, in transparent brown glass, with
opaque orange stripes; *right* in opaque orange glass.
1970, h. 8 in.
DM John H. Cook (England): blown by him at Venini of
    Murano, Italy

International Modern Glass

231 Hand-blown vase with the help of a wire mould to form some parts of the shape. Silver foil fused in the surface, 1968
DM Pavel Hlava (Czechoslovakia)

232 Crystalline composition, sculpture in glass, 1960, h. 22 in.
DM Edvin Öhrström (Sweden)

233 Glass bubble, freeblown in pink glass, with painted birds, clouds and waves in white and blue enamels, fired in a ceramic kiln, 1974
DM Ulrica Hydman-Vallien (Sweden)

Shapes

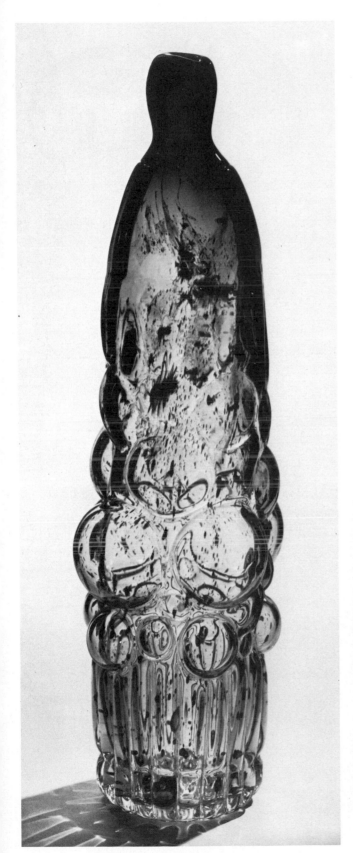

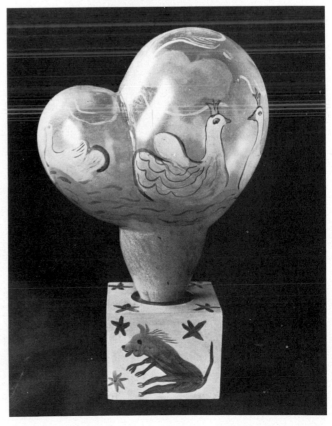

234 Blown glass globe, 1970
DM Michael Boylen (U.S.A.)
O Corning Museum of Glass, New York

235 Blown form, h. 8 in., length 18 in., 1970
DM Marvin Lipofsky (U.S.A.)
   Made at Leerdam Glassvormcentrum with the aid of its
   glass master L. Van der Linden

236 Mounted free form on a limestone base, 1966
DM William H. Boysen (U.S.A.)
   Exhibited in the first Toledo Glass National, 1966

International Modern Glass

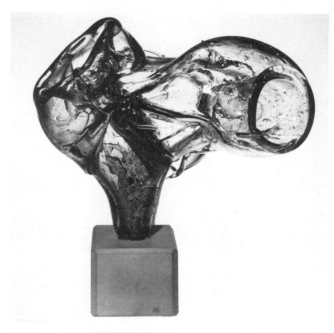

237 Freehand-blown vases, colour speckled, 1970
DM Colin Walker (England), while a student at the Royal
   College of Art, London

238 American glass, 1966–9. *left to right:* air sculpture,
cobalt glass, encasing gold veil, containing central forms
of silver; vase and tall pitcher, copper-red glass, integral
handles, clipped and tooled; bottle-vase, ruby red, cobalt
blue and white design between layers of pale cobalt blue;
and sculpture, titled 'Blue Lady', copper-blue glass
DM Dominick Labino (U.S.A.)

Shapes

239 Freehand-blown bottles, 1969, h. 15 in.
DM Bertil Vallien (Sweden)

240 Glass sculpture, titled 'Form III', 1969
DM Samuel Herman (U.S.A.: working in England)

241 Glass sculpture, titled 'Form IV', 1970
DM Samuel Herman (U.S.A.: working in England)

International Modern Glass

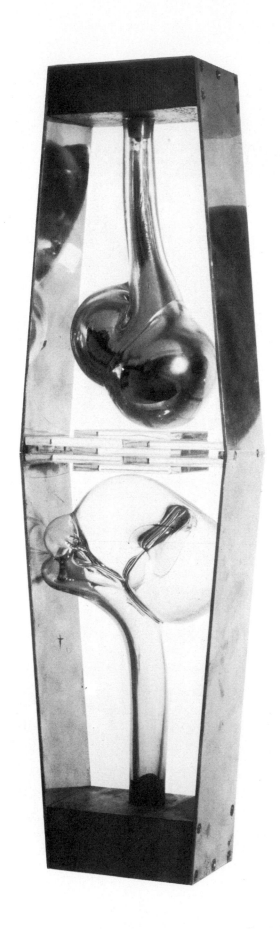

242 Freehand-blown form into a complex wire mould, 1970
DM Jiri Suhájek (Czechoslovakia), while a student at the Royal College of Art, London

243 Two bowls, blown purple glass with solid transparent additions, h. 8 in., 1974
DM John Cook (England)

244 Freehand-blown people shapes, with applied colour handles, threads, legs and finials, 1970
DM Wayne Filan (U.S.A.), while a student at the Royal College of Art, London

Shapes

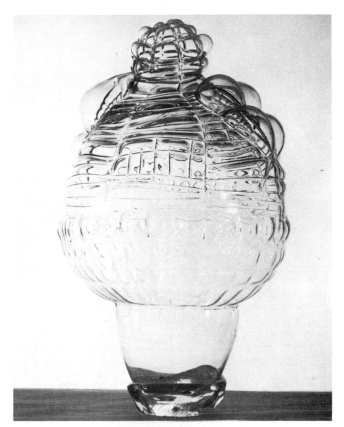

245 Freehand-blown bottles, 1969, h. 16 in. and 13 in.
DM Bertil Vallien (Sweden)

International Modern Glass

246 Plate, white enamel fused in clear glass, 1959,
dia. 15⅞ in.
DM Maurice Heaton (U.S.A.)
O Corning Museum of Glass, New York

247 Bowl, freehand-blown with encased enamel in clear
bubbly glass, c.1954, h. 3½ in.
DM Toshichi Iwata Glass, Tokyo, Japan

O Corning Museum of Glass, New York,
Inv. 55,6.15

248 Vase, shaped in thick yellowish glass with abstract
pattern in blue and black, 1950, h. 9⅞ in.
DM Paolo Venini (Italy)
O The Toledo Museum of Art,
Inv. 54.49. Gift of the Italian Government

Colour: splashes, fusings, enamels

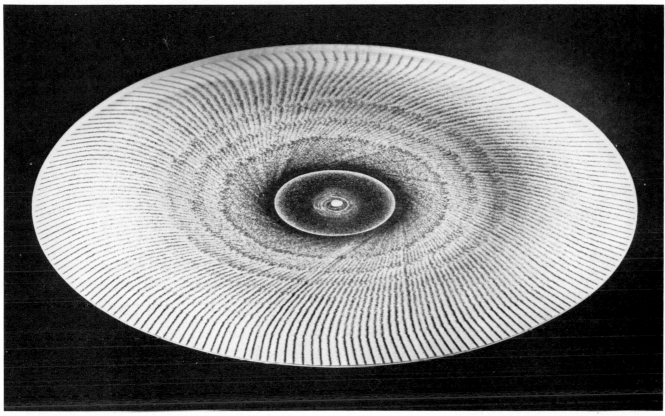

249 Vase, cased and cut through layers, 1963, h. 6 in.
D Mona Morales-Schildt (Sweden)
M Kosta Glass, Sweden
O Corning Museum of Glass, New York,
Inv. 63.3.61

250 Bottle, blue with purple coloration, 1960, h. 14 in.
D Andries D. Copier (Holland)
M Royal Leerdam Glass, Holland. A 'Unica' piece
O Boymans-van Beuningen Museum, Rotterdam

251 Lampshade, white, overlaid with yellow, red and
white stripes, 1959, h. 12 in.
DM Paolo Venini (Italy)

252 Vase, clear crystal with colour bubbles and striations,
1967
D Sybren Valkema (Holland)
M Royal Leerdam Glass, Holland

International Modern Glass

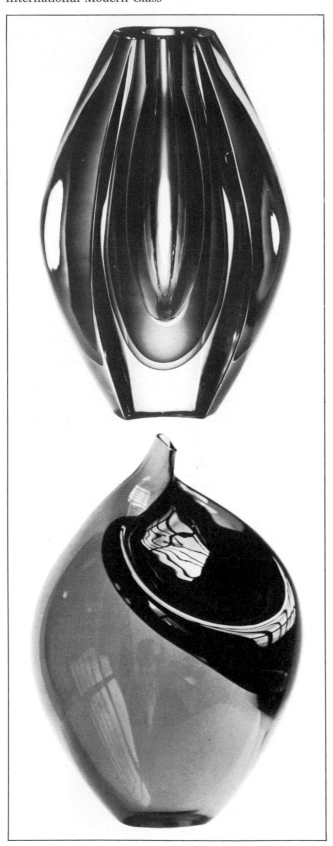

253 Dish, clear glass with leaf design in blue, green and amber, 1959, dia. (maximum) 11½ in.
D   Floris Meydam (Holland)
M   Royal Leerdam Glass, Holland

254 Vase, clear glass, with encased enamel patterning of flecks and spots, 1959, h. 4½ in.
D   René Roubiček (Czechoslovakia)
M   Nový Bor Glass, Czechoslovakia

Colour

255   Bottle, freeblown in light blue, green and grey glass, h. 14 in., 1969
DM Roland Jahn (U.S.A)
O   Murray Weiss Esq.

256   Pitcher, with overlay colour threads and 'tesserae' pattern, 1951
D   Ercole Barovier (Italy)
M   Barovier & Toso, Murano, Italy
O   Victoria & Albert Museum, London

International Modern Glass

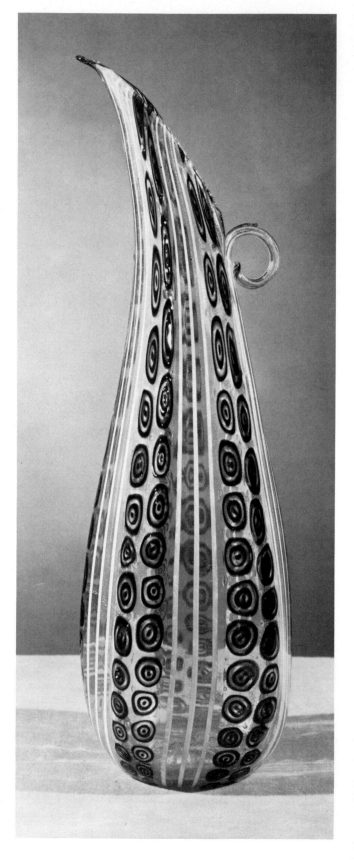

257 Vase, cylindrical, in freehand-blown glass, yellow with black and fumed iridescence, 1967, h. 4 in., dia. 3¼ in.
DM Erwin Eisch (Germany)
O The Toledo Museum of Art,
Inv. 68.85

258 Vase 'silver-schmelz' glass, freehand formed, 1967
DM Dominick Labino (U.S.A.)

259 Vase, freehand-blown in opaque copper red glass, swirled, 1966, h. 6½ in.
DM Harvey K. Littleton (U.S.A.)
O The Toledo Museum of Art,
Inv. 66.133. A Purchase Award at the first Toledo Glass National

Colour

260 Vase, blown 'Lava glass', 1970: speckled oxide
colours with free forming of undulations
D   Per Lütken (Denmark)
M   Kastrup-Holmegaards Glass, Denmark

261 Laminated sculptural form enclosing gold leaf, 1968
DM Heather Cowburn (England), while a student at
     The Royal College of Art, London

International Modern Glass

262 Bowl, blown with thin blue-green colour trails and bubbles encased, 1968
D Andries D. Copier (Holland)
M Royal Leerdam Glass, Holland. A 'Unica' piece

263 Bowls, in frosted and blue glass, 1966
The pattern is doodled on to the inside of the bowl in resin. This then protects the blue 'cup' of glass while the inside is sand-blasted to the clear glass. The outside of the bowl remains smooth and clear reflecting the intricate pattern of blue within.
DM Bertil Vallien (Sweden)

Colour

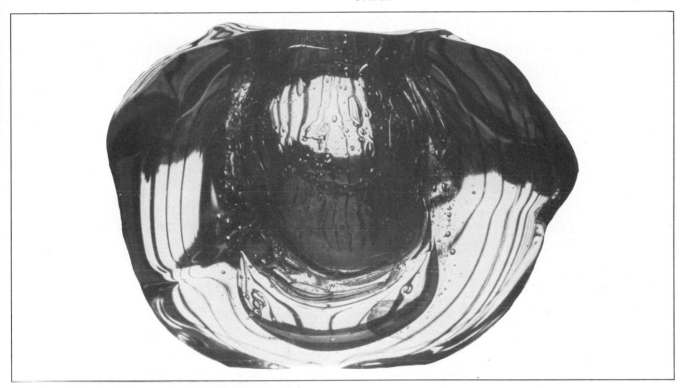

264   Vase, cased and cut, with fused-in silver colour according to a technique invented by Jaromir Špacĕk
D   Pavel Hlava (Czechoslovakia)
M   Exbor Studios at Nový Bor, Czechoslovakia

265   Bowl, freehand-blown, with opaque glass overlaid, 1969
D   Kaj Franck (Finland)
M   Notsjoe Glass (Wärtsilä), Finland

266   Vertical lamination with molten glass in low relief. Titled 'Source', 1967
DM   Edris Eckhardt (U.S.A.). Exhibited in her retrospective exhibition at The Corning Museum of Glass, New York, 1968

International Modern Glass

267   Vase, hand-moulded lead crystal, 1967
D   V. Žahour (Czechoslovakia)

268   Vase, hand-pressed, 1969
D   Rudolf Jurnikl (Czechoslovakia)
M   Rudolfova Huť, Czechoslovakia

Moulded and pressed

267   Vase, hand-moulded lead crystal, 1967
D   V. Žahour (Czechoslovakia)

268   Vase, hand-pressed, 1969
D   Rudolf Jurnikl (Czechoslovakia)
M   Rudolfova Huť, Czechoslovakia

269   Plate, hand-pressed, 1968
D   Adolf Matura (Czechoslovakia)
M   Rudolfova Huť, Czechoslovakia

International Modern Glass

270 Plate, hand-pressed, 1968
D František Pečný (Czechoslovakia)
M Heřmanova Huť, Czechoslovakia

271 Ashtray, moulded in a wood-faced mould, 1966,
dia. 14 in.
D Timo Sarpaneva (Finland)
M Iittala Glass, Finland

Moulded and pressed

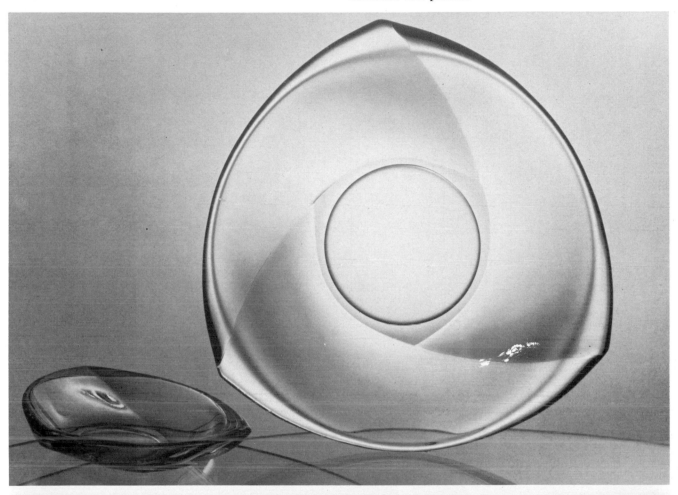

272 Bottle, mould-blown glass, 1969
D Willem Heesen (Holland)
M Royal Leerdam Glass, Holland

273 Cast paperweights, 1967
D Erik Höglund (Sweden)
M Boda Glass, Sweden

274 Vases, mould-blown, 1967, h. 8½ in., titled 'Old
Manor' collection: *left* 'Busy Lizzy', *right* 'Lock'
D Helena Tynell (Finland)
M Riihimäen Lasi Oy, Finland

International Modern Glass

275 Glass-wagon, cast parts in silica powder, 1966,
h. 18 in.
DM Bertil Vallien (Sweden)
Vallien starts with a wood box packed with slightly damp fine-grind English silica. He presses out the forms he wants with his hands or templates of any hard material, and fills the void with molten glass up to the level of the sand. An empty bottomless box is put on top of the first one, packed with the silica, and a new imprint (which must have an adequate opening to the cast piece below) is made and filled with more hot glass. Another empty box is added and the process repeated box by box until there are several layers. For Vallien, seven or eight castings are not unusual, but it is most important that the connection between the glass castings be substantial enough to bear the weight of the crystal mass below, which it is to support. When the last layer of crystal is cast, the boxes and sand are carefully removed and the sculpture cooled slowly in a kiln at 500°C.
– Dido Smith writing of Vallien's glass in *Craft Horizons*, (New York) September/October 1967, p. 46

Moulded and pressed

276 Bowls and glasses, blown into a metal mould in which the decor motif is engraved, titled 'Flora', (current)
D   Oiva Toikka (Finland)
M   Notsjoe Glass, (Wartsilä) Finland

277 Two vases, Nos. 9667–8, moulded with patterned faces, 1966, h. 10½ in.
D   Geoffrey Baxter (England)
M   Whitefriars Glass, Wealdstone, England

278 Vase, hand-moulded lead crystal, 1967
D   Ladislav Oliva (Czechoslovakia)
M   Bohemia Glass at Poděbrady

279 Decanter and glasses in clear glass. Titled 'Snowstar', 1973
D   Nanny Still McKinney (Finland)
M   Riihimäen Lasi Oy, Finland

International Modern Glass

280   Glass screen, abraded; being a detail of the Angel of the Resurrection, Great West Screen, Coventry Cathedral, 1952–61. The screen, part of the Cathedral complex designed by Sir Basil Spence, consists of ninety panels which were worked in this way.
DM John Hutton (New Zealand: working in England)

Abraded: sandblast and acid

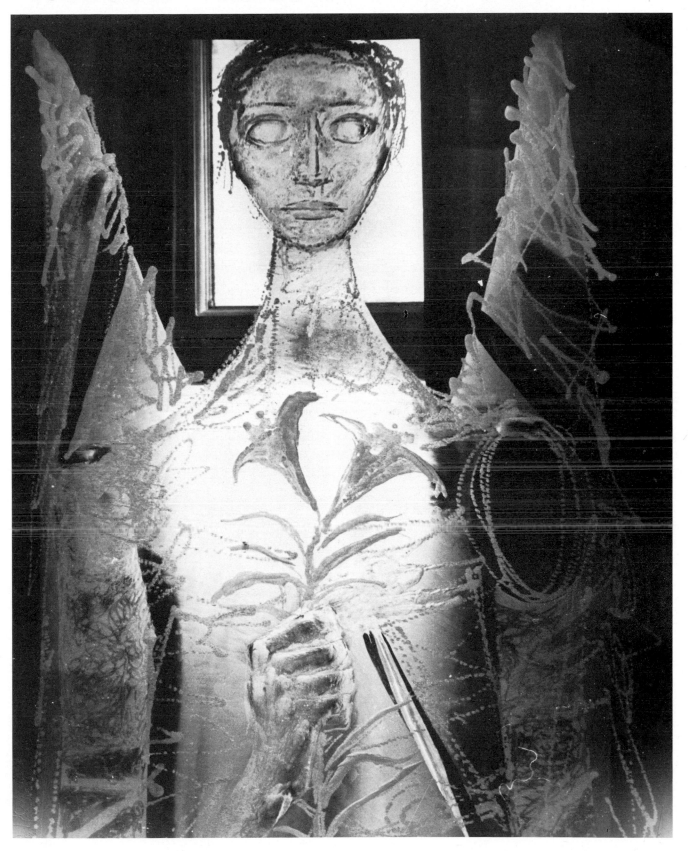

281 John Hutton in a photograph which shows the electrically driven flexible drive fitted with a rubber wheel on which has been glued a strip of emery cloth. He uses this to polish over areas which have been more coarsely ground with rougher wheels. Bent back from the flexible drive is a small sponge which is used when grinding wet

282 Detail of engraved panel, one of five depicting 'Flying Angels', west front entrance doors, Wellington Cathedral, New Zealand, 1972, h. 8 ft. 4 in. × 6 ft.

283 Three sheets of glass, with sand-blast decoration, mounted in a polished metal base, 1967
DM Eric Hilton (England)
    Exhibited in the 'Four British Schools, Designs in Glass' exhibition at The Corning Museum of Glass, New York, 1967–8

284 Detail of engraved glass panel representing 'King Lear', one of nineteen figures worked by John Hutton at The Shakespeare Centre, Stratford-upon-Avon

International Modern Glass

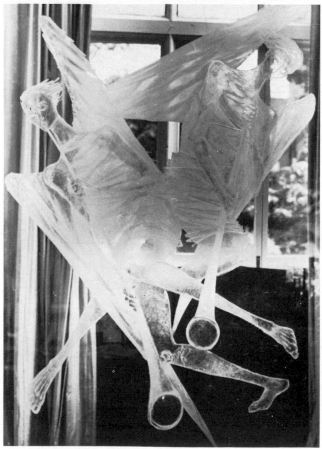

285   Vase, sand-blast decoration 1969, h. 15 in.
D   Ladislav Oliva (Czechoslovakia)
M   Exbor Studios at Nový Bor, Czechoslovakia

286   Vase, cut lead crystal, sand-blasted with a quotation from a poem by Milhály Váci, 1969
DM Julia Báthory (Hungary)

287   Bottle, sand-blast and acid decoration, 1967, h. 22 in.
DM Bertil Vallien (Sweden)

Abraded

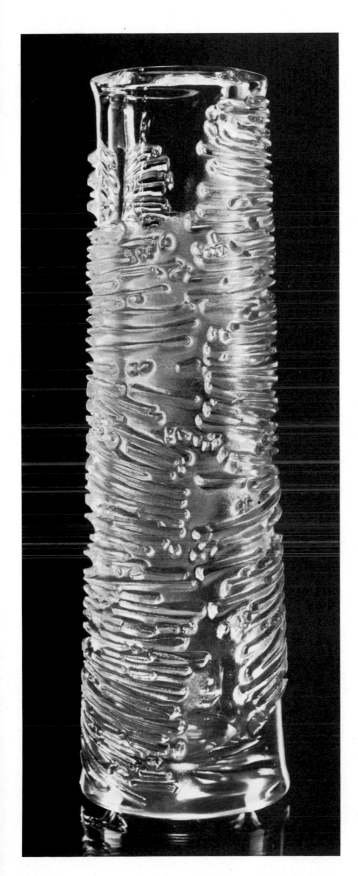

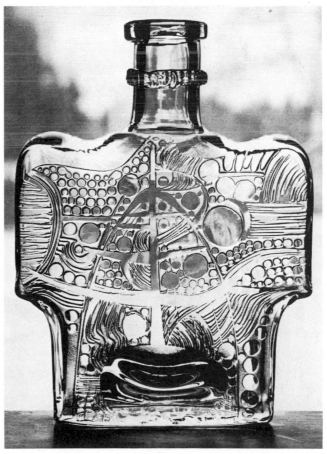

167

288 Plate-glass door, sand-blast decoration, symbolising
interests of the owners, done to the artist's design.
D   William Meadows (England)

International Modern Glass

289　Glass Mask with colour protrusions
D　Max Ernst (Germany)
M　Sculpture in Glass of the 'Fucina degli Angeli', Venice
O　Peggy Guggenheim Foundation, Venice
　The recreation in glass of the masterpieces of Picasso,

Ernst, Arp, Cocteau and many others to their complete satisfaction is the achievement (since 1963) of Egidio Constantini and the glass-blowers of Fucina degli Angeli. Their work has been widely exhibited in Europe, and in America (by Adria Art of Madison Avenue)

Sculptures and 'fun' glass

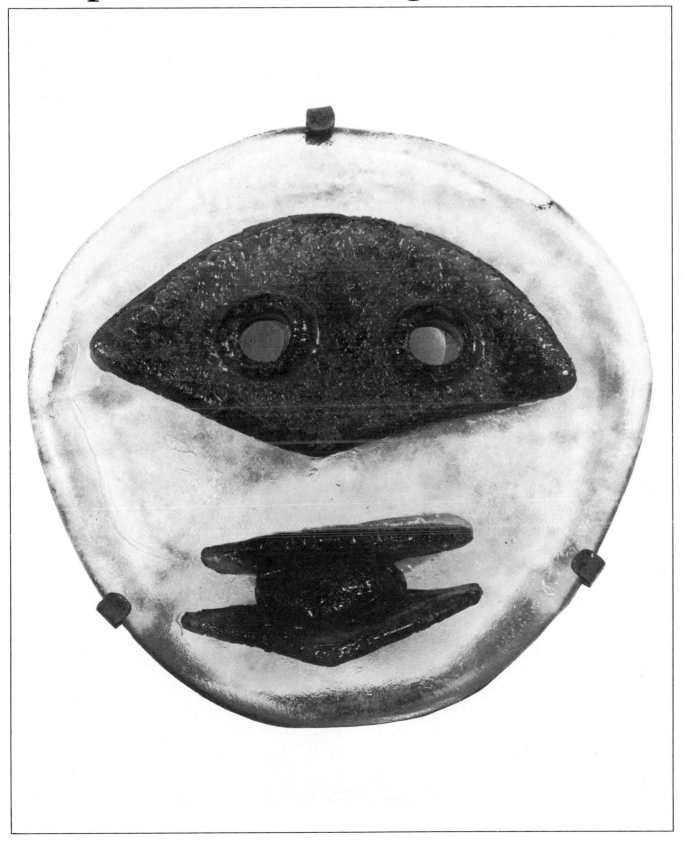

290 Sculpture, lead crystal, titled 'Totem Pole', 1968
D   Vicke Lindstrand (Sweden)
M   Kosta Glass, Sweden

International Modern Glass

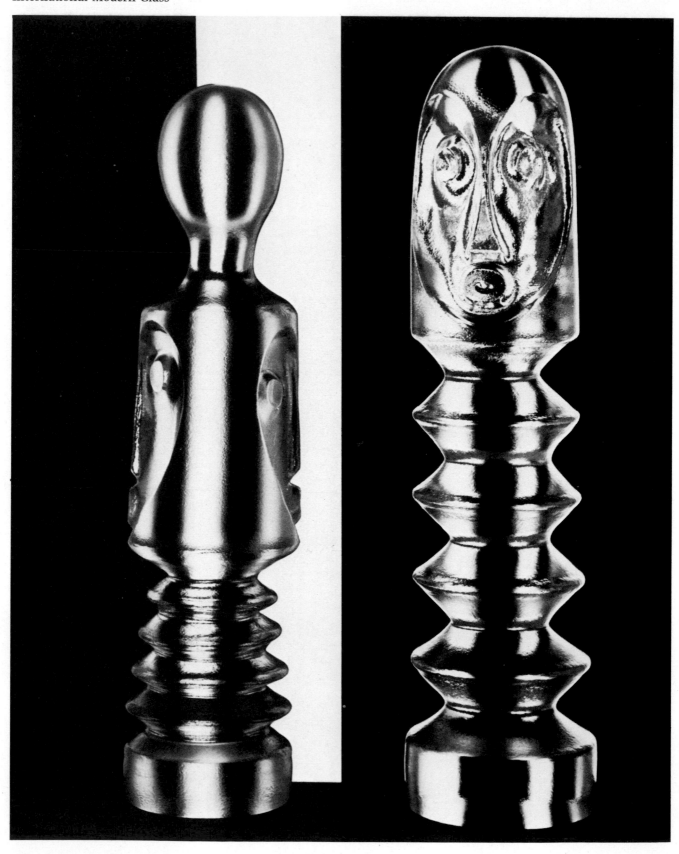

291   Mobile with glass medallions, titled 'The Fish'
D   Alexander Calder (U.S.A.)
M   Sculpture in Glass of the 'Fucina degli Angeli', Venice
O   Peggy Guggenheim Foundation, Venice

292   Glass sculptures
D   René Roubiček (Czechoslovakia)
M   Exbor Studios at Nový Bor, Czechoslovakia

Sculptures and 'fun' glass

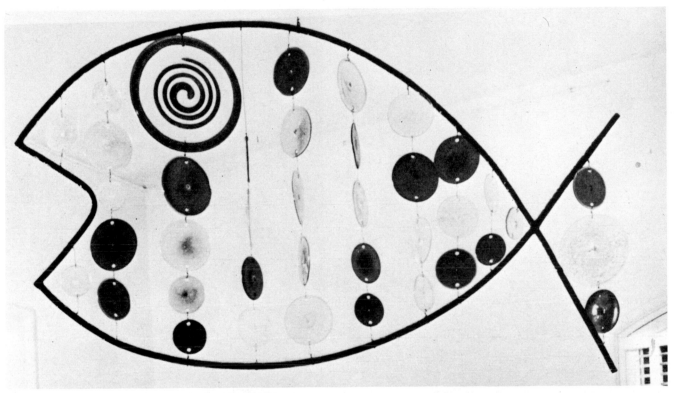

293 Glass Figure, one of two of the group 'Man and Wife'
D Jean Arp (1888–1966, France)
M Sculpture in Glass of the 'Fucina degli Angeli', Venice
O Peggy Guggenheim Foundation, Venice

294 Glass sculpture, clear with trailed decoration in aquamarine, h. 15 in.
D Angelo Barovier (Italy)
M Barovier & Toso, Murano, Italy

295 Sculpture, cast crystal, titled 'Victoria Regia', 1967, dia. 20 in.
D Helena Tynell (Finland)
M Riihimäen Lasi Oy, Finland

International Modern Glass

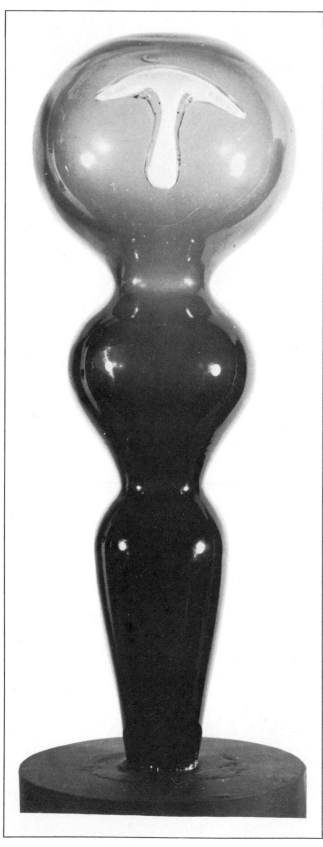

296   Sculptures in glass, made by the lost wax process, 1967
DM Edris Eckhardt (U.S.A.)
     Exhibited in 'Edris Eckhardt, Artist in Glass: A Retrospective Exhibition', Corning Museum of Glass, New York, Summer 1968

Sculptures and 'fun' glass

297 Sculpture, crystal glass, titled 'Torso'
D Miroslav Klinger (Czechoslovakia)
M Železný Brod Trade School, Czechoslovakia

298 Plates in the form of fried eggs, yellow and white, 1969
D Rolf Sinnemark (Sweden)
M Kosta Glass, Sweden

299 Glass sculptures, blown into a wood-faced mould and then free-formed, 1967, h. 16–35 in.
D Timo Sarpaneva (Finland)
M Iittala Glass, Finland

International Modern Glass

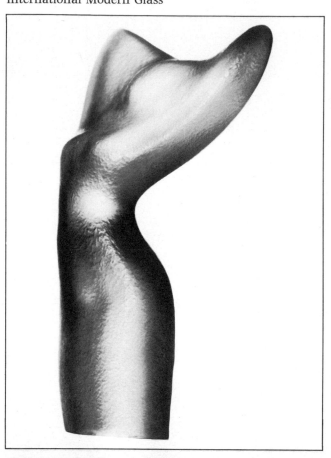

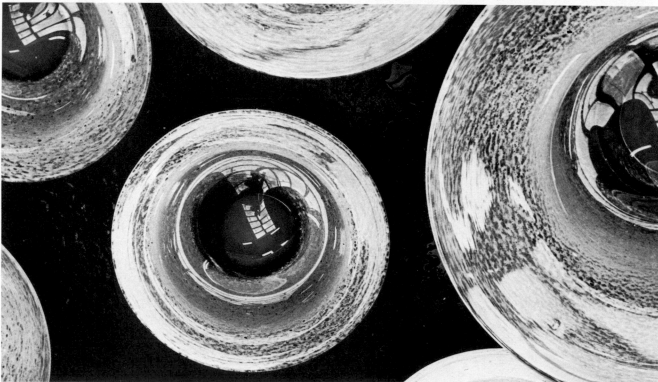

300 Glass sculptures, blown in graphite moulds, 1967
D   Lars Hellsten (Sweden)
M   Skrufs Glass, Sweden

Sculptures and 'fun' glass

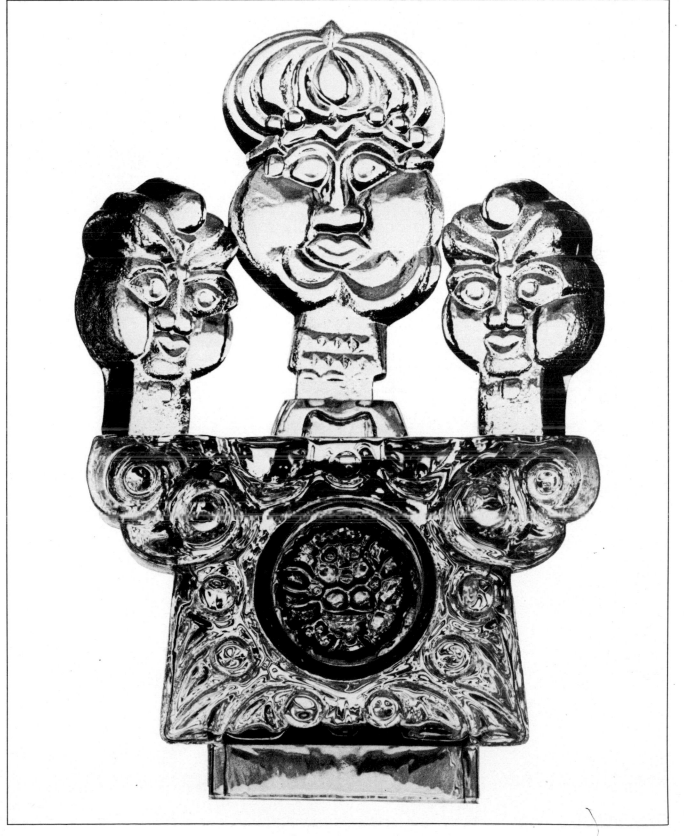

175

301 Glass sculpture, 1968
DM Renato Toso, (Italy).
   Renato Toso of Vetreria Fratelli Toso at Murano designed
   some sculptures and multiples in glass, and these were
   exhibited in 1969 at the Galleria del Cavallino, San
   Marco, Venice

7 Glass sculpture, blown form, unique item. 1969. Ht 14 in.
D Oiva Toikka (Finland)
M Arabia Glass, Finland

International Modern Glass

8 Three glasses from 'Polaris' suite, 12520
  D Tapio Wirkkala (Finland)
  M Rosenthal AG, Germany, 'Studio Line'.

9 Sundae glass, from 'Lotus' suite 24000
  D Richard Latham (glass). Relief decoration by Bjørn Wiinblad.
  M Rosenthal AG, Germany, 'Studio Line'.

302 Sculpture, titled 'Capricorn', 1969
DM Břetislav Novak (Czechoslovakia)
   at the Železný Brod Trade School

303 Glass sculpture 'Le Coq', (current)
D Michel Daum (France)
M Cristallerie de Nancy: Daum, France.
   Daum have long been noted for the limpid
   simplicity of their glass sculptures

304 Figurines, hand-blown, representing 'Cockerel' and
'Cat'
D Jaroslav Brychta (Czechoslovakia)
M Železný Brod Trade School, Czechoslovakia
   Brychta's figurines have long been a notable
   feature of the Železný Brod production, and many
   students are taught to make them

Sculptures and 'fun' glass

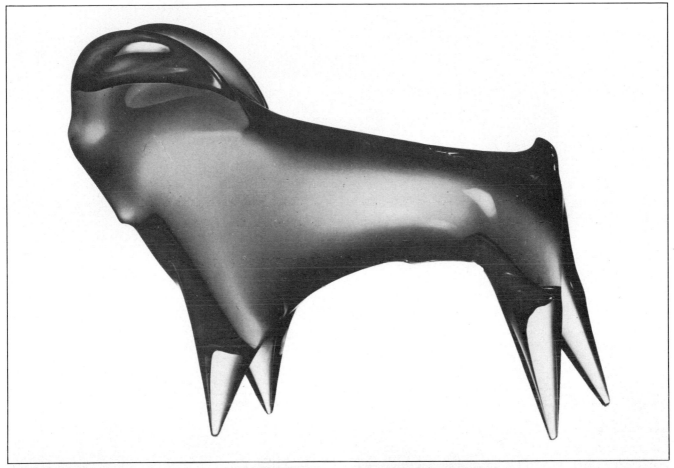

305 Figurine, hand-blown in laboratory glass, 1969,
titled 'The Cat'
DM Věra Lišková (Czechoslovakia)

International Modern Glass

306   Sculpture, titled 'Lake Palace', 1969, h. 25 in.
A study in the various possibilities of clear glass and in
the combination and juxtaposition of compact glass and
free air, with the feeling of the fragility of glass emphasised
D   Oiva Toikka (Finland)
M   Notsjoe Glass (Wärtsilä), Finland

Sculptures and 'fun' glass

307   Wine glass fantasy sculpture, 1969
D   Erik Höglund (Sweden)
M   Boda Glass, Sweden

308   Group of stylised birds, free-formed, 1969
D   Luciano Gaspari (Italy)
M   Salviati & C, Venice, Italy

International Modern Glass

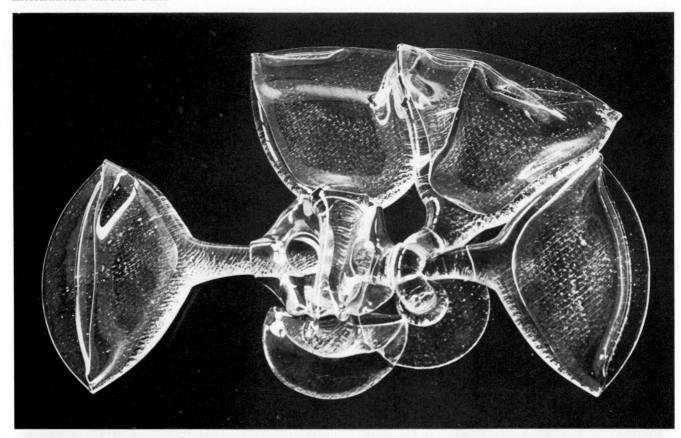

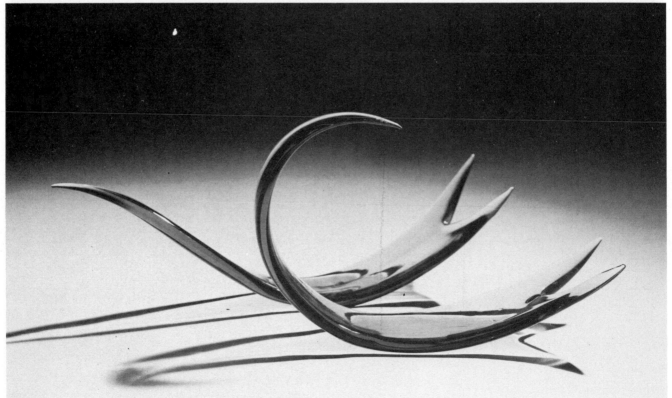

309   Glass sculpture, free standing, free-formed, cobalt
blue with air enclosures, 1969, h. 10 in.
DM Dominick Labino (U.S.A.)

Sculptures and 'fun' glass

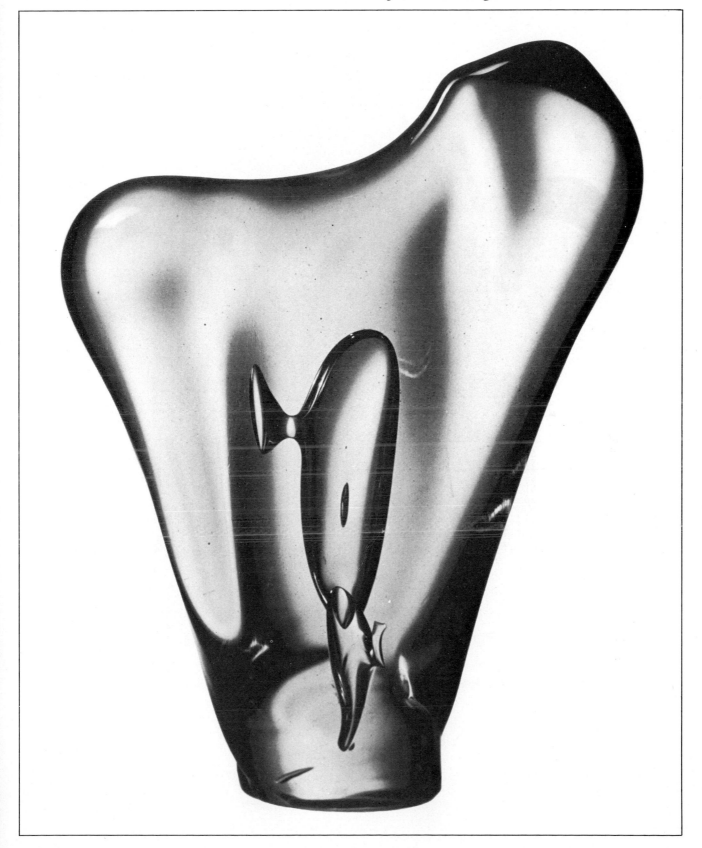

310 Blown glass unique form, titled 'Truncated
Movement', 1969, h. 22 in., w. 12½ in.
DM Harvey K. Littleton (U.S.A.)
  As exhibited by the Lee Nordness Galleries in New York

International Modern Glass

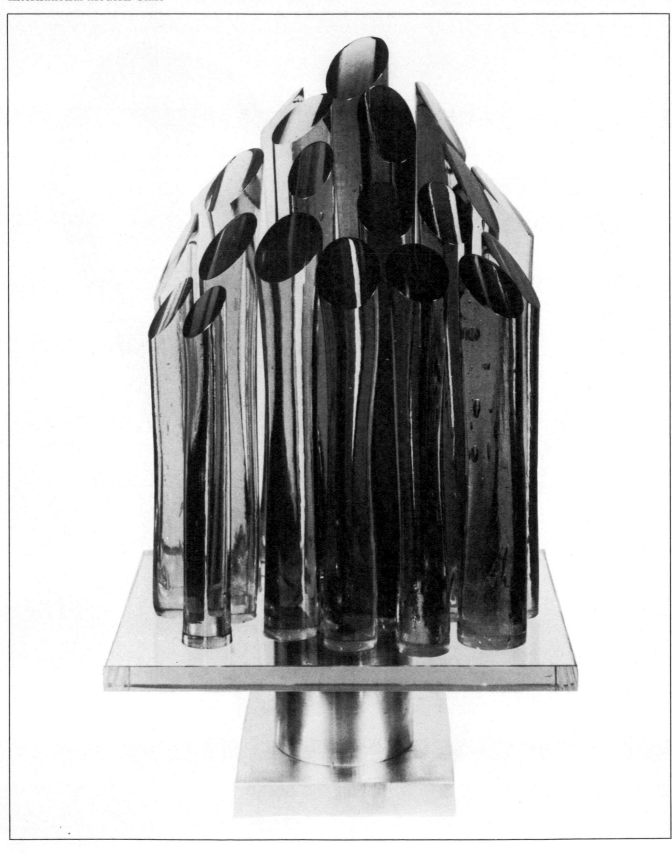

311 Unique glass sculpture, 1965
DM Edvin Öhrström (Sweden)

312 Sculpture, toughened glass and steel, titled 'New Toy', 1967, h. 9 in., w. 11 in., length 24 in.
DM Harry Seager (England)
O   M.R. Whitley, Esq.

Sculptures and 'fun' glass

313 Blown glass 'Flower', 1969
D   Rolf Sinnemark (Sweden)
M   Kosta Glass, Sweden

International Modern Glass

314   Glass construction in 'Pyrex' boro-silicate glass, 1972.
h. 12 in., dia. 12 in.
DM Alan G. Thomson (England)

Sculptures and 'fun' glass

315   Detail of blown glass sculptures, titled 'The
Utilitarian Junction', 1969. The complete sculptures are
about 48 in. high with a thrown ceramic base
DM L.E. Rudge (England)

International Modern Glass

316 Blown glass sculpture, mounted on wooden base, length 24 in.
DM Samuel Herman (U.S.A.: working in England)

317 Blown glass unique form, titled 'Crystal Section', 1968, 7 × 4 × 4 in.
DM Harvey K. Littleton (U.S.A.)

Sculptures and 'fun' glass

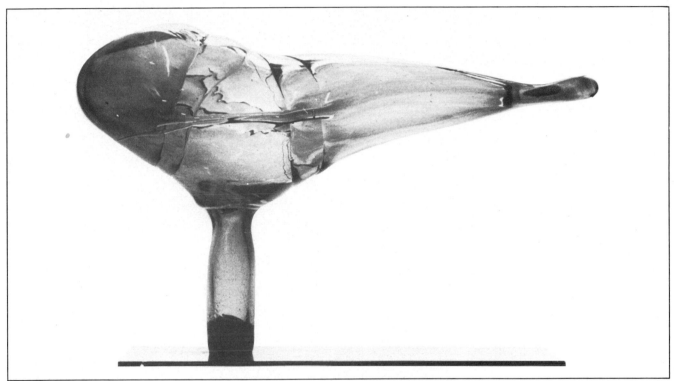

318   Glass sculpture, titled 'Ice Forms'
DM Dominick Labino (U.S.A.)
O   The Cleveland Institute of Art, Cleveland, Ohio, U.S.A.

International Modern Glass

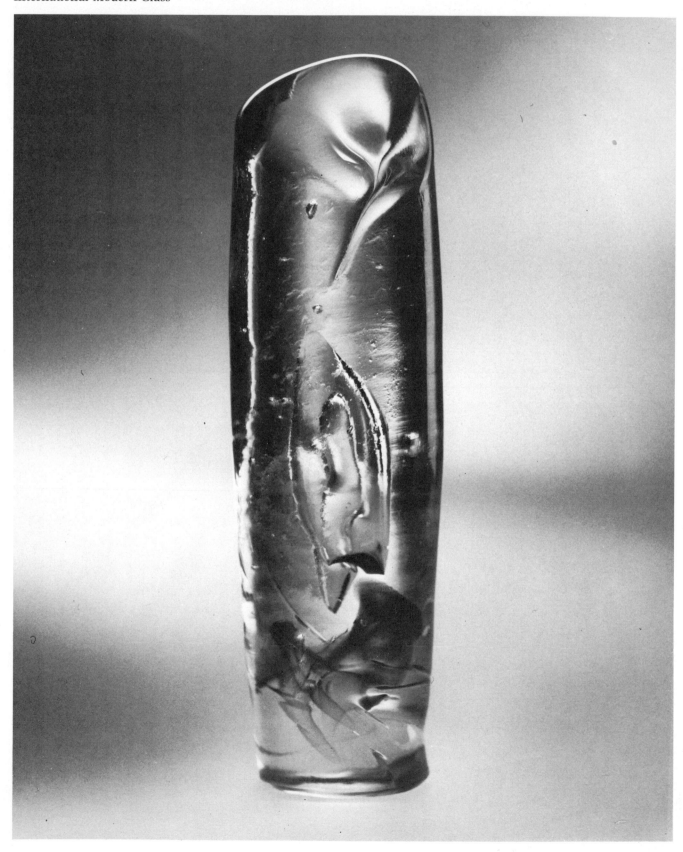

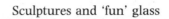

319 Crystal coil structure, 1965, one of a series ranging
from 12 to 30 in. high
DM Willem Heesen (Holland)

Sculptures and 'fun' glass

320 Glass form. h. 14 in., length 28 in. in red clear glass.
Titled 'Nuutajärvi, Suomi, Finland series', 1970
DM Marvin Lipofsky (U.S.A.) made in Finland

321 Freeblown figures of ducks, hand-painted in
enamels and fired in a ceramic kiln, 1974
DM Ulrica Hydman-Vallien (Sweden)

International Modern Glass

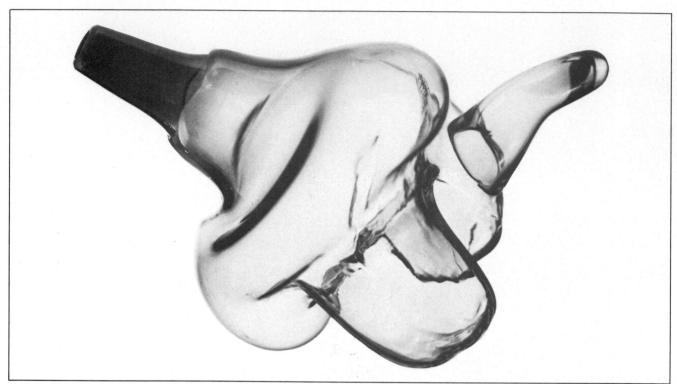

322 Blown glass clear form, with platinum and copper
lustres, and multi-lustred painting on the surface.
Title 'The Pill', 1969, h. 14 in. × dia. 6 in.
DM Joel P. Myers (U.S.A.)

Sculptures and 'fun' glass

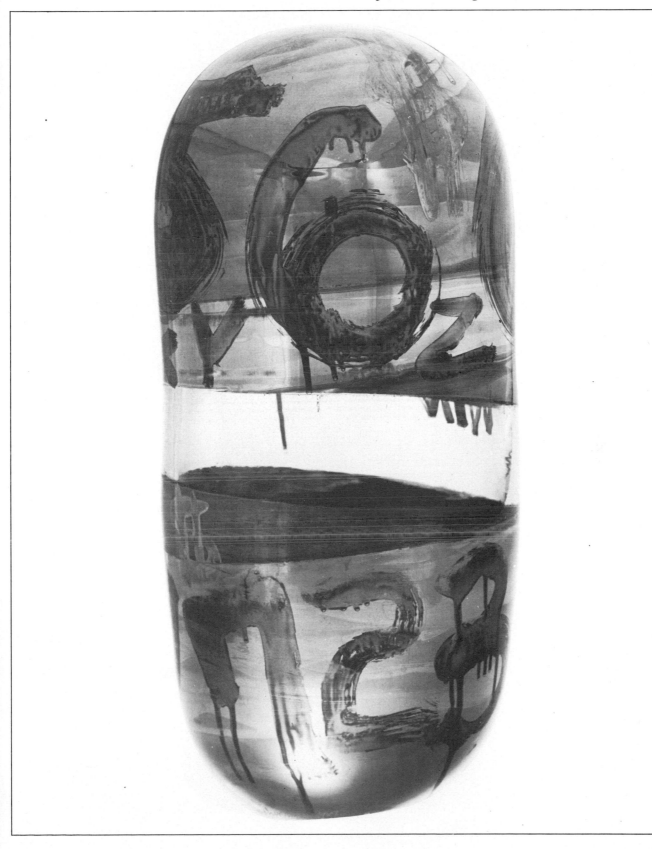

323 Blown glass form in opaque orange, with white
band and red stripes, and orange prunts, 1970, h. 14 in.
DM John Cook (England). Blown at Venini, Italy

International Modern Glass

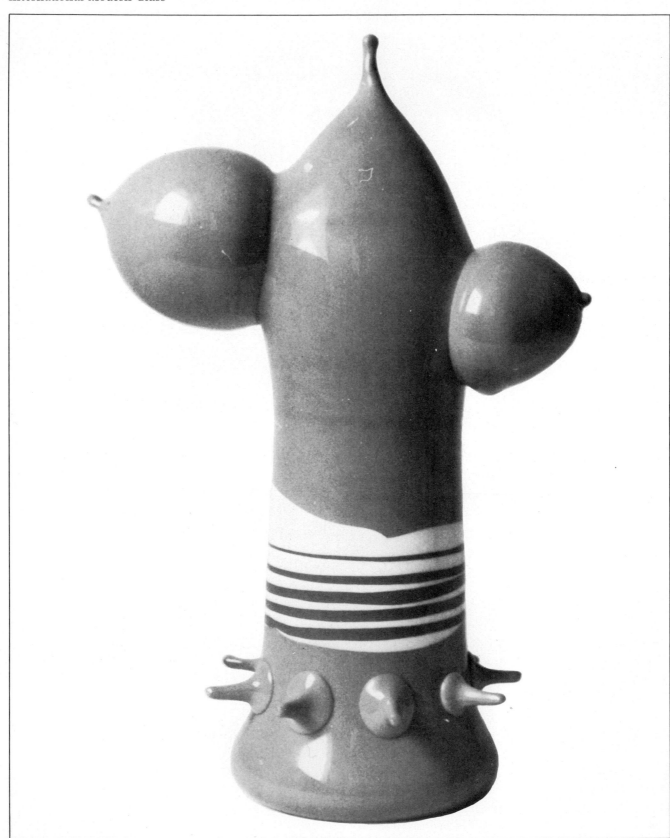

10 Blown glass shapes, 1974. Ht 5–8 ins.
DM Pauline Solven, at The Glasshouse, London

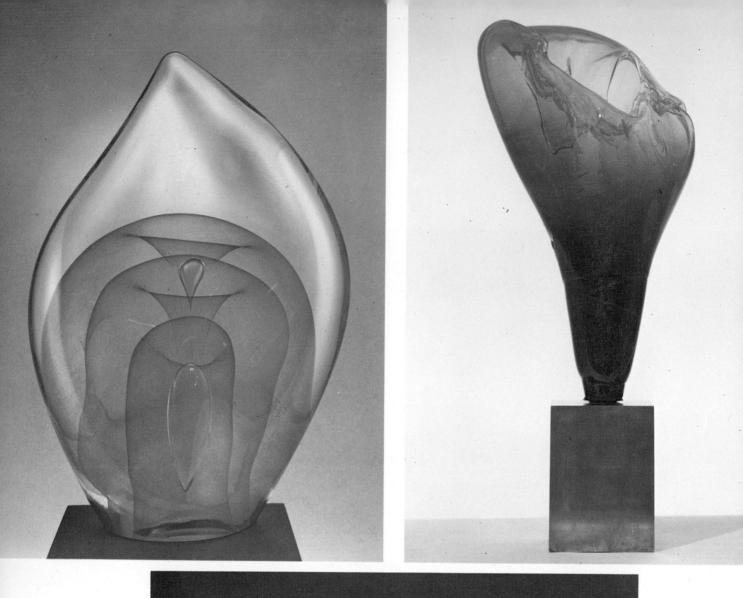

11 Glass sculpture, 10 × 7 in. 1973. Titled: 'Emergence XV'
DM Dominick Labino (U.S.A.)
O   Victoria & Albert Museum, London

12 Blown glass sculpture. Titled 'Butterfly Wing', 1969. Ht
15 in.
DM Harvey K. Littleton (U.S.A.)

13 Glass 'landscape', titled 'Celestial journey end', lead crystal,
lacquered wood, 25 × 25 × 10 in. 1974
DM Bertil Vallien (Sweden)

324 Blown glass construction, platinum lustred stripes
with silver lustre areas, 1969, h. 19¼ in., dia. 10 in.
DM Joel P. Myers (U.S.A.)

Sculptures and 'fun' glass

325 Multi-positional glass sculpture, ⅜ in. clear float
glass, wire and rope, 1974, h. 24 in., length (fully
extended), 161 in. Titled: 'Flexing Screen'
DM Harry Seager (England)

International Modern Glass

326   Installing the glass and concrete panels of one of
Erik Höglund's 'stained glass' windows made by him at
Boda Glassworks, Sweden

Screens and 'architectural' glass

327   Section of glass wall for the City Hall of Vasterås,
Sweden, 1965, seen in construction in the designer's
studio
DM Edvin Öhrström (Sweden)
    The complete sculpture forms one whole wall between
    the stair well and the reception hall

International Modern Glass

328 Screen, worked and decorated by hand and composed without joints or links, titled 'Laguna', (current)
D Renato Toso (Italy)
M Vetreria Fratelli Toso, Murano, Italy
   These screens can be adapted to many uses, particularly illumination, decoration of rooms and as light curtains

329 Decorated glass mirrors installed in 1969 at Sweden House in Stockholm
D Monica Backström (Sweden)
M Boda Glass, Sweden

Screens and 'architectural' glass

330 Multicoloured fused glass panel, titled 'Under-water
Landscape', 1959, h. 31 in., length 38½ in.
D   Michèle Lanoir (France)
M   Les Gémmaux de France

International Modern Glass

330 Multicoloured fused glass panel, titled 'Under-water
Landscape', 1959, h. 31 in., length 38½ in.
D   Michèle Lanoir (France)
M   Les Gémmaux de France

331   Detail of fused silica panel, 1968
D   Stephen J. Edwards (England)
M   Thermal Syndicate Ltd., Wallsend, Northumberland.
These coloured vitreous silica panels are colour fast
for ever and withstand extremes of heat and cold
without cracking or crazing. They have infinite uses
in the form of internal or external murals, wall-
cladding and flooring.

Screens and 'architectural' glass

332 Detail of lighting screen shown below

333 Lighting screen of coloured relievo glass, 1968,
length 36 ft.
DM Professor György Z. Gács (Hungary)

International Modern Glass

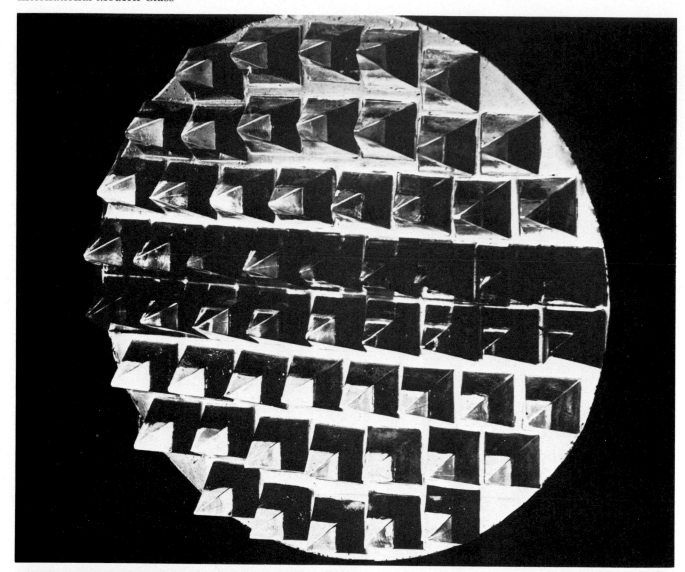

334 Glass Curtain, of linked glass shapes
D   Betha and Teff Sarasin (Switzerland)
M   Salviati & C, Venice, Italy

Screens and 'architectural' glass

335 A 'stained glass' window formed by mounting coloured glass blocks in resin or concrete and setting convenient sections within angled iron frames.
DM Erik Höglund (Sweden)

International Modern Glass

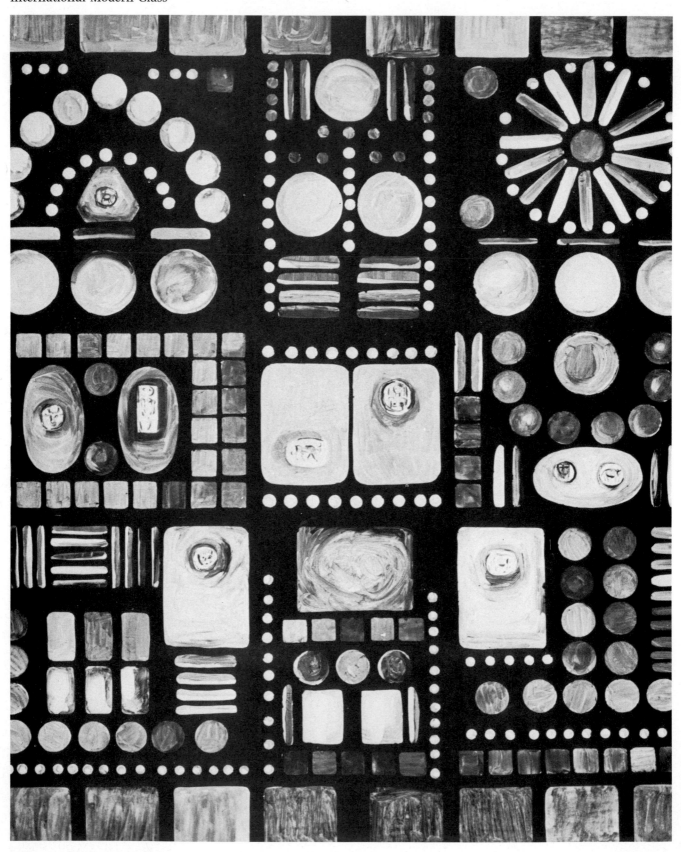

336 Stained glass panel, of coloured glass and lead strip, 1968, h. 39 in., w. 28 in.
DM Fritz Hans Lauten (Germany)
O Landesgewerbeamt, Baden-Württemberg Museum, Stuttgart, Germany

Screens and 'architectural' glass

337   Illuminated ceiling for the Banca Antoniana – Bank
of Padua, Italy, formed of prismatic blue and gold squares
D   Alberto Rosselli (Italy)
M   Salviati & C, Venice, Italy

338   Two of the crystal blocks used in the glass wall
(opposite)

International Modern Glass

339 Detail of the crystal blocks, forming the free-standing glass wall 'Light and Dark' in the Union Internationale des Télécommunications at Geneva. The wall is formed from 200 blocks of grey and white cut crystal, interspersed with blocks of 'Ravenna' glass in which warm glowing colours are 'locked' within the glass.
D   Sven Palmqvist (Sweden)
M   Orrefors Glass, Sweden

Screens and 'architectural' glass

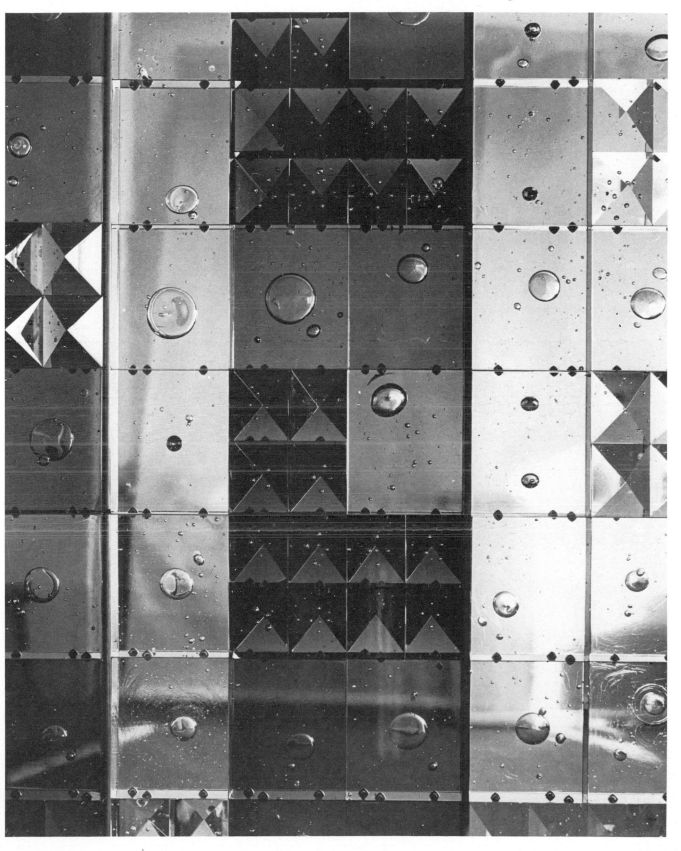

340 Composition of cast glass, titled 'Square', 1968,
6 ft. square
D Stanislav Libenský and Jaroslava Brychtova
(Czechoslovakia)
M Železný Brod Trade School, Czechoslovakia.
This husband and wife team have earned an
international reputation for their architectural
compositions and vitrails

341 The Sergelstorg development in Stockholm showing
the position of Edvin Öhrström's monumental glass
sculpture (see plate 342)

International Modern Glass

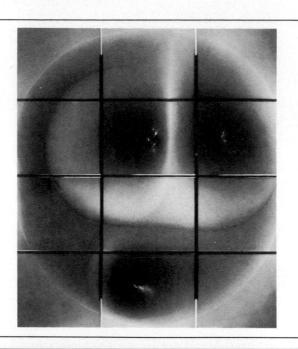

342 Section from the 120 ft. high sculpture in glass and stainless steel for Sergelstorg Square in the City of Stockholm, 1969
DM Edvin Öhrström (Sweden)

Screens and 'architectural' glass

343 Silvered glass engraving, titled 'Moses', 1970
DM John Hutton (New Zealand: working in England)

344 Window decoration, clear and coloured glass
unique, 1974
D   Oiva Toikka (Finland)
M   Arabia Glass, Finland

International Modern Glass

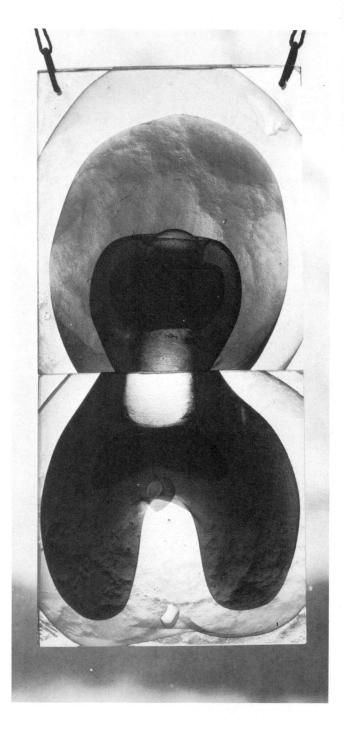

A select list of glass manufacturers

There has been no attempt to include every name associated with glass manufacture or design in this list. What is presented is a cross-section of the famous, the known, and the comparatively young and unknown names spanning a period from the late nineteenth century to the present time – some 300 names. While every attempt has been made to verify the information – often, in the case of contemporary workers, by correspondence and meetings – there will inevitably be some errors. I shall be glad to hear of corrections, and in compiling the list have been conscious many times of some words attributed to Dr. Johnson: 'It is impossible', he said, 'for an expositor not to write too little for some, and too much for others. He can judge what is necessary for his own experience, and how long soever he may deliberate will at last explain many lines which the learned will think impossible to be mistaken, and omit many for which the ignorant will want his help. These are censures merely relative and must be quietly endured.'

Abbreviations which occur frequently

Beard, 1968
Geoffrey Beard, *Modern Glass* (Studio Vista, and E.P. Dutton, London and New York, 1968).

Corning, 1959
'*Glass 1959*', catalogue of a 'Special Exhibition of International Contemporary Glass' (Corning Museum of Glass, New York, 1959).

Hilschenz, 1973
Helga Hilschenz (ed.), *Katalog des Kunstmuseums Düsseldorf, Glassammlung Hentrich Jugendstil und 20er Jahre* (Düsseldorf, 1973).

Liège, 1958
'*Aspects de la Verrerie Contemporaine*', catalogue of exhibition at Musée Curtius (Liège, 1958).

Paris, 1925
'*Les Années 25*', catalogue of exhibition at Musée des Arts Décoratifs (Paris, March–May 1966).

Polak, 1962
Ada Polak, *Modern Glass* (Faber & Faber, London, 1962)

AB Åfors Glasbruk, Sweden
Founded in 1876, Åfors is now part of the successful Kosta group (q.v.). It has always concentrated on art and domestic glass, and most of its current designs are the work of the talented Bertil Vallien (*see* Biography section). Its modern factory employing about 150 people is situated at Eriksmåla in Småland.

Arabia Glass, *see* **Nuutajärvi-Notsjö**

Baccarat, France
The 'Cristalleries de Baccarat' was founded in 1765 at Baccarat, near Nancy, and in Paris. The factory made both clear and coloured glass in the nineteenth century but was world-famous for its paperweights by the mid-century. It still produces limited editions of these (usually with enclosed sulphide portraits of prominent statesmen, etc.) and has an extensive table-glass production.

Barovier & Toso, Murano, Italy
This firm traces its origins back to the fourteenth century. It was revived in the nineteenth century, merged with the Toso family in 1936, and is now under the active direction of Ercole Barovier and his son, Angelo (*see* Biography section). It produces decorative, domestic table and lighting glass, and a number of unique glass sculptures.

Boda Bruks AB, Sweden
Boda, now part of the Kosta Group, was founded in 1864 in southern Sweden. Of recent years under the leadership of designers Fritz Kallenberg, Erik Höglund and his wife, Monica Backström, an effective range combining metal, wood and glass has been developed. The main production is of table and decorative glass formed in several different ways and usually characterised by Höglund's pressed medallion prunts of bold simple outline and clear, brown and green colour ranges.

Bohemia Glassworks, Poděbrady, Czechoslovakia
In July 1965 all the manufacturers of lead crystal in Czechoslovakia were merged into a single enterprise bearing the name *Bohemia* Glassworks. Its administrative centre, and a glassworks, was set up at Poděbrady, a spa town some thirty-five miles from Prague. The uniform management of production, flexibility in handling orders, financial control, quality control – all can be more satisfactorily achieved. In

its evolution of design, Bohemian cut lead crystal has already brought a number of progressive results and its designers, Ladislav Oliva and Vladimir Žahour, in particular, have had their exciting work widely shown in international exhibitions. With technical innovations such as automatic chemical polishing of the glass with acid, the traditional product is always being improved and enhanced.

Borské sklo (Nový Bor) National Corporation, Czechoslovakia
Glass production, which has been developing for several centuries in the Nový Bor region, led to the formation of a glass-making school there in 1856 at Kamenický Šenov. The school founded in 1870 in Nový Bor itself was concerned with commercial purposes. The artistic ideas found their expression in the Exbor Studios which Nový Bor set up. After 1945 a considerable number of outstanding glass artists (of the calibre of René Roubíček and Ladislav Oliva) realised their ideas here, and the Studios rank among the first in artistic glass production of all kinds, in Czechoslovakia. Most of the important international exhibits are prepared here and the Lobmeyr traditions of perfect artistic and handicraft creation (stemming from the days when the region was part of the Austrian Empire) is continued.

Daum, France
The 'Cristalleries de Nancy: Daum' was founded in 1875 and achieved considerable importance in the late nineteenth century when the Daum family came under the influence of Emile Gallé (*see* Biography section).

Harrachov Glassworks, Czechoslovakia
There was a glassworks on the estate of the Count of Harrach as early as 1712, and records imply that the works had been built much earlier. From the beginning, it attempted to produce glass of a higher quality than its predecessors, and achieved outstanding results in producing crystal glass. All the making and decorating shops were concentrated at Harrochov and a wide range of coloured and engraved glass was produced. It was among the first in Bohemia to make cased coloured glass and to enclose sulphide portraits. Harrachov exhibited at the 1851 Exhibition in London and at all the major shows to 1900 — some twenty-two. At each one it won prizes for its products and established extensive contacts with free-lance designers.

Today, Harrachov produces blown and hand-sculptured glass, drinking sets, all kinds of vases, ashtrays, bowls and jardinières. The same concentration on a wide colour range is apparent in all its pieces.
Designer: Milos Metelák.

Iittala Glass, Finland
Finland has had over sixty glassworks established in a long history but only three, Nuutajärvi (now Arabia Glass), Iittala and Riihimäki have stayed the course. Iittala was founded in 1881 and there are still those living in the Häme countryside who just recall the electric generators and electric light being installed in the cutting shops and offices of 1895. With an early concern for technical and economic progress, Iittala began to train the local people as glassmakers. However, the difficulties of the First World War — particularly the shortage of materials — caused the manager, Claes Norstedt, to sell out to Karhula Oy in 1917. This company, part of A. Ahlström Oy, initiated a period of great modernisation. Mechanically made glass was concentrated at Karhula and Iittala specialised in blown glass.

With early designs from Goran Hongell, Alvar Aalto and Gunnel Nyman, the firm steadily increased its range and production. Its liaison with the leading contemporary Finnish designers, Tapio Wirkkala and Timo Sarpaneva, and its continued success in exhibitions such as the Milan Triennales and Expos has done much to ensure international recognition for Finnish glass.

Jenaer Glaswerk Schott & Genossen, Mainz, Germany
Founded in Jena in 1884, this company has always concentrated on chemical and laboratory glassware and that in which the boro-silicate heat-resistant formulae can be used. The firm moved into West Germany in 1945, and erected a new factory at Mainz in 1951–2. It is now one of the largest producers of glass for optics, lighting, electronics, cooking and laboratory use. They use designs by the free-lance German designer, Heinz Löffelhardt, and he has done a great deal to produce clean functional lines in a glass which needs no decoration.

Jobling, James A. & Co. Ltd., Sunderland, England
Sunderland, in north-east England, is an old-established glass-making centre and in 1885 the Wear Flint Glass Works, which had been in existence since 1858, was taken over by James Augustus Jobling. The factory specialised in pressed domestic

glass, which made progress inevitable. The intervention of the First World War, with the consequent shortage of labour, even allowed for the installation of more labour-saving equipment. In 1921 Ernest Jobling-Purser negotiated with the Corning Glass Works in America for the right to manufacture their 'Pyrex' boro-silicate glass in England. This move led to great expansion of the Jobling business. The installation of even more efficient automatic presses and increases in factory area and staff brought them from a small business to a great modern factory. They have shown a consistent concern for good design and have collaborated with free-lance designers.

Kastrup Og Holmegaards Glasvaerker A/s, Denmark
The Wendt family of glassmakers from Norway established the first furnace at Holmegaard's Moor in November 1825. Since then glass has been produced continuously in the same place, originally using peat for fuel. In 1847 other glassworks were built, the first at Kastrup, near the coast of Copenhagen. The two enterprises had the same management until 1873 when Kastrup was sold. It prospered, amalgamated with other smaller firms in 1907 and came to control the total Danish production of industrial glassware. It turned to fully automatic bottle-making – then its staple concern – in 1912.

All this time Holmegaard's carried on and completely dominated the production of service glass. They co-operated with the Royal Danish Porcelain Factory with the purpose of designing service sets matching the porcelain sets. This led in 1924 to the employment of the first artist, O.J. Nielsen, who was later succeeded by the architect, Jacob E. Bang (see Biography section). More than any other, Bang contributed to the creation of modern Danish art glass.

In July 1965 Holmegaard's and Kastrup were blended into the one company. They now employ about two thousand persons distributed in four glassworks. With modern machines and plants they produce about 350 million bottles and glasses each year. In addition, Per Lütken's design team creates a full range of designs for mouth-blown glassware.

Kosta Glasbruk AB, Kosta, Sweden
In the Nordiska Museet in Stockholm is a hand-made glass which bears the explanation 'Made at Kosta in 1742'. Kosta, founded in that year, is the oldest Swedish glassworks still in production. Its early makers were also skilled – a Kosta chandelier with twelve arms dating from about 1760 hangs in the church at Herrakra, ten miles from the present factory.

The whole story of Kosta can be traced in its extensive archives, and more easily in the book issued on its bicentenary in 1942. From the turn of the present century it started its association with good designers – Wennerberg, Wallander, Ollers, Branzell, Dahlskog, Erixson, Skawonius, Bergh, Lindstrand, Morales-Schildt, Wärff, Sinnemark – all have merited biographical inclusion and several illustrations in this book. The Kosta group now includes the sister factories of Boda and Åfors, so it is hardly surprising that few glass factories anywhere can exceed the achievements of Kosta.

Lalique & Cie, France
The 'Cristal de Lalique' was founded by René Lalique in 1909 at Combs-la-Ville. When René Lalique died in 1945 (see Biography section), the business was carried on by Marc Lalique. Together with his daughter, Marie-Claude Lalique, they have laid stress on fine table glass and on glass for architectural and interior decoration purposes. The firm has splendid showrooms at 11 rue Royale, Paris, and makes its glass at a factory at Wingen-sur-Moder on the German border which René Lalique acquired in 1918.

N.V. Vereenigde Glasfabriek Leerdam, Leerdam, Holland
Established in 1765, Leerdam did not enter its important phase until its contact with members of the Dutch De Stijl group about 1915. Encouraged by the efforts of H.P. Berlage and K.P.C. de Bazel, Leerdam asked them for glass designs. This close collaboration between artist and industry has always continued. Under A.D. Copier's design leadership, the company (which as Glasfabriek Leerdam merged with N.V. Vereenigde – the United Glassworks – in 1937) founded its unique series of free-formed glass, called 'Unica', and more recently a glass-training school (1940) and a 'Glasvorm-centrum' (1968).

In the National Glass Museum at Leerdam the development of the company is clearly illustrated.

Lobmeyr, J. & L., Austria
Founded in Vienna in 1823 as a glass-selling and engraving shop Lobmeyr specialised in engraved decorative and table glass. Some of this was of a pure form. A branch firm was established at Steinschönau in 1918 and the firm was led with great distinction from about 1900 by Stephan and Hans Harold Rath (see Biography section). In the 1925 Paris Exhibition, Rath was said to have 'availed himself of the best

modern artists. They on their part have knowledge of the medium into which their designs have been translated. Their crystal or muslin glass, and the designs made for them by Jaroslav Horejc have earned Lobmeyr a lasting place in glass history.

LIT: R. Schmidt, *100 Jahre österreichische Glaskunst Lobmeyr: 1823–1923* (Vienna, 1925); Polak, pp.63–4.

Moser Glass, Czechoslovakia
When Ludvik Moser established his works at Karlovy Vary in 1857 he concentrated on providing luxurious glass for table use. With its 'Maria Theresa', the 'Splendid', the 'Royal Set', and other aptly named table services Moser has tried to originate glass which is both attractive and functional. With many of Czechoslovakia's free-lance designers working for it, and with its resident designers Oldřich Lípa and Luboš Metelák designing cut and engraved glass, Moser's original aim is maintained.

LIT: *Czechoslovak Glass Review*, 1967, No.7.

Nuutajärvi-Notsjö Glass (Arabia Glass), Finland
Urjala, a couple of hours' car ride from Helsinki, is the home of Nuutajärvi-Notsjö Glass, founded in 1793 and the oldest glassworks still functioning in Finland. In its early years, the factory had difficulty in finding enough glass-blowers and, in common with all glassworks, has had its years of boom and slump. The development of its art glass programme owed much to the talented Finnish designer Gunnel Nyman (1909–1948). The glassworks' economic problems ran good and bad until it was turned into a joint stock company in 1949, but within months a tragic fire destroyed the workshops and the shareholders had no alternative but to sell to the great industrial concern of Wärtsilä. This has been entirely to its advantage, bringing complete modernisation, new machines, good press and public relations (Wärtsilä also owns the leading ceramic factory 'Arabia') and new buildings to blend with those of the old ones which had survived.

This fusion of old and new can be seen in a production which covers blown and pressed household and decorative glass and individual works of art. It is fortunate for this factory, and for Finnish glass, that it is led in design terms by Kaj Franck and Oiva Toikka, who have international reputations for the excellence of their work, and the clarity of thought to which it bears witness. Each object is fully 'thought through' all its stages to produce work of very high quality and aesthetic standard. This is particularly true of the ranges of pressed-glass goods.

Orrefors Glasbruk AB, Orrefors, Sweden
Of more recent foundation (1898) than nearby Kosta (1742), Orrefors has nevertheless maintained the same high standards and insistence on good design. This process was started by the employment in the 1910–30 period of Simon Gate and Edward Hald. Their superb designs for engraving, the development of 'Graal' glass (page 25), and their technical and aesthetic brilliance put the firm foremost in the important exhibitions such as that at Paris in 1937. They also started the training of some of the present designers, particularly Nils Landberg, Sven Palmqvist and John Selbing. With their colleagues Ingeborg Lundin, Gunnar Cyrén and Carl Fagerlund the group produced many important series of glass ('Ravenna' and 'Fuga') and still excels at the production of table-glass, lighting glass and unique design items. Its subsidiary at Sandviks concentrates on technical, domestic and window glass.

Peill and Putzler, Düren, Germany
The firm of Peill was founded in 1903 and merged with the lampshade firm of Putzler in 1947. Employing over a thousand employees, it is best known for its lead crystal. All articles are mouth-blown and hand-cut but some interesting variations have been achieved. By varying the direction of the cut, abrading the surface in other areas to contrast the design, applying bas-reliefs of platinum film and achieving a myriad of other relief effects, Peill has produced something new in lead crystal. It also knows how to market and describe it in attractive terms. Some of their designs are by the Bauhaus-trained designer, Wilhelm Wagenfeld.

Riihimäen Lasi Oy, Finland
The idea of founding the Riihimäki glassworks in a town which became one of Finland's most important rail junctions was that of M. A. Kolehmainen and his son. As Technical Director of Karhula Glass he knew his subject, and in 1910 set up at Riihimäki, and rapidly expanded the manufacture. He held a competition in design for artists in 1913 and industrial designing of glass was begun there in the early 1920s. The great Riihimäki glass competition of 1928 was the first real venture in this field. Its aim was to produce some new designs for everyday cheap soda glass: no cutting or engraving being

allowed, the shape was supposed to dominate. The competition was won by Henry Ericsson (1898–1933), the first of a succession of talented artists to be associated with Riihimäki. Designs came from Arttu Brummer (1891–1951) and Gunnel Nyman (1909–1948) and ensured that Riihimäki kept its place in the international race.

Today the same ideals are the concern of the designers Helena Tynell, Nanny Still McKinney, Tamara Aladin, Aimo Okkolin and Erkkitapio Siiroinen.

Rosenthal AG, Selb, Germany
A description of the successful design policy of this firm and its employment of internationally-known designers and teams of selectors is given on page 41.

Saint-Louis, France
The 'Cristalleries de Saint-Louis' was founded as the 'Verrerie Royale de Saint-Louis' in 1767, and with Baccarat is among the oldest glass factories in France. It has traded under its present name since 1829, and was famous in the mid-nineteenth century for its production of paperweights. It now concentrates on tableware and lamps.
LIT: Paul Hollister, *Encyclopedia of Glass Paperweights* (Clarkson N. Potter, New York, 1969).

Salviati & Co., Venice, Italy
The great revival of Murano glassmaking in the nineteenth century was in part owing to Antonio Salviati, who founded his own firm in 1859. Its exhibit at the Paris 1867 Exhibition marked an important step in the revival and in the following years Salviati's production was awarded much acclaim. The company obtained the first prize at the 1933 Milan Triennale and again at the 1937 Paris Exhibition. In the post-war period it has continued to win awards for its decorative items, table sets and for important works in the field of lighting fixtures.

Sèvres, Cristallerie de, France
The Sèvres glassworks was built in 1725 on land belonging to the Duke of Orléans. In 1756, Madame de Pompadour had it moved to buildings situated in her park at the Château of Bellevue, in Meudon. At her death it was managed (until 1777) by her brother, and the King's counsellor, the Marquis de Marigny. After the Revolution it was worked for more than forty years by a master glassmaker, Jean Casadavant. He

made goblets, flasks and remarkable translucent opalines. Some of these pieces are exhibited in the Meudon Museum.

Later the works was taken over by the joint Sèvres works at Choisy-le-Roi, which specialises in making vases, lamps and ornamental objects in crystal and opaline. Its subsidiary produces commercial glass for the chemical, optical and jewellery trades.

Steuben Glass, New York, U.S.A.
Steuben Glass was established in 1933 as an outgrowth of an older company. Thirty years earlier an English glassmaker, Frederick Carder (1863–1963), had gone to America to establish a glass factory at Corning, New York, naming it after Steuben County in which the city of Corning lies. His factory was acquired in 1918 by that great company. Thereafter it became the Steuben Division of the Corning Glass Company, producing handmade glass in a wide variety of shapes and colours.

In 1933 Arthur A. Houghton Jr. took over the Steuben Division. As a scholar and aesthete he wanted to produce crystal glass to the highest standards of design, quality and workmanship. For overall direction Houghton turned to the architect, John Monteith Gates, and with Sidney Waugh as first designer a start was made. A formal design department was established in 1936. In the intervening forty years or so to the present Steuben, with the help of many younger designers, and with whole series in crystal created by guest designers, has achieved an international reputation for limited editions and unique pieces.

In 1951 the Corning Glass Center was built at Corning, New York. Steuben Glass is made there, and the Center also houses the splendid Corning Museum of Glass. This provides an international service to historians and visitors by its exhibitions, permanent collections, annual *Journal*, publications and conferences. The high standards of material and workmanship which go into Steuben Glass cannot be faulted. The designs, with decoration mostly for the engraver to work, are not to everyone's liking, but there is abundant evidence of care, thought and, on occasion, virtuosity.
LIT: James S. Plaut, *Steuben Glass* (New York, 1951); *The Story of Steuben Glass* (company issue, 1964).

Stevens & Williams Ltd., Brierley Hill, England
This famous works is the descendant of that founded in the eighteenth century by descendants of the Huguenot glass-

makers who settled in the Stourbridge district in the early seventeenth century. By 1796 it was working nine pots for the Honeyborne family. Then in 1824 they transferred ownership to Joseph Silvers and Joseph Stevens and the partnership became Stevens & Williams in 1846.

The nineteenth-century manufacturing history of the firm — which can be traced in the firm's own museum and in the neighbouring Brierley Hill Municipal Collections — was bound up with the careers of John Northwood and his son (*see* Biography section). They also employed the architect, Keith Murray, as a designer in the 1930s, and have concentrated on full lead crystal tableware. Their Moor Lane works, on land bought by Robert Honeyborne in 1732, was reconstructed in 1870 and again in 1945, and is still under direction of descendants of the Silvers–Stevens partnership.

LIT: John Northwood II, *John Northwood I, His Contribution to the Stourbridge Glass Industry* (Stourbridge, 1958); D.R. Guttery, *From Broad Glass to Cut Crystal* (Leonard Hill, London, 1956).

Stuart & Sons Ltd., Stourbridge, England

Again, this leading lead-crystal manufacturer owes its origin to descendants of the Huguenot glassmakers who settled in the Stourbridge district, and whose genealogy is still intertwined with its history. By 1796 the Red House Glassworks was established (to be followed by the adjacent White House) and in 1827 the Stuart family had entered the industry. Through Frederick Stuart a partnership was formed, and from the first the firm specialised in cut glass. This partnership with the Mills family was dissolved in 1881 and four years later the title of the firm was changed. Frederick Stuart, who died in 1900, had seven sons so appropriately it became Stuart & Sons. The cone of the Red House works still stands above the present factory, the Stuart family are still in charge, and the demand for its lead crystal continues unabated.

Stumf, Touvier, Violette & Cie., Cristallerie de Pantin, Pantin, Seine, France

The 'Cristallerie de Pantin' was established as such *c.*1900, having produced work as Stumf, Touvier, Violette et Cie from 1851. Some of their work, often incised and gilded, was designed by the Dutch architect, H.P. Berlage (1856–1934), and by the designer 'FP'. They also had connections with Legras (q.v.) and exhibited at Paris, 1878 and 1900, and Turin, 1911. They ceased to work about 1937.

COLL: Conservatoire des Arts et Métiers, Paris; Kunstmuseum, Düsseldorf.
LIT: Polak, 1962, p.52; B. and H. Blount, *French Cameo Glass* (Des Moines, Iowa, 1968), p.22; Hilschenz, 1973, p.353.

Tiroler Glashütte — Claus Josef Riedel K.G., Austria

Established in Bohemia by the Riedel family in 1756. From this time until 1945 the business has been transferred from father to son. By 1860 Josef Riedel (1816–1894) had 1250 men working in his factory. His son, Josef (1862–1924) discovered that selenium dyed glass ruby-red in colour. The present factory in the Austrian Tyrol was set up in 1957 by Walter Riedel (b.1895) and his son, Claus Josef Riedel (*see* Biography section). Its 'Exquisit' glass was chosen by two of the selectors of the 1959 Corning Glass Museum exhibition 'Glass 1959' as displaying 'evidence of superior ability in the art of glassmaking and decorating'.

Val-Saint-Lambert, Belgium

In May 1826 François Kemlin and August Lelièvre (who had been assistant to Aimé Gabriel d'Artigues when he controlled the Cristalleries de Saint-Louis, q.v., in Lorraine) lit the first furnaces of the glass factory at Val-Saint-Lambert. One of the first principal shareholders was King William of Orange. By 1846 the factory had been extended to seven furnaces and a new cutting shop had been opened. Lelièvre returned in 1863 but expansion continued with the acquisition of the Namur company. Further acquisitions in 1883 allowed the company to reorganise financially and become constituted as it is today — the 'Cristalleries du Val-Saint-Lambert'.

Despite problems in both world wars the factory has maintained a traditional manufacture of lead-crystal table glass, and a production of cement-jointed stained-glass windows.

Designers: George Graffart from 1926 to 1958; René Delvenne from 1922 to 1967.

LIT: Joseph Philippe, *Le Val-St-Lambert*, Librarie Halbert, Liège, 1974.

Vereinigte Farbenglaswerke AG, Zwiesel, Germany

Established in 1870, 'Zwiesel' combined with two glassworks in Saxony and Czechoslovakia in 1898. After World War II its facilities were used by Jenaer Glass (q.v.) until they restarted their own production in 1953. Using the free-lance designer Heinz Löffelhardt, 'Zwiesel' won a gold medal at the XIth

Triennale for its crystal wine glasses (Series 1007 + 1011).
LIT: *Zeitschrift Kunst & Handwerk*, 1964, No.1.

Waterford Glass Ltd., Waterford, Ireland

Waterford began to develop as a centre for cut glass in the early eighteenth century and was given greater encouragement to develop when John Hill took Stourbridge glassmakers there later in the century. After a high reputation in Regency times the factory declined and closed in 1851. In 1947 a small training factory was opened again at Waterford and in 1951 a much larger building was completed. By 1952, after a lapse of a hundred years, lead crystal was again being produced in Waterford! The factory has, however, done little to break from traditional lead crystal — could not a little of the design skills of the Kilkenny workshops be introduced?

Webb Corbett Ltd., Stourbridge, England

Huguenot glassmakers working the Coalbournhill site, the intervention of John Hill (who later set up the Irish Waterford industry), the success of the Stevens family in taking over from Hill: there are many confusing strands of history to take into account in the history of this lead-crystal enterprise. The name of Webb had long been important in the local industry and the present firm of Thomas Webb & Corbett (subsequently named Webb Corbett) was constituted in 1897. The inevitable energy and expansion allowed acquisition of the Tutbury Glass Works in 1906, and production has continued at both Stourbridge and Tutbury. The Webbs still manage and the firm has struck out with adventurous design policies (using the services of Lord Queensberry). It has also consolidated its position by becoming part of the Doulton Fine China Group.
Designer: I.M. Stevens (now Stourbridge College of Art staff); David Smith.

Webb, Thomas & Sons, Stourbridge, England

In 1837, as Queen Victoria came to the throne, Thomas Webb acquired the Platts Glasshouse. He worked it until 1856 when his expanding business caused him to transfer to the nearby site of Dennis Park, still the headquarters of this famous lead-crystal firm. In his rebuilt works Thomas Webb and his sons concentrated on a wide and colourful variety of table glass — won a Grand Prix at the 1878 Paris Exhibition, and took the famous cameo-engravers George and Thomas Woodall into their employ.

In 1920 the works was bought by Webb's Crystal Glass Co., and developed under the Swedish-trained managership of Sven Fogelberg. Still concentrating on tableware they developed subsidiary interests elsewhere in electric lamp-bulb- and valve-making, and cathode-ray tube-blowing for television receivers. In 1921 they acquired the Edinburgh and Leith Flint Glass Works, which consolidated their position in traditional markets. They are now part of Crown House Investments trading as Dema Glass and have carried out much rebuilding and re-equipping of their Dennis Hall site.
Designer: David Hammond.

Whitefriars Glass Ltd., Wealdstone, England

The original Whitefriars works stood near St Paul's Cathedral in the City of London and was established in 1680. It had a succession of owners as a flint house, and became James Powell & Sons in 1835. They concentrated on domestic tableware, and also showed chandeliers in their 1851 Crystal Palace exhibit. The main development in these years, however, was the employment of Philip Webb as designer in making table glass for William Morris (plate 1). The purity of line in glass of the 1860s was not equalled elsewhere for many years. Powell's continued with well-designed glass under the direction of Harry J. Powell, the glass historian (*see* Bibliography). The company also produced stained glass and coloured glass for mosaic work.

At new premises in 1923 at Wealdstone, Harrow, the firm took the title of 'Whitefriars Glass'. Having occupied their City premises for almost 250 years they had traditions to maintain and a brazier mounted on a cart carried the fire from London to Harrow to light the new furnaces. Their reputation has grown under the direction of W.J. Wilson, a pioneer in the revival of diamond-point engraving, and Geoffrey Baxter.

Železný Brod Glass, Czechoslovakia

The corporation of Železnobrodské sklo is now among the largest of the Czechoslovak glass-producing enterprises. With its seven plants it ranges over the whole field of glass production and works in close liaison with the School of Glassmaking Art at Železný Brod (founded 1920). There is some specialisation in costume jewellery, but it was really the widespread interests of the school and its designers, resulting in the setting up of small workshops, which led to the merging of them all in 1948 as the 'Železný Brod Glass, National Corporation'.
LIT: *Czechoslovak Glass Review*, 1966, No.3

A select list of designers

Aalto, Hugo Henrik Alvar b.1898   Finland
Professor, member of the Finnish Academy, Aalto graduated in architecture in 1921 and has had his own office since 1923. As Finland's most distinguished contemporary architect, he has been involved in numerous schemes and has designed furniture, light-fittings, glass and textiles, often as part of bigger works. His Savoy vases (1937) are still in production by Iittala Glassworks.
EXH: (glass), Paris, 1937; New York World Fair, 1939
LIT: Gerd Hatje (ed.), *Encyclopedia of Modern Architecture* (London, 1963), pp.28–32 (references cited).

Aladin, Tamara b.1932   Finland
Has worked for Riihimäen Lasi Oy in Finland since 1959. In her designs is observance of simple shape above all else. The blown glasses and vases in clear and grey-red contrast with the moulded glass for everyday use. Also works in ceramics.
Plate 133

Alberius, Olle b.1926   Sweden
Studied at Konstfackskolan, Stockholm 1952–6. Worked for various potteries in Sweden. Joined Orrefors in 1971.
COLL: Nationalmuseum, Stockholm.

Ander, Gunnar b.1908   Sweden
Working as an architect he has designed in metals and ceramics, and in glass for Lindshammars and its sister company, Alsterbro.

Argy-Rousseau, Gabriel b.1885   France
Besides exhibiting pâte-de-verre pieces at the salons of the 1920s he also made delicate bowls and a series of lamps.
LIT: Ernest Tisserand, 'La pâte-de-verre', *L'Art Vivant* (1929), pp.484–6.
Ray and Lee Grover, *Art Glass Nouveau* (1967), pl.36; Martin Battersby, *The Decorative Twenties* (Studio Vista, London, 1969); Hilschenz, 1973, p.148.

Åsélius-Lidbeck, Catherina b.1941   Sweden
Studied ceramics at Stockholm Konstfackskolan, 1962–6, and practised in glass at Orrefors and Kosta. At Gullaskrufs Glass since 1967.

Asti, Sergio b.1926   Italy
Trained as an architect, graduating in 1953, Asti has been much involved with the Triennales at Milan (in which city he was born). Organised the Industrial Design Exhibition at the 1957 Triennale (gold medal), and was Commissary for Industrial Design at the 1960 Triennale. Has done a considerable amount of product design for various Italian firms, and has designed glass for some years for Salviati of Venice.
Plate 140

Atkins, Lloyd b.1922   U.S.A.
Born in New York and educated at the Pratt Institute. Designer with Steuben Glass. His work is in public collections as far from New York as Rangoon and Teheran.

Awashima, Masakichi b.1914   Japan
Studied at the Design Department of the Art School of Japan. Worked with Kozo Kagami, a pupil of Wilhelm von Eiff, from 1935 to 1946, and with the Hoyar Crystal Glassworks from 1946 to 1950. The Awashima Glass Design Institute, founded in 1950, became the Awashima Glass Company in 1956.
EXH: Pilkington Glass Museum, 'Artists in Glass', 1969, No.8
Plates 108, 142

Backström, Monica b.1939   Sweden
Studied at the Konstfackskolan, Stockholm, 1959–64. Designed at Boda from 1965. Noted for introducing small nails, copper-thread and bits of metal into molten glass, silvering the surfaces and creating new shapes. The glass partitions which she designed, with the collaboration of her husband, Erik Höglund (q.v.), at Boda were installed in the new Sweden House (1969) in the Hamngaten, Stockholm, and form a particularly attractive setting.
EXH: Växjö, Smålands Museum, summer 1965
LIT: *Form*, No.9, 1965, pp.608–9
Plates 112, 139, 329

Bang, Jacob E. 1899–1965   Denmark
Began work as an architect and sculptor after training at Royal Academy of Fine Arts. Important design influence in Denmark with firm of Holmegaards, subsequently joined to Kastrup, which he had entered in 1955. His work at Holmegaards was mostly engraved by the Swedish engraver, Elving Runemalm.
EXH: Liège, 1958, Nos.233–8; Corning, 1959, Nos.55–7.
LIT: G.M. Heddle, *Manual on etching and engraving glass*

(Tiranti, London, 1961), pl.31; Polak, 1962, pp.51, 73, 83, pls.47b, 94a.

Bang, Michael b.1944   Denmark
Son of Jacob E. Bang (*above*) he was educated as a ceramics artist and designed for the Royal Porcelain Factory, Copenhagen. He had his own model workshop from 1964 to 1966. Having designed for a time for Ekenas Glass in southern Sweden, he returned to the Odense department in Denmark of Kastrup-Holmegaards Glass. He has specialised in attractive ranges of table-lamps.

Bar-Tal, Ariel b.1920   Israel
Born in Budapest, he trained as a painter at the Budapest Academy. At the German occupation of Hungary he was, as a Jew, imprisoned and spent over four years in concentration camps. Towards the end of the war he succeeded in escaping to Italy where he studied and worked as a sculptor. In 1950 he came to Israel and was particularly successful at improving on ancient shapes and colours of glass he studied in the Haaretz Museum.
EXH: New York, America–Israel Culture House, March April 1968.
LIT: Elka Schrijver, *Glass and Crystal* (Merlin Press, London, 1964), p.87.

Barovier, Angelo b.1927   Italy
Son of Ercole Barovier (*below*), Angelo is a widely exhibited painter and glass designer as well as export manager of the Barovier & Toso Company, one of Murano's leading glass companies.
COLL: Corning Museum, New York; National Glassmuseum, Leerdam, Holland.
EXH: Corning Museum, 1959, No.168; Paris, Salon des Artistes Décorateurs, regular exhibitor; Verona, 1960.

Barovier, Ercole b.1889   Italy
Inherited the firm 'Artisti Barovier' from his father after the First World War. In 1936 he founded a new factory, Barovier & Toso, with the brothers Artemio and Decio Toso, whose family also traced their glass traditions back to the seventeenth century. As an artist and chemist Ercole Barovier is, after forty years, still the chief designer of his firm. During his career he has created and exhibited more than 25,000 different models of vases, bowls, chandeliers, figurines, etc.

He has discovered new technical processes and developed new compounds for colouring.
COLL: Victoria & Albert Museum, London; Louvre, Paris; Corning Museum, New York; Curtius Museum, Liège; National Glassmuseum, Leerdam, Holland, etc.
EXH: Has been represented at most important art exhibitions from 1925 onwards, including the Venice Biennales, Milan Triennales and the Universal Exhibitions in Brussels, New York, Paris, Berlin and Montreal.
LIT: Liège, 1958, Nos.264–6.
Plate 256

Báthory, Julia b.1909   Hungary
Studied in Germany at the Schule für Angewandte Kunst, 1929, at Dessau. Worked from 1932 to 1939 (with some interruptions) in Paris. Organised the glass section of the Secondary School of Fine and Applied Art in Budapest in 1952 and led this until her retirement in 1969. In 1957 she was awarded the Munkacsy Prize and in 1969 the Silver Degree of the Order of Work.
COLL: Musée des Arts Décoratifs, Paris; Musée du Verre, Liège; Iparművészeti Museum, Budapest; Bakonyi Museum, Veszprém.

Baxter, Geoffrey P. b.1922   England
Studied at Guildford Art School and the Royal College of Art, graduating as Des. R.C.A. Joined James Powell & Sons (Whitefriars) Ltd., in 1954 and has designed many successful lines. With the excellent lead given by the firm's former managing director, William J. Wilson (q.v.), Whitefriars Glass Ltd. (as it is now called) has done much for England's sad design reputation in glass. The company's work challenges and often surpasses the best in Scandinavia. Geoffrey Baxter has recently spent much time introducing a range of *mille-fiori* paperweights which rival the best of French nineteenth-century production.
Plate 277

Bergh, Elis 1881–1954   Sweden
The usual schools of industrial-art training in Stockholm led Bergh into the office of the architect Agi Lindegren, 1903–4. In 1905 he received an official scholarship to study in Munich. From 1906 to 1915 he designed at Böhlmarks lamp factory, making many designs for the Pukebergs glassworks. He worked from 1916 to 1921 as factory manager at Herman

Bergman's metal-casting factory, and from 1921 to 1928 as designer for Hallbergs Gudsmeds AB in Stockholm. In 1929 Kosta Glass invited him to be director of design, a post he held until his retirement in 1950. The purity of form and swirling designs for cutting which characterise Bergh's work have seldom been equalled.

COLL: Kosta, factory collection; Nationalmuseum, Stockholm; Toledo Museum of Art (Inv. 40.41).

Plates 67, 76

Berndt, Viktor b.1919   Sweden
Studied at Källströms, and then in Murano. Has designed for Flygsfors Glass since 1950.

COLL: Corning Museum, New York; Curtius Museum, Liège.

EXH: Växjö, Smålands Museum, June–September 1964 and 1968.

Blomberg, Kjell b.1931   Sweden
Studied at the Stockholm Konstfackskolan. Has travelled in Europe and been with Gullaskruv Glass since 1954.

COLL: Nationalmuseum, Stockholm; Nordiska Museum, Stockholm; Nordenfjeldske Museum, Trondheim.

Bohnert, Gertrude *fl.*1945–60   Switzerland
Ranked by many as the finest diamond-point engraver on the continent. Self-taught, she excelled at the depiction of animals and insects in line and stipple and influenced the early work of Phyllis Boissier (q.v.).

LIT: G.M. Heddle, *A manual on etching and engraving glass* (Tiranti, London, 1961), pls.66–8.

Boissier, Phyllis *fl.*1946–70   England
Taught herself to engrave in diamond-point in 1946. Works directly and only does preliminary drawings for portraits. Was influenced in her early work by that of Gertrude Bohnert (q.v.).

COLL: Victoria & Albert Museum, London; Manchester City Art Gallery; Corning Museum, New York.

EXH: Corning, 1959, No.60; Steuben International Glass Exhibition (principal U.S.A. cities), 1960; Royal Festival Hall, London, 1963, with Laurence Whistler and Shiela Elmhirst (q.v.); Paris, 1st International Congress of Diamonds.

LIT: *Pottery and Glass*, November 1957, p.347; *Pottery Gazette*, September 1958, p.1124.

Plates 189, 191

Borgström, Bo b.1929   Sweden
Ceramist and glass designer with Aseda Glassworks, Sweden, since 1955. Has studied in Europe and America after training at Stockholm.

Borgström, Carl-Einar b.1914   Sweden
Studied sculpture. Has worked in several media and done glass-designing for Bjorkshults Glass.

Boylen, Michael b.1935   U.S.A.
Educated at Yale University, and the University of Wisconsin.
    Like most of Harvey Littleton's pupils Boylen has had an active exhibition and teaching programme since graduation.

COLL: University of Wisconsin; Corning Museum of Glass, New York; Museums at Cleveland; Delaware; Bennington; Dartmouth Art College; University of Vermont; Milwaukee Art Center.

EXH: Frequent, one-man, invitational, national and regional juried exhibitions, including Toledo Glass Nationals.

Plate 234

Boysen, Bill H.   U.S.A.
Educated at the Universities of Washington and Wisconsin, Boysen is one of the younger group of American glass artists whose work is to be found in most significant exhibitions of hand-blown glass.

Plate 236

Brandt, Åsa b.1940   Sweden
Trained at the Konstfackskolan, 1962–7, she studied at the Gerrit Rietveld Academie in Amsterdam and the Royal College of Art in London, 1967. Now has her own glass studio at Torshalla, Sweden.

COLL: Nationalmuseum, Stockholm; Craft Museum, Copenhagen, Gothenburg and Eskilstuna Museums, Sweden.

EXH: Form Design Center, Malmö, 1969; Eskilstuna Konstmuseum, 1969; Varbergs Museum, 1970, etc.

LIT: Dansk Brugkunst, Vol.41 (3) 1969, pp.73–5 (review of Malmö exhibition).

Branzell, Sten 1893–1959   Sweden
Studied at the schools of industrial art in Stockholm. Thereafter worked for the architect Ragnar Ostberg and in 1919

went to Gothenburg. Helped Ernst Torulf with his designs for 'Göte platsen' and the Gothenburg exhibition in 1923. Travelled and studied in many countries and from 1926, as Gothenburg City Architect, led a busy varied life. His design activities included work for Kosta Glass from 1922 to 1930.

Bratt, Monica b.1913   Sweden
After training at the Konstfackskolan in Stockholm she joined Reijmyre Glass as designer in 1937.
EXH: Liège, 1958, Nos.373–5.
LIT: *Form*, 1951, pp.40–1.

Brocard, Philippe-Joseph d.1896   France
His work in imitation of Islamic lamps, in multi-coloured glass adorned with enamel paints, became very fashionable in France in the late nineteenth century. He first gained attention at the Paris Exhibition of 1867. The importance of French glass, until at least the end of the century, meant that Brocard's work was both appreciated and sought after. His activities in glass were c.1880–5.
COLL: Musée des Arts Décoratifs, Paris; Royal Scottish Museum, Edinburgh; Kunstmuseum, Düsseldorf.
LIT: James Barrelet, *La verrerie en France* . . . Paris 1953, pp.140, 145, 171.
Polak, 1962, pls.14, 15a & b; Hilschenz 1973, p.155.
Plate 7

Brörby, Severin b.1932   Norway
Engaged by Hadelands Glassworks in the engraving department in 1948. From 1952 to 1955 he trained at the State School of Applied Arts and Crafts in Oslo and since 1956 has been a designer for Hadelands. He was awarded the 'Badge for Good Design' in 1966, and in 1967 the City of Oslo Scholarship, which enabled him to travel and study in Canada and America.
EXH: Corning, 1959, No.221; Milan Triennale XII, 1960.

Brummer, Arttu 1891–1951   Finland
Set up his own interior design office in 1913. He designed glass for Riihimäki Glassworks, taught at the Central School of Industrial Design, and was Curator of the Museum of Crafts and Design, Helsinki, and Chairman of the Association of Designers, Ornamo. A creator and innovator in Finnish art glass, Brummer was involved in many important commissions. His chalice 'Breaker' was presented to the President of France at the 1937 Paris World Fair. In 1961 his chalice 'Finlandia', designed for Sibelius's eightieth birthday, was chosen as the 'Work of the Decade'.
LIT: Kerttu Niilonen, *Finnish Glass* (Tammi, Helsinki, 1966), pp.17–18.

Brychta, Jaroslav b.1896   Czechoslovakia
Studied at the Artisan School at Litomyšl and then for seven years, 1912–19, at the Industrial Art School in Prague under Professor Drahoňovský. In 1920 he began a period of practical work at the glassmaking trade schools at Bor and Kamenický Šenov, and from that year taught at the glassmaking trade school at Železný Brod. He specialised in small glass sculptures.
LIT: *Czechoslovak Glass Review*, No.3, 1966; No.6, 1966, pp.188–91.
Plate 304

Brychtová-Zahradniková, Jaroslava b.1924   Czechoslovakia
From 1945 to 1950 at the School of Applied Art in Prague working under Professor K. Štipl, and Academy of Fine Arts in Prague. Since 1950 she has been employed as industrial artist at the Železný Brod Glassworks of the National Corporation. With her husband, Stanislav Libenský (q.v.), she has achieved a considerable reputation for glass spatial works at such exhibitions as the São Paulo Biennale (No.8, 1965) where they were awarded a gold medal for 'Grey Composition' and 'Blue Composition'. Their glass 'architectural screens' for the International Railway Union in Paris testify to their profound talent and all-round understanding of glass. Both are State Prize Laureates.
EXH: Expo '58, Brussels; São Paulo (*see above*), 1965; Expo '67, Montreal; Expo '70, Osaka, 'The Glass River of Life' exhibit.
LIT: *Modern Bohemian Glass*, Artia, Prague, 1963; *Czechoslovakia Glass Review*, No.4, 1966, p.125; Vol. XXIV, 1969, special 'Art in Glass' issue.
Plate 338

Burian, Ivan b.1939   Czechoslovakia
Read architecture at Prague University, then joined the Academy of Applied Arts to study glass and sculpture; he is tutor of art history and glass design at Železný Brod.
EXH: Major Czech exhibitions; Exp '70, Osaka; Heal's, London, February, 1970.
LIT: *Czechoslovak Glass Review*, June 1965, pp.5, 9.

Burton, John   U.S.A.
A native of Yorkshire, England, he first worked for the steel industry in Sheffield where he acquired a practical knowledge of chemistry and metallurgy. In 1921 co-founder of the Sheffield Educational Settlement where he served as director of art and crafts. In 1927 he decided to settle in California and during the thirties he lectured at many western universities and colleges. In 1942 he became an American citizen. As a glassworker he excels at lamp-work.
COLL: Victoria & Albert Museum, London; Corning
       Museum, New York.
EXH: Fisher Art Gallery, University of S. California, 1957;
      Toledo Nationals, etc.
LIT: *Craft Horizons*, November/December 1960; John
      Burton, *Glass, Handblown, Sculptured, Colored;
      Philosophy and Method* (Pitman, London, 1969).

Čabla, Bohurnil b.1926   Czechoslovakia
Trained 1945–7 at the Glassmaking Trade School at Kamenický Šenov and 1947–51 at the Pedagogical Faculty, section of plastic art education, at Olomouc. Since 1957 he has worked as a teacher at the Glassmaking Trade School. Specialises in painted and etched glass, and hand-modelled glass.

Cappellin, Giacomo b.1887   Italy
Produced glass in a simple style and is best known for his copies of sixteenth-century Venetian glass, some produced in liaison with Paolo Venini who joined him in 1921. In this year their firm 'Vetri Soffiati Muranesi Cappellin-Venini & C.' was started, but their main patron, Andrea Rioda (whose furnace they had taken over), died soon after. Venini left the firm in 1925, the year they exhibited at Paris.
LIT: Polak, 1962, p.55; Exhibition Catalogue 'Vetri di
      Murano, 1860–1960', Verona, spring 1960;
      information from Professor G. Mariacher.

Carder, Frederick 1863–1963   U.S.A.
Born in England, he worked his way through the ranks of local pottery and glass manufacturers. Finally became a designer for Stevens & Williams of Brierley Hill. Left England in 1903 to help found the famous Steuben Glassworks in America. As designer and experimenter, Carder produced some splendid coloured glass and superb pieces embodying great technical skills.

COLL: Corning Museum, New York; Toledo Museum of Art.
LIT: H.J. Haden, 'Frederick Carder – designer, technologist
      and centenarian', *Glass Technology*, 5, No.3. June
      1964, pp.105–9; T.S. Beuchner, *Connoisseur Year
      Book*, 1961; long-playing record 'Conversations with
      Carder on Steuben: his American Art Glass'
      (Philpot, Glenbrook, Connecticut, 1963); Ray and Lee
      Grover, *Art Glass Nouveau* (Chas. E. Tuttle & Co.,
      Vermont, 1967), pp.145–52.

Černý, Jan b.1919   Czechoslovakia
Trained 1935–7 at the State Graphic School, Prague, and 1935–42 at the School of Applied Art, Prague. Since 1951 he has lectured at the latter school.

Chevalier, George b.1894   France
Trained at the École Nationale des Arts Décoratifs. Worked at the Maurice Dufrène Studio and obtained his professor's diploma from the École des Beaux Arts. Designed some important glass for the Cristalleries de Baccarat in 1925 (now in the Musée des Arts Décoratifs, Paris).
EXH: Corning, 1959, No.96.
LIT: *France Actuelle*, VIII, January 1959, pp.3–8.

Clarke, Dillon b.1946   England
Trained at Stoke-on-Trent and Hornsey College of Art; Royal College of Art, 1967–70. Interested in studio glass work and free-lance design work in glass.
EXH: Primavera, London, 1969; Portsmouth Art Gallery,
      1969; Glasshouse, London (permanent exhibition).

Cook, John Heald b.1942   England
Started full-time training in 1960 on the pottery course at Harris College of Art, Preston, followed by the course in industrial design at Leeds College of Art. Specialised in glass at the Royal College of Art, 1965–8, and the School of Applied Arts in Prague, Czechoslovakia. In 1968, worked as visiting designer at the Venini Glassworks at Murano and also spent some time there in 1970 blowing his own glass.

Set up the glass-making course at the School of Industrial Design, Leicester Polytechnic and is now in charge of Ceramics, Silver and Glass Studies.
COLL: Victoria & Albert Museum, London.
EXH: Expo '70; Sweden, America, Japan, Germany,
      Edinburgh; various galleries in Great Britain.
Plate 230, 243

Copier, Andries Dirk b.1901   Holland
Attended the School of Graphic Arts at Utrecht and the
Academy of Art at Rotterdam, 1917–25. Also joined Leerdam
Glass in 1917 as an apprentice and soon started to turn out
glass with new forms and techniques. Was awarded a silver
medal at the Paris Exhibition of 1925. His first major exhibition
of 'Unica' pieces was at Stuttgart in 1927, and through his
later initiative in opening a glass school and his splendid and
gifted artistic direction, Leerdam glass enjoys a foremost position in Europe. Its 'Unica' pieces, as well as its household glass,
are much revered.
EXH: Landesgewerbemuseum, Stuttgart, 1927; Liège, 1958,
       and many others including a Retrospective, Hague
       Gemeentemuseum, May–July 1969, later at Leerdam.
COLL: Most national museums: important collections at the
       Glassmuseum, Leerdam, and the Municipal Museum,
       The Hague.
LIT: A.D. Copier, 'Interplay of technology and design in
       glass' in *Proceedings of the 8th International Congress on
       Glass* (London, 1968), pp.29–38; *Craft Horizons*
       (September/October 1969), p.53.
Plates 74, 129, 250, 262

Cros, Henri 1840–1907   France
Started as a pupil of Etex, the sculptor. He was also a painter
and tried to combine both arts by modelling in coloured
waxes. He then turned to encaustic decoration and made
painted terracottas and experimented to find a substance
which could be used for polychrome sculptures like the ancient
examples in the Louvre. 'Plastic glass' was an old secret and
after endless research Cros succeeded in creating small
medallions. In 1891 a furnace at Sèvres was allocated to his
use and here Cros produced some of his great decorative relief
panels. In 1900 these were considered 'one of the finest discoveries known in the art of glass' and his great six-foot-high
relief *L'histoire du feu* formed the centrepiece of the Sèvres
stand at the exhibition in Paris in that year.
   Cros' process, as described by Janneau in 1931,
      consists in placing in a hollow mould of refractory clay
      a mixture in a soft pasty condition – made from an
      original model of wax or plaster – a sort of paste of
      powdered glass, mixed with a proportion of oxide and
      diluted with a fusion mixture. This paste is allowed to
      dry for a time. Then it is taken, either uncovered, like
      fragile porcelain (with which it has close affinities), or

in its mould, to the muffle furnace which fuses it into
glass. The mould of fireclay falls away in powder, and
the baked shape is ready to be polished or wiped clean.
   Cros, whose work was greatly admired by his contem-
poraries, particularly Antonin Daum, was often helped by his
son, Jean.
COLL: Musée des Arts Décoratifs, and Musée des Arts
       Modernes, Paris
LIT: M.P. Verneuil, 'Les Pâtes de Verre', *Art et Décoration*
       (1909); G. Janneau, *Modern Glass* (The Studio,
       London, 1931), pp.30–1.
Plate 29

Cummings, Keith b.1940   England
Educated University of Durham, B.A.Hons. (Fine Arts). Then
worked on experimental projects at Whitefriars Glass, 1963–4.
Developed fused glass as an architectural medium and
designed and produced commissions in this, as well as a range
of pressed glass slabs for interior screens. After teaching at
Blackpool School of Art, 1964–7, he joined the staff of Stourbridge College of Art where he is presently a Senior Lecturer
with responsibility for flat glass and surface techniques, casting
processes and history of glass. He is a consultant, and a
member of one of the advisory panels of the Council for
National Academic Awards.
EXH: Design Centre, London; Heal's, London; British
       Council U.S.A. tour; Ulster Museum; Usher Gallery,
       Lincoln, etc.

Cyrén, Gunnar b.1931   Sweden
Studied silver-smithing at the Stockholm Konstfackskolan and
worked and travelled extensively in Germany (under Professor Elisabeth Treskow at the Cologne Art School), Egypt,
Spain, Italy, Turkey and Greece. Glass designer at Orrefors
1959–70 and a Lunning Prize winner in 1966.
Plate 124

Daden, Frederick *fl.*1940–70   England
Began in 1942 at the Whitefriars Glass Company and became
a Master Glassworker in 1961. Demonstrator in glass at the
Royal College of Art in 1968. Is interested in hand-formed
tableware and in repairing antique pieces.

Dahlskog, Ewald 1894–1950   Sweden
Started work as a lithographer and thereafter studied at both

the School of Decorative Art and the School of Art in Stockholm. Set up as a painter and held his first one-man exhibition in Stockholm in 1918. Like Edvin Ollers (q.v.) he was one of the leaders in the 'Optimists' group. Dahlskog also worked for films and theatre. Helped in the interior decoration of important buildings and concert-halls in Gothenburg and Stockholm, and the Swedish–American Line ship *M/S. Stockholm*, 1938.

During 1926–9 Dahlskog made glass designs for Kosta and rejuvenated classical cutting by new methods and styles.
Plate 49

Dammouse, Albert Louis 1848–1926   France
Born in Paris, he trained as a sculptor and in later years worked as a potter. His work in glass (dating from 1898) is difficult to define as such: what he really made, as Janneau noted, was a 'soft porcelain, extremely delicate and diaphanous with the enamel set between minute castings of harder enamel . . . He transformed, and improved upon, the ancient and curious craft of the glass-workers of Nevers.' The glass was designed with sensitivity but pieces of it are rare and confined to major museums.
COLL: Musée des Arts Décoratifs, Musée Galliéra, Paris;
   Musée de Limoges; Kunstmuseum, Düsseldorf.
LIT: M.P. Verneuil 'Les Pâtes de Verre', *Art et Décoration*
   (1909); G. Janneau, *Modern Glass* (The Studio,
   London, 1931), p.33; Hilschenz, 1973, p.162.
Plates 31(a), 31(b)

Daum family 19th/20th centuries   France
Jean-Louis-Auguste and Jean-Antonin Daum came from Lorraine and set up their first factory at Nancy in 1875. Their early artistic efforts were in gold ornamentation on glass based partly on Arabian designs. Their cameo glass, produced about 1890, when it was at its peak in England, ranks among the best of its kind. During Gallé's direction of the École at Nancy, and later under Maurice Marinot's direction, the Daums played an active part in the furtherance of high standards of craftsmanship in French glass manufacture. Exhibitions and medals follow in rapid succession: Paris (1889), Chicago (1893), Lyon (1894), Brussels (1897) and a Grand Prix at Paris in the important exhibition of 1900. The Daums were fully immersed in the sensuous Art Nouveau style, but about 1920 when Paul Daum entered the firm, simpler forms began to make their appearance. They had an important exhibit at the 1925 Paris Exhibition.

The signature 'Le Verre de France' or 'Le Verre Français' which appears on some French glass of the 1920s has been credited to Daum, but there is also a claim that it was made by Schneider at his factory at Epinay-sur-Seine.

Today, under the direction of Michael Daum (b.1900), a clean sculptural quality is evident in much of the glass.
COLL: Musée des Arts Décoratifs, Paris; Kunstmuseum,
   Düsseldorf
EXH: Paris, 1925 (jury reports by Antonin Daum); Liège,
   1958, Nos.246–54.
LIT: *Jardin des Arts*, Nos.97–8., February 1963; Paris,
   1925, pp.64, 76; Hilschenz, 1973, p.170. (cites
   extensive bibliography).
Colour plate 3 and plates 19, 225, 303

Décorchement, François-Émile 1880–1971   France
Born at Conches, Eure, where he lived all his life. His first works, like those of Despret (q.v.), were in a fine but opaque substance. From 1904 onwards he made his own glass and introduced metallic oxides for colour effects. When he returned from war service, about 1920, he found a formula for a hard translucent substance from which he formed the pieces which won Antonin Daum's praise (as recorder of the Glass Section at the 1925 Paris Exhibition) for 'their style, their form, and their sober magnificence'. Composed of crystal, the oxide colours were combined with silica. Placed in a deep mould and baked for twenty hours in an oil furnace which he had invented, Décorchement's work emerged ready for the polishing of certain parts. He became in effect a 'glass-potter', working with glass rather than the paste beloved by Cros, Dammouse and others.
COLL: Musée des Arts Décoratifs, Paris; Toledo Museum of
   Art; Musée Galliéra, Paris; Musée de la Manufacture
   Nationale de Sèvres; Kunstmuseum, Düsseldorf.
EXH: Paris, 1925, Paris, 1966, Nos.718–23.
LIT: René Chavance, 'Les Pâtes de Verre de Décorchement',
   Art et Décoration, XLIX, 1926, p.78; G. Janneau,
   Modern Glass (1931), p.32; René Chavance 'François
   Décorchement' *Mobilier et Décoration*, 1947, No.3,
   pp.49–56; Polak, 1962, pl.17; Hilschenz, 1973, p.216.
Plate 42

Delvenne, René b.1902   Belgium
Joined the Cristalleries du Val-St-Lambert in 1919 and became

a designer in 1922 working under Charles Graffart (q.v.). When Graffart retired in 1958, Delvenne succeeded him as 'Chef du Service des Creations' until his own retirement in 1967.

EXH: Liège, 1958, Nos.195–8.

Despret, Georges 1862–1952   France
Exhibited at Paris in 1900 some bowls in the *pâte de verre* technique popularised by Henri Cros (q.v.) and others, including Gallé. He had begun his experiments the year before, working with a dense opaque-coloured paste which produced jewel-like results. But Despret did not continue in Cros' steps and this vogue gradually died out because of the technical difficulties it presented.

EXH: Paris, 1900; Turin, 1911.

LIT: *L'Art Décoratif*, 17, 1907; G. Janneau, *Modern Glass* (1931), pp.31–2; Polak, 1962, p.33; Hilschenz, 1973, p.224.

Drahoňovský, Josef 1877–1938   Czechoslovakia
Attended the Turnov Jewelry School 1890–4 where he was taught to cut precious stones and glass. In 1896 he obtained a scholarship to Prague School of Applied Art, becoming an Assistant Professor there in 1904, and Professor in 1911. In 1914 he set up workshops for stone-engravers.

Drahoňovský concentrated on producing large plaques of several layers of glass and in 1930 he revived the old techniques of engraving framed glass panels. His main work in glass was the St. Wenceslas Cup, presented by Czech Catholics to Pope Pius XI in 1930 (Prague, Museum of Arts and Crafts). Drahoňovský did little work on glass itself, except for rock-crystal 'cameos', and entrusted most of the work to pupils. He is associated primarily with stone-cutting and with training a succession of highly competent pupils.

LIT: Jindřich Čadík, *Dílo Josefa Drahoňovského* (Prague, 1933); *Josef Drahoňovský* (Zikes, Prague, 1939); H. Vollmer, *Künstler . . . Lexikon* (1953).

Dreiser, Peter b.1936   Germany (working in England)
Born in Cologne, Dreiser was accepted in 1951 as a student of glass-engraving at the State Glass Crafts School in Rheinbach near Bonn. This school, the first technical school of its kind in Europe, was first set up in 1856 at Steinschonau in northern Bohemia where the well-known firm of J. & L. Lobmeyr was later to establish a glassworks. After the Second World War the school reopened in Rheinbach (1948) under its old director, Professor Alfred Dorn. Dreiser took his final examinations in 1954, qualifying as an engraver, designer and glass-cutter. He came to England in April 1955 and later worked as an engraver with his own shop for Thomas Goode's of London. In June 1970 he set up as a free-lance engraver and is a member of both the Crafts Centre and the Society of Designer Craftsmen.

Plates 170, 176, 180

Drobník, Antonin b.1925   Czechoslovakia
Trained 1940–3 at the Glassmaking Trade School, Železný Brod; 1943–9 at the School of Applied Art in Prague. Since 1951 he has worked as plastic artist at the Železný Brod Glassworks of the National Corporation. He has also done fused-glass sculptures, hand-cut glass and etched flat glass. His animal sculptures are cut from a single piece of glass.

LIT: *Czechoslovak Glass Review*, Vol.XIX, 1964, special issue, pp.35–7.

Durand, Victor 1870–1931   U.S.A.
The Durand family came originally from Baccarat in France. In 1897, with his father's assistance, Durand leased the Vineland Glass Manufacturing Co., and was soon producing commercial and scientific glass. In 1924 he invited several important craftsmen to join him at Vineland to produce art glass, and by 1926 they had won the first prize (gold medal) at the International Exposition in Philadelphia. In rich iridescent shades and with spider-webbing decoration, Durand's glass is prized by collectors.

LIT: A.C. Revi, *Nineteenth Century Glass* (Thos. Nelson & Sons, New York, 1960), p.230; Ray and Lee Grover, *Art Glass Nouveau* (Chas. E. Tuttle & Co., Vermont, 1967), pp.128–34.

Eckhardt, Edris b.1929   U.S.A.
A native of Cleveland, was a graduate of, and has been a faculty member of the Cleveland Institute of Art. Before developing an interest in glass she achieved considerable renown for her ceramic sculptures. Her earliest glass experiments (in 1953) concentrated on rediscovering the methods used by late Roman glassmakers in the manufacture of gold glasses. Her studies were aided by fellowships from the Guggenheim Foundation and a Tiffany Foundation Award, 1959. Though her techniques, which have had a significant

impact on the making of glass in America, are somewhat related to those used, for example, by Henri Navarre (q.v.), she has developed them independently.

EXH: Corning, 1959, Nos.272–4; Corning Museum, New York, May–October 1968 (Retrospective 1953–68).

LIT: *Craft Horizons* (December 1956), pp.12–15; (November/December 1956 and 1962); (November/December 1968), p.38 (review of Corning Exhibition).

Plates 266, 296

Edenfalk, Bengt b.1924   Sweden

Born at Karlskrona, he attended the Konstfackskolan from 1947 to 1952. Russel Lynes Jr described him as 'a sculptor of considerable ingenuity and wit who obviously delights in his material . . .' when choosing Edenfalk's bubble-pattern bottle as one of the three objects most 'interesting' or 'important' from the 1800 or so exhibits in the major 1959 exhibition ('Glass') at the Corning Museum, New York. Joined Skrufs Glassworks as chief designer in 1953.

EXH: Corning, 1959, Nos.259–62; Växjö, Smålands Museum, 1965.

Eiff, Wilhelm von 1890–1943   Germany

Originally set out to be a painter but abandoned this to spend four years as an apprentice in the Württemberger Metallwarenfabrik. Then went to Paris to concentrate on glass and stonecutting. He completed his studies in Stuttgart where he settled as a freelance artist in 1913, specialising in glass and stonecutting. His output was large and often rapidly executed. In his relief portraits he reached his creative peak.

After service in the First World War, Eiff was appointed Professor in the new experimental workshops for glass and stonecutting at the Stuttgart School of Art and Crafts, working there until his death. Among the techniques he developed here was that of glass-etching using electrical tools. These allowed him great artistic freedom on large undivided glass windows (the majority of these were destroyed in the Second World War). Many of his pupils, e.g. Hanns Model, Konrad Häbermeier, Helen Monro-Turner and Nora Ortlieb, have become competent glass-engravers and teachers.

COLL: Museums at München, Stuttgart; Metropolitan Museum, New York.

LIT: Nora Ortlieb, *Wilhelm von Eiff* (Bamberg, 1950); biography in *Neue Deutsche Biographie*, Vol.4, 1959.

Eisch, Erwin b.1927   Germany

The son of a glass-engraver and chief designer for his family's factory in Frauenau, Bavaria. He studied at the Academy of Fine Arts in Munich and is now an active experimenter and important figure in the revival of glass-blowing by designers. For him the 'artist must hold and feel the moving form in the hot glass'.

COLL: Toledo Museum of Art (Inv. 68.85).

LIT: 'Glass by Erwin Eisch', *Craft Horizons* (May/June 1963); Erwin Eisch, 'Glass with a claim on good design', in *Studies in Glass History and Design*, papers read at VIIIth International Congress on Glass, July 1968 (1970) pp.111–12; *Craft Horizons* (October 1972), p.120.

Plate 257

Elliott, George b.1934   England

Trained at Stourbridge College of Art and the Royal College of Art. Worked for a time in glassworks in Denmark and Norway, and in England at Stevens & Williams. It is however as a teacher, adviser and exhibitor that his career has advanced. Having advised on the setting-up of the glass-blowing areas at Exeter and Birmingham Colleges of Art, building and supplying tank furnaces to glass-blowing studios in Suffolk and Kent, he now lectures at the Stourbridge College of Art. He also has his own glass studio in Bewdley Museum.

EXH: Victoria & Albert Museum, London, Craftsmen's Exhibition, 1972; Design Centre, London, 1974.

Elmhirst, Shiela b.1920   England

Has been engraving with diamond-point on glass since 1951. Began her artistic training at the Slade School in 1946, but it was the chance discovery of eighteenth-century engraved Dutch vases at the British Museum which led her to take up glass engraving. Discovered for herself (as did Phyllis Boissier) the technique of engraving on glass with a diamond. Most of her work is commissioned for presentation to distinguished individuals and organisations.

COLL: Royal College of Arms; Corning Museum, New York; Churchill College, Cambridge; Christchurch Museum, Ipswich, etc.

EXH: Corning, 1959, Nos.61–2; Steuben International Glass Exhibition, 1960 (major cities in U.S.A.); Royal Festival Hall, London, 1963; Foyle's Gallery, London, 1966; Pittsburgh, U.S.A., 1968.

LIT: Shiela Elmhirst, 'The Aesthetic and Practical Application of Diamond-Point Glass Engraving', paper read at VIIIth International Congress on Glass, Brussels, June–July 1965.
Plates 186, 190, 191, 201

Englund, Eva b.1937   Sweden
Trained at the Konstfackskolan, Stockholm 1959–62. With Pukebergs Glass 1964–74. Joined the Orrefors design team in 1974. Won the Stockholm City Art scholarship.
COLL: Växjö, Kalmar and Varbergs Museums; various in America.
EXH: Växjö Smålands Museum, June–September 1968.

Ericsson, Henry 1898–1933   Finland
Studied at the Central School of Industrial Design and in Paris and Rome. Won first prize in the important Riihimäki Glassworks Competition in 1928 and has also worked as a painter and graphic artist.
EXH: Barcelona, 1929 World Fair.
LIT: Kerttu Niilonen, *Finnish Glass* (Tammi, Helsinki, 1967), p.33.

Erixson, Sven b.1899   Sweden
Having trained at the schools of industrial art in Stockholm he travelled extensively, exhibited as a painter in Gothenburg and became a professor at the School of Arts in Stockholm (1943). His work is in most of the Swedish museums. He worked on some glass designs for Kosta, 1929–31, including an amusing 'aqua-vitae bottle' in animal form (1930).

Fagerlund, Carl b.1923   Sweden
As a lighting architect, Fagerlund joined the Orrefors design team in 1946. He has attracted attention for his monumental lighting arrangements in public premises in Sweden and abroad, mainly in America, but is equally adept at designing simple, subtly shaded lamps for the home. Some idea of the scale of a grand Orrefors chandelier may be given by that which was installed in 1968 at the new offices of General Motors in New York: weight, 2 tons; diameter, almost 11 feet; 372 lights consuming 12,000 watts. The eighteen chandeliers in the Kennedy Center, Washington, D.C., are also to Fagerlund's design and are 15 feet high.

Fedden, Bryant b.1930   England
Educated at Bryanston and Clare Colleges, Cambridge, he now concentrates on sculpture, letter-cutting and glass-engraving.
Plate 205

Filan, Wayne b.1946   U.S.A.
Trained at Philadelphia Art College, then (1970) at the Royal College of Art, London. Received a Craftsmen's Award from the Philadelphia Council of Professional Craftsmen.
EXH: Corning, 1969, Jury prize.
Plate 244

Filip, Miloš b.1926   Czechoslovakia
Trained 1947–50 at the Glassmaking Trade School, Kamenický Šenov; 1950–6, School of Applied Art in Prague. Since 1959 has worked as a plastic artist in the Institute of Housing and Clothing Culture in Prague. Specialises in pressed, cut, engraved and painted glass.

Franck, Kaj b.1911   Finland
Born in Viipuri. Studied furniture design at the Institute of Industrial Art in Helsinki, 1929–32. Both as a ceramist and as a glass designer he soon became a revolutionary force in his native country where utilitarian articles had long been neglected. Has done pioneering work in the ceramic industry: with a keen appreciation of the demands of articles in everyday use, he has created a series of extremely simple and low-priced table services consisting of single pieces which complement each other. His household ceramics are just as useful and handsome in the kitchen as they are on the dining-table. The individual pieces are made in vivid colours.

Franck used vivid colours in his household glassware, too, but he often used a discreet smoke colour or a delicate oyster grey for his artistic glassware. The latter ranges from simple vases in material as thin as soap bubbles to bowls and minor glass sculptures, fishes and birds, executed in heavy glass filled with air bubbles and fused-in metal particles. He has worked for Taito Oy (lighting fixtures) in Helsinki, for the Associated Woollen Mills in Hyvinkää (fabrics), for Te Ma Oy (furniture) in Helsinki, and for a glass factory in Italy. From 1946–61 he headed the design department at Arabia Glass, and from 1950–73 was the Art Director of Nuutajärvi Glass. As a teacher at the Institute of Industrial Art in Helsinki he was nominated Professor and has relinquished his post as Art Director to Oiva Toikka (q.v.). He travelled on a scholarship from the state of

Finland to Scandinavia in 1939; on a scholarship from Svenska Kulturfonden to Germany and Italy in 1949; on a Fulbright grant to the United States and as a Lunning prize-winner to Mexico, Japan and Thailand in 1955.

EXH: Gold Medal in Milan, 1951; Diplôme d'Honneur in Milan, 1954; Grand Prix in Milan, 1957; Compasso d'Oro in Milan, 1957; Corning, 1959, Nos. 94–5; Cultural Award by 'Stockholms Tidningen' (Sweden), 1961; Gold Medal in Sacramento, 1961; Eugen-Medal granted by the King of Sweden, 1965.

LIT: Factory literature such as Arabia's *Ceramics and Glass* (especially No.1, 1966, and centenary issue, 1973).

Colour plate 6 and plate 265

Fritz, Robert C. b.1945   U.S.A.
Educated at San José State College, Ohio State University, California College (Oakland) and University of Wisconsin. Has exhibited widely in America.

EXH: Dallas, 'Art, Light, Form: New American Glass', May–June 1967, cites career details.

LIT: *Craft Horizons*, May–June 1968, p.60.

Gács, György Z. b.1914   Hungary
Studied painting at the Academy of Fine Arts, Budapest, and took part in national exhibitions. An artist of considerable talents, Professor Gács has been in charge of the Glass Faculty at the High School for Applied Arts in Budapest since 1967. He designs windows, decorative architectural glass, enamelled panels, tapestries, mural decorations in concrete, ceramics, glass and sculpture. He was awarded the Munkácsy Prize in 1956 and 1970.

Plates 322, 333

Gallé, Emile 1846–1904   France
The most important name associated with French glass, Gallé was born at Nancy of a glass-blower's family. He attended the Lycée at Nancy and then travelled in Germany, 1862–6. The Franco-Prussian War caused him to return to France and he started to make pottery. In the early 1870s he studied in London – particularly in the museums and botanical collections – and returned to Nancy in 1874. He then set up his glassworks and spent the next thirty years designing and making glass. With subtle colour shading and exact delineation of such items as flowers and insects, each piece was a work of art and therefore signed. Dr Ada Polak has recorded that:

> *'it seems obvious that he came to enjoy the signing of his glass very much. It meant yet another outlet for his explosively inventive mind; and as he was not modest, the spreading of his name all over the world obviously gave him great personal satisfaction . . .'*

His fame was established by the 1889 exhibition in Paris, and he was at the height of his reputation by that of 1900. After his death, with Victor Prouvé as Manager, his workshop continued to produce objects in Gallé's style up to 1913. The firm ceased to exist in 1936.

COLL: Musée des Arts Décoratifs, Paris; Musée de l'École de Nancy; Victoria & Albert Museum; Corning Museum, New York; Kunstmuseum, Düsseldorf.

LIT: Louis de Forcaud, *Emile Gallé* (Paris, 1903); Emile Gallé, *Ecrits pour l'art* (Paris, 1908); James Barrelet, *La verrerie en France* (Paris, 1953), p.175; Ada Polak, 'Gallé Glass, Luxurious, Cheap and Imitated', *Journal of Glass Studies*, V, 1953, pp.105–15; Gabriella Gros, 'Poetry in Glass. The Art of Emile Gallé', *Apollo*, November 1955; Ada Polak, 'Signatures on Gallé Glass', *Journal of Glass Studies*, VIII, 1966, pp.120–3; R. Dennis, 'The Glass of Emile Gallé', *Antiques International* (Michael Joseph, London, 1966), pp.182–92; Hilschenz, 1973, p.233 (cites extensive bibliography).

Plates 5, 20, 23–28

Gaspari, Luciano b.1913   Italy
Teaches art at the Academy of Fine Arts in Venice and is a painter and versatile designer. Has exhibited his glass frequently both in Italy and abroad. Designs glass articles for Salviati of Venice and was awarded the Enapi Prize at the 1959 Milan Triennale.

EXH: Corning Museum, New York, 1959, No.181; Venice, Biennale, most years from 1932.

Gate, Simon 1883–1945   Sweden
When in about 1916 the Swedish Society of Arts and Crafts started an agency to create contacts between artists and industry, one of the first results was the employment by Orrefors of Simon Gate. Together with master glass-blower Knut Bergqvist (1873–1953) and with the help of fellow designer Edward Hald (q.v.) Gate developed new techniques such as the multi-coloured 'Graal' glass, and 'Ariel', which utilised air

bubbles to give an added dimension. The almost art-nouveau shapes of some of Gate's work, rivalled by the rich, almost Byzantine shape of his great covered cups and bowls covered with stylised engraving, won many international prizes.
EXH: Gothenburg, 1923; Paris, 1925.
LIT: Arthur Hald, *Simon Gate: Edward Hald* (Norstedts, Stockholm, 1948); Elisa Steenberg, *Modern Swedish Glass* (Lindqvists, Stockholm, 1949).
Plates 62, 63

Gehlin, Hugo d.1953   Sweden
Best known for his free furnace work at Gullaskruf, a factory near Orrefors in southern Sweden he worked at from 1930. His vessels often had plaited glass threads and other colour prunts and frills applied to them. He also designed some double-walled bowls and basins, trapping a layer of air between the inner and outer surfaces.
COLL: Nationalmuseum, Stockholm.
LIT: Polak, 1962, p.71, pl.75a.

Gentili, Giorgio b.1928   Italy
An architect, trained in Venice, and with professional experience in England, Switzerland and Sweden. He has collaborated with Vetreria Vistosi of Murano on the design of lamp-fittings.

Gordon, Ernest b.1926   England
A graduate of the Royal College of Art, he is best known for the work he did at Kosta Glass in Sweden from 1953.
Plate 227

Goupy, Marcel b.1886   France
Designed glass between 1918 and 1936 while working for Rouard, the French dealer in fine glass and ceramics. Exhibited ceramics at Paris in 1925.
COLL: Musée des Arts Décoratifs, Paris, Inv. No. 21822; enamelled glass, Paris 1966, No.734.
LIT: 'La Parure de la Table et Marcel Goupy', *Art et Décoration* (1934), pp.300–5.
Plate 46

Graffart, Charles 1893–1967   Belgium
Joined the Cristalleries du Val-St-Lambert in 1906 to work as an engraver and spent fifty-two years in their service. Became a designer in 1926 and 'Chef du Service des Créations' in 1942.

COLL: Musées Royaux d'Art Brussels.
EXH: Liège, 1958, Nos.175–81.

Gundersen, Jon b.1942   Norway
Trained at the Oslo State School until 1967. Employed as a designer at Hadelands from this time and has participated in group and Society of Young Artists exhibitions.

Gunther, Alfred b.1906   Germany
Born in Bohemia, he studied at the School of Arts for the Glass Industry at Steinschönau. He has latterly designed for Ischendorfer Glashütte, near Cologne.
EXH: Corning, 1959, Nos.119–21.

Häbermeier, Konrad b.1907   Germany
Trained as an apprentice in the Württemberg metalware factory at Stuttgart/Geislingen. He then studied at the School of Arts and Crafts and the Academy of Fine Arts in Stuttgart. His studies completed, he took a teaching post at the Academy as an assistant to Professor Wilhelm von Eiff (q.v.) and was later appointed Professor and Head of the Department of Glass at the State Higher Technical School at Schwäbisch Gmund.
    A designer of glass (and a stone carver), an industrial designer and frequent exhibitor, Häbermeier has co-operated with many international organisations. His work in glass has been made in his own school and by Gralglashutte GmbH at Dürnau/Göppingen. Much of his work is in the great engraving traditions set down by his teacher, Eiff, but in addition he also uses sand-blasting techniques to etch windows.
LIT: 'Konrad Häbermeier und das Glas', *Werkkunst*, 2, 1963, issued by Landesgewerbeamt, Baden-Württemberg (Museum), Stuttgart.
Plates 94, 143

Hald, Edward b.1883   Sweden
One of Sweden's most revered designers, and a distinguished painter who studied with Henri Matisse in Paris. Hald's 'partnership' with designer Simon Gate, glass-blower Knut Bergqvist (1873–1953) and engraver Gustav Abels at Orrefors is part of the country's glass tradition. Their collection has been well documented and the museum at the Orrefors factory (designed by Simon Gate's son, Bengt Gate) has many examples of their joint work from 1916–17. The seal of international approval was set on their efforts at the 1925 exhibition in Paris.

COLL: Nationalmuseum, Stockholm; Orrefors, Glass Museum.
LIT: Arthur Hald, *Simon Gate, Edward Hald* (Norsteds, Stockholm, 1948); O. Lyndquist, 'Edward Hald', *Glass och Porslin*, 1943, No.6, p.7.
Plates 61, 64

Hammond, David b.1931   England
Studied at the Stourbridge College of Art (1945–51) and the Royal College of Art (1953–56). He is now designer to Thomas Webb & Sons of Stourbridge and Edinburgh, lead-crystal glass manufacturers and part of the Dema Glass group.
Plates 90, 116

Heaton, Maurice b.1907   U.S.A.
Born in Switzerland into a third generation of stained-glass craftsmen, he moved with his father, Clement Heaton, to the United States in 1914. He made church windows, glass murals and lighting fixtures from 1931 and developed a technique of fusing enamel to glass in 1947. Later, in 1961, he adapted this technique to lamination, whereby the coloured enamel is fused between two to six pieces of glass.
COLL: Metropolitan Museum; Corning Museum, New York; Museum of Contemporary Crafts, New York; etc.
EXH: Many exhibitions in America and Canada sponsored by the State Department, Museum of Modern Art, New York, the Smithsonian Museum, Washington, D.C. etc. Also in South America, India and Europe. Boston, Society of Arts and Crafts, October 1964; Corning, 1959, No.281.
LIT: *Craft Horizons*, June 1954; November/December 1964, p.45 (reviewing Boston exhibition); 'The Laminated Panels of Maurice Heaton', *Craft Horizons*, August 1970, pp.25–6.
Plate 246

Heesen, Willem b.1925   Holland
Became a trainee at the glass school at Leerdam in 1943 and is now a chief designer of Royal Leerdam. He has been an important influence in the revival of diamond-point engraving in Holland. He has also made remarkable glass windows, both in sand-blasted, and the so-called triplum technique in which glass dyes are smelted together between two or more layers at high temperatures. The escaping gases from the dyes cause air-bubbles. In his glass structures he has made full use of the transparent glass and of its prismatic and reflective qualities.

Heesen also designs a wide range of utility glass for daily use.
EXH: Museum Bellerive, Zurich, 1972.
LIT: *Craft Horizons*, January/February 1965, pp.34–6; ibid., October 1972, p.12.
Plates 220, 272, 319

Hellsten, Lars b.1933   Sweden
After the usual thorough Konstfack training under Stig Lineberg in Stockholm (1957–63), Hellsten won the Royal Foundation Scholarship in 1963 and then joined Bengt Edenfalk at Skrufs Glassworks at Skruv in 1964. He specialises in unique glass-sculptures and his work is widely exhibited in Sweden. It may be seen at the Växjö Stadshotell, the Swedish Embassy in Washington, D.C., the Esso motel at Jonkoping, in the Nationalmuseum, Stockholm and the museums at Norrkopings and Gothenburg. He later won Government scholarships in 1969 and 1970 and in 1972 transferred from Skrufs to the Orrefors design team.
LIT: *Form*, No.9, 1965, pp.610–11: 'Moebel', *Interior Design*, September 1966, p.59.
Plates 118, 300

Hennix, Erik b.1941; *and* **Margareta** b.1941   Sweden
A husband-and-wife team whose best work was done for Johansfors Glass. Some of Margareta's gold-decorated bowls are very effective and vaguely reminiscent of Aztec treasure. They have both worked extensively in ceramics.
EXH: Växjö, Smålands Museum, 1965, 'Seven Designers'.
LIT: *Form*, No.9, 1965, pp.612–13.

Herman, Samuel J. b.1936   U.S.A.
Until his move to Australia in 1974 Herman was one of the leading influences in glass instruction in England. Born in Mexico City. Educated at Western Washington State College and on Harvey Littleton's course at the University of Wisconsin, 1964–5. Graduated with Master's degree. A Fulbright grant, and a Graduate Special Fellowship from Wisconsin sent him to London in 1966, where he eventually became Senior Tutor in charge of the Glass Department of the School of Ceramics and Glass at the Royal College of Art. There he successfully introduced the free-hand blowing initiated in America. In 1969 Herman joined with Graham Hughes, Artistic Director of the Worshipful Company of Goldsmiths, to set up the Glasshouse in Neal Street, London WC2, where artists can make and sell their own glass.

COLL: London County Council, Education Authority;
Leicester Museum; Victoria & Albert Museum;
Edinburgh College of Art; University of Wisconsin;
Jablonec Museum, Czechoslovakia; Kunstinvstri
Museum, Oslo; Röhsska Museum, Gothenburg.
EXH: Various, including Jablonec, Czechoslovakia;
Gemeentemuseum, Arnheim; Gothenburg; Primavera
Gallery, London; Design Centre, London; Victoria &
Albert Museum, London, February/March 1971;
Boymans Museum, Rotterdam; Museum Bellerive,
Zurich (1972).
Plates 240, 241, 316

Hilton, Eric b.1936   England
Started on staff of Stourbridge College of Art. Then established
the glass department within the Faculty of Three-Dimensional
Design at Birmingham College of Art, 1967. Later Assistant
Professor, Division of Visual Arts, University of Victoria,
Canada.
LIT: Beard, 1968, p.92; Eric Hilton, 'Investigating glass on
a minimum of equipment' in *Studies in Glass History
and Design*, papers read at the VIIIth International
Congress on Glass, July 1968 (1970), pp.113–15.
Plate 283

Hlava, Pavel b.1924   Czechoslovakia
Trained 1939–42 at Glassmaking Trade School, Železný Brod;
1942–8, School of Applied Art in Prague. From 1956 he
worked at the Institute of Housing and Clothing Culture in
Prague. He has won an international reputation with his use
of Jaromir Špaček's method of fusing-in silver to vases, and for
his glass sculptures blown into a wire mould.
EXH: Expo '58, Brussels, with Matura and Filip (q.v.), (gold
medal); Leipzig Trade Fair, 1965 (gold medal), Expo
'67, Montreal.
176, 230, 262

Höglund, Erik Sylvester b.1932   Sweden
A Swedish sculptor born at Karlskrona and educated at the
Konstfackskolan, Stockholm, 1948–53. Was a Lunning Prize
winner in 1958 and has designed at Boda Glass since 1953.
His wife, Monica Backström (q.v.), also designs for the firm.
Represented in the Nationalmuseum, Stockholm, and in other
museums in Sweden and abroad. His bronze free-sculpture
can be seen in Trelleborg, Borås, Stockholm, Karlskoga,

Sandviken and Växjö. He has designed mural glass windows for
Växjö Cathedral, Lessebo Church, Eskilstuna Town Hall, etc.
Only the briefest indication can be given here of Höglund's
amazing versatility. The illustrations broaden the picture.
EXH: Växjö, Smålands Glassmuseum, summer 1967;
Museum Bellerive, Zürich, July 1972.
Plates 110, 131, 146, 163, 273, 307, 329, 335

Holmgren-Exner, Christel b.1940   Austria (working in
Denmark)
Trained at the Academy in Vienna in industrial design.
Formerly employed at the Austrian Design Centre in Vienna
and the design studio of Bernadotte and Bjørn in Copenhagen.
Joined Kastrup-Holmegaards Glass as a designer in 1968, and
is married to Christer Holmgren (*see below*).

Holmgren, Christer b.1933   Sweden (working in Denmark)
Was educated at the State Design School in Gothenburg.
Joined Kastrup-Holmegaards Glass as a designer in 1957 and
has participated in the Company's exhibitions in Denmark and
abroad, as well as in member exhibitions of the Society of
Danish Arts and Crafts.
Plate 114

Hongell, Goran b.1900   Finland
Studied decorative art at the Central School of Industrial
Design and taught decorative painting in later years. Became
artistic assistant at Karhula Glassworks in 1940. Was at his
peak at the end of the thirties, when he created heavy clear
crystal bowls of pure form. Was also involved in designing
utilitarian pressed and blown glass.
Plate 75

Hopper, David b.1948   U.S.A.
Student at San José State College under Robert Fritz (q.v.).
EXH: William Sawyer Gallery, July/August 1969
LIT: *Craft Horizons*, September/October 1969, p.55.

Horacek, Vaclav b.1928   Czechoslovakia
Trained 1943–7 at the Glassmaking Trade School, Železný
Brod; 1949–58, School of Applied Art in Prague. Specialises
in the design of cut glass.

Horejc, Jaroslav b.1886   Czechoslovakia
Was born in Prague where he attended the Arts and Crafts

School. He graduated in 1910 and became a Professor at the Prague Academy of Applied Arts in 1918. Horejc was more a sculptor than a glass designer and his name is best known in glass history for the series of four beakers he made, 1921–4, for Stephan Rath's Lobmeyr studio. Three copies of each of the four subjects were made, although replicas have since been made in 1960 at Borské sklo. In 1924 Horejc gave up engraving glass but his work had a considerable influence on Swedish productions of the time.

COLL: Metropolitan Museum, New York; Nationalmuseum, Stockholm; Musée des Arts Décoratifs, Paris; Museum of Applied Art, Prague.

EXH: Paris, 1925; Paris 1966, No.744.

LIT: Most of his work after 1911 is illustrated by Karel Herain 'Oz dobne sklo' ('Decorative Glass') in the journal *Umeni II* (Prague, 1929), pp.381–406; Z. Pésatová, *Bohemian Engraved Glass* (Prague and London, 1968).

Plates 47, 48

Houston, James b.1921   Canada

Canadian painter, graphic artist, book designer and illustrator who has studied in Canada, Paris and Tokyo. Houston joined the Steuben Glass design team in New York as an Associate Director of Design in 1962. One of his first tasks was the design of 'Seraph Raphael', for the Joseph P. Kennedy Foundation. Houston also acts in an advisory capacity to the Canadian Eskimo Arts Council and the National Gallery of Canada.

LIT: 'Poetry in Crystal', 1963; 'Islands in Crystal', 1966 (Steuben exhibition catalogues).

Plate 168

Hunebelle, André *fl.*1920s   France

His vases and bowls in slightly frosted glass and decorated with formalised flowers and spirals were a feature of French glass exhibits of the twenties. In 1927 he opened a shop in Paris and his style turned towards the geometric shapes encouraged by Cubist artists.

LIT: *Art et Décoration*, 1931, pp.51–8; *Studio*, 1931, 102, p.97; Martin Battersby, *The Decorative Twenties* (London, Studio Vista, 1969), p.69.

Hutton, John b.1906   New Zealand

Abandoned law studies to take up painting and emigrated to England in 1935. Became particularly interested in mural painting, working for the 1937 Paris Exhibition and on mural paintings for the Orient liner *Orcades*. During the Second World War he was a camouflage officer, afterwards continuing with large-scale paintings for the 'Britain Can Make It' exhibition, 1947, and the Festival of Britain, 1951. Taught mural painting at Goldsmiths College School of Art for some years. Since 1952, when he began designing the ninety panels of the great west screen of Coventry Cathedral, he has been engaged mostly on glass engraving. From 1972–4 he was engaged on a commission for Wellington Cathedral in his home country of New Zealand.

John Hutton uses several different grindstones attached to a flexible drive (plate 281). The range of tones that he can thus achieve extend from an opaque chalky white to a highly polished transparency. His drawings are made with white chalk on black paper. He has also recently done some silvered-glass engraving, and stained-glass windows composed of appliqué with engraving.

COLL: Victoria & Albert Museum, London; Royal Scottish Museum; Corning Museum, New York; Pilkington's Museum of Glass, St Helens, Lancs.; National Library of Canada; Sudeley Castle, Glos.; Wellington Cathedral, New Zealand; Kirkby Stephen Church, Cumbria.

EXH: March 1969, Commonwealth Institute, London (one-man show); July 1970, Cambridge Festival; October 1970, Ashgate Gallery, Farnham (one-man show); touring, New Zealand, 1973; Portsmouth Art Gallery, 1974.

LIT: Commonwealth Institute, Exhibition Catalogue, March 1969.

Plates 280, 281, 282, 284, 343

Ingrand, Max 1908–69   France

An alumnus of the École des Beaux Arts and the École Nationale Supérieure des Arts Décoratifs. His training completed, he set up a studio in Paris for making stained-glass windows, and working glass into various shapes and forms. He was highly versatile and hard-working, and numerous examples of his art are to be found not only in France, but in most European countries (including England), the United States, Canada, the Middle East, and even India and Japan. As an interior designer he was partly responsible for the decoration of the S/S French Line ship *Normandie* and was the *maitre*

Brighton School of Art. Professor of Art at the University of Wisconsin. He is involved with glass at many levels: as a prime mover in the important Glass Nationals at Toledo Museum of Art; as technical investigator and tireless worker for the advancement of the profession; and as artist. In 1957 he went to Europe to study for eight months and spent most of the time at glass factories in Italy. The French craftsman Jean Sala (q.v.) taught him a few techniques but it was only by repeated experiment (assisted by the Toledo Museum of Art and the University of Wisconsin) that he was finally able to set up the successful Wisconsin course which broke through to new realms of form and colour.

COLL: Museum of Modern Art, New York; National Collection of the Fine Arts, Smithsonian Institute, Washington, D.C.; Corning Museum, New York; Toledo Museum; Victoria & Albert Museum, London, etc.

EXH: Corning Museum, 1964; Milan Triennale XIII, 1964; Toledo, 1966 (purchase award); Lee Nordness Gallery, New York, 1969; Zürich, 1972.

LIT: Dido Smith, 'Offhand Glass Blowing', *Craft Horizons*, January/February 1964, pp.22–3; Harvey Littleton, 'Artist-produced glass: a modern revolution', in *Studies in Glass History and Design*, papers read at the VIIIth International Congress on Glass, July 1968 (1970), pp.109–10. Harvey Littleton, *Glassblowing: A Search for Form*, New York, Van Nostrand & Reinhold, 1972.

Colour plate 10 and plates 259, 310, 317

Löffelhardt, Heinz b.1901   Germany

Trained in silver; then studied with George Kolbe and Wilhelm Wagenfeld (q.v.) at the Vereinigte Lausitzer Glaswerke until the Second World War. Since then he has designed free-lance for Jena and the Farbenglaswerke, Zwiesel.

EXH: Corning, 1959, Nos.122–4.

LIT: Beard, 1968 pp.148–9.

Plates 125, 154

Luce, Jean b.1895   France

Proprietor of a specialist shop selling ceramics and glass, and a creator of unique pieces and decorations in glass, faience and porcelain. May be said to have contributed by his efforts to the promotion of good design in contemporary tableware.

EXH: Paris, 1925; Paris, 1966.

LIT: René Chavance, 'Les Verreries de Jean Luce', *Art et Décoration*, 1928, pp.17–24; Polak, 1962, p.43.

Lundgren, Tyra   Sweden

Best known as a potter, whose work is well illustrated in French and Swedish literature, Tyra Lundgren did some interesting glass designs, 1934–40, for the Italian firm of Venini and also worked in ceramics for Arabia Glass in Finland in the 1920s.

Lundin, Ingeborg b.1921   Sweden

After training at the Swedish State School, she began working with glass in 1947 and joined Orrefors where she stayed until 1970. Her designs of these early years called for unexpected bulges in the classic glass bubbles, but her skill and artistry soon won complete respect from the glassmakers. The keynote of her compositions is movement, often the result of inspiration she has derived from watching the rhythmic movements of the workers. She has said that she is most content when creating free and fantastic forms in glass, but also enjoys the challenge of designing a new piece or set of utility glass. She was awarded the premier Scandinavian design award, the Lunning Prize, in 1954, and a gold medal at the XIth Milan Triennale of 1957.

Plates 121, 149, 183, 222

Lütken, Per b.1916   Denmark

Was educated at the Danish School of Arts, Crafts and Industrial Design in Copenhagen, until 1937. Started work with Holmegaards Glassworks A/S in 1942. Study tour to Italy in 1954.

COLL: Museum of Applied Art, Copenhagen; Victoria & Albert Museum, London; Landesgewerbemuseum, Stuttgart; Corning Museum, New York; Museum für Kunst und Gewerbe, Hamburg; Neue Sammlung, München; House of Denmark, San Diego, California; Danische Institut, Dortmund; Museum Haaretz, Tel Aviv; Stadtische Gallerie, Oberhausen; Formsammlung der Stadt Braunschweig, Brunswick; Musée du Verre, Liège.

EXH: Design in Scandinavia, U.S.A., 1954–7; Neue Form aus Dänemark, Germany, 1956–7; Formes Scandinaves, Paris, 1958; The Arts of Denmark, U.S.A., 1960–2; (all official Danish artware exhibitions). Organiser of the exhibition 'The Drinking

Glass' at Louisiana in 1963.

LIT: Liège, 1958, p.50; Corning, 1959, Nos.43–54; *140 years of Danish Glass*, circulated in U.S.A. by the Smithsonian Institution, Washington, D.C., 1968–70.
Plates 100, 260

Luxton, John b.1920   England
Trained at Stourbridge School of Art, 1936–9; and entered the Royal College of Art in 1939. His studies were interrupted by six years in H.M. Forces. In 1946 he resumed his studies at the Royal College and graduated as an Associate in 1949. In that year he joined Stuart & Sons Ltd. of Stourbridge as designer, was engaged in the design of crystal tableware of all kinds and played an active role in the training of the factory's apprentices.

McCutchen, Earl b.1933   U.S.A.
Was educated at Iowa State College, Ohio State University and the Institute of Art in Florence. Has exhibited widely in America since 1966, notably in exhibitions of contemporary glass at the Smithsonian Museum and at Dallas, May/June 1967. McCutchen trained as a potter and is intrigued by the inter-relationships and contrasts of glass and clay.

McKinney, Nanny Still b.1926   Finland
Trained at the Institute of Industrial Arts, 1945–9, and joined Riihimäen Lasi Oy in 1949. Nanny Still (who, since her marriage, has taken her husband's name of McKinney) is a versatile designer, working in glass, porcelain, wood, steel, plastics, jewellery and light-fittings. She was awarded Swedish and French scholarships in 1954 and 1957 and has made many study trips. She was awarded Diplomas of Honour at the Milan Triennales of 1954, 1957 and 1960; International Design Award, U.S.A., 1965; and Pro Finlandia prize, 1972.

COLL: Victoria & Albert Museum, London; Corning Museum, New York; Museum of Modern Art, New York; Metropolitan Museum of Art, New York; Nordenfjeldske Museum, Trondheim; Neue Sammlung, München.
EXH: São Paulo, 1958; London, 1969; Brussels, 1960, 1963, 1968; Paris, 1964.
Plates 97, 119, 137

Marinot, Maurice 1882–1960   France
Born at Troyes, son of a merchant in cotton goods. Went to Paris in 1901. From 1905–12 studied in the Atelier Corman at the École des Beaux-Arts, and exhibited paintings with the Fauvist group. In 1911 returned to Troyes and started to learn glassmaking, exhibiting his work at the Salon des Indépendants in that year. He continued to make and exhibit glass until 1937 when he returned to painting. All his drawings and paintings were destroyed in the 1944 bombing of Troyes, but his daughter, Florence, has presented important collections of his work to the Victoria & Albert Museum, London, and to the Metropolitan Museum, New York.

He explained in his unpublished autobiography what he set out to achieve:

> *To preserve, within a given form, the robust nobility of the hot, thick glass ready to be blown, and while blowing it, to let the nature of the glass assert itself, to control its natural tendencies without denying them; while the glass is at the height of its incandescence to coax from it forms that are plump and yielding, and then to incorporate into them other pieces evoking still or running water, or cracking and melted ice.*

His total production was about 2,500 pieces and falls into four categories: 1911–23, clear glass decorated in enamels, at first in brilliant *'fauve'* colours, then in white; 1920 and after, 'naked and muscular pieces' blown by Marinot himself; thirdly, sculptures in glass etched in acid or shaped by wheel; 1927 and after, objects in moulded glass. It is however difficult to date his pieces precisely, but each one bears his signature and lives up to André Derain's words: 'I have never seen anything so beautiful, which is at once so elaborate and so simple.'

EXH: Paris, 1925; Musée de Lyon, 1965; Paris, 1966.
COLL: Musée Municipal, Sète, France; Metropolitan Museum, New York; Victoria & Albert Museum, London (gifts from Marinot's daughter); Musée des Arts Décoratifs, Paris.
LIT: Ami Chantre, 'Les verreries de Maurice Marinot', *Art et Décoration*, January/June 1920, p.144; Gaston Quénioux, *Les Arts Décoratifs Modernes* (Librairie Larousse, Paris, 1925), p.246; Guillaume Janneau, Introduction to 1925 Exhibition at Paris, in *Art et Décoration*, January/June 1925, p.174; G. Janneau, *Modern Glass*, 1931, pp.93–4; Polak, 1962, p.41, pl.22; Robert Charleston, 'The Glass of Maurice Marinot', Victoria & Albert Museum *Bulletin*, Vol.1, No.3, July 1965, pp.1–8; *Realities*, March 1968, pp.56–9.
Colour plate 4 and plates 57–60

Marsh, Honoria Diana b.1923   England
First experimented in glass engraving in 1950, following a chance meeting with the late L.G. Siese, a craftsman very knowledgeable about the technicalities of this medium. She had already exhibited drawings and paintings, both as an amateur and as a professional. She was elected to the British Society of Master Glass-Painters in 1950–1. Her work has been reproduced in all the major art periodicals and most European magazines. All her work is privately commissioned. She specialises in very large goblets engraved with diamond point, in line and stipple, and her work is always fully signed. She works freehand from her own scale drawings, after copious research before beginning the engraving.
EXH: London, Archer Gallery, November 1970.
LIT: Cyril Ray, *Lafité*, London, 1968; *The Connoisseur*, April 1968; November 1970.
Plates 207, 208

Martens, Dino b.1923   Italy
Studied at the Venice Academy of Art as a painter and has designed for Vetreria A. Toso of Murano, and Salviati of Venice.
EXH: Liège, 1958, Nos.272–4; Corning, 1959, Nos.201–2.
LIT: Polak, 1962, pp.57, 68; *Craft Horizons*, September/ October 1964, p.45.
Plates 127, 128

Matura, Adolf b.1921   Czechoslovakia
Trained 1938–40 at the Glassmaking Trade School, Železný Brod; 1940–7, School of Industrial Art, Prague; 1954–9, Central Plastic Art Centre of Glass Industry, Prague. Since 1960 he has been at the Institute of Housing and Clothing Culture, Prague. He has designed glass for Bohemia Poděbrady, Exbor Studios, and Moser Glass. His table suite 'Montreal' (No. 26560) was particularly successful at Expo '67 in Montreal.
Plates 182, 269

Meadows, William b.1926   England
Educated Sherborne School and Corpus Christi, Cambridge. Started engraving glass by diamond-point stipple method. This, in 1964, became a full-time occupation, together with lecturing and writing.
LIT: 'Some comments on diamond-point engraving from the point of view of the collector and artist' in *Studies in Glass History and Design*, papers read at VIIIth International Congress on Glass, July 1968 (1970), pp.97–9.
Plates 211, 288

Maude-Roxby Montalto di Fragnito, David Howard b.1934
Born in England, educated in England, Australia, France and Italy. From 1957 to 1961 he studied painting at the Academy of Fine Arts in Florence. In 1961 he started diamond-point stipple engraving on glass. After working in ceramic design in Italy he returned to England in 1964 to undertake commissions for diamond-stipple engraved glass in which he specialises.

Metelák, Luboš b.1934   Czechoslovakia
Son of Alois Metelák (b.1897, glass designer and teacher at Železný Brod). From 1949–53 at the Glassmaking Trade School, Železný Brod, and from 1954–9 at the School of Applied Art, Prague. Now an engraver with Moser Glassworks.
EXH: Heal's, London, February 1970; all principal exhibitions of Czech glass.
Plate 86

Meydam, Floris b.1919   Holland
Was employed by Royal Leerdam in 1935 as assistant in the design department. In 1943 he became a trainee at the Leerdam Glass School, where he was appointed a teacher in 1944. At the same time he joined the design department, and is now, with Willem Heesen (q.v.), a chief designer. His abstract crystal shapes, which sometimes owe their final appearance only to bevelling, are cut from one lump of crystal and fully utilise the possibilities of reflection. Meydam has also designed the 'Unica' pieces for which Leerdam is renowned. These are free forms more or less spontaneously created from the red-hot material. Has more recently (1969–70) designed a number of glass sculptures, given a new form by receding and cutting-in.
EXH: Liège, 1958, Nos.298–322.
Plates 91, 93, 253

Model, Hanns b.1907   Germany
Was a pupil of Wilhelm von Eiff (q.v.) from 1928 to 1933. He then started his own workshop in Stuttgart where he still lives.
EXH: Corning, 1959, p.161.
LIT: *Kunst und Kunsthandwerk*, Vol.4, 1958, pp.17–22.
Plate 223

Monro, Helen (Mrs W.E.S. Turner) Scotland
Studied glass-engraving in the Glass Department of Professor Wilhelm von Eiff (q.v.) at the Kunstgewerbeschule, Stuttgart, 1938–9. Under her guidance the Department of Glass Design at Edinburgh College of Art grew from small beginnings in 1941 to become one of the best equipped in the United Kingdom. In 1956 she established the Juniper Workshop as a base for her own work, and for a time as a point of contact for graduate students. One of the most talented copper-wheel engravers in Great Britain, Helen Monro-Turner has always been interested in architectural applications of glass, both interior and exterior; some of her work can be seen on the main staircase of the National Library of Scotland, and over the main doorway of the Life Offices Association, Aldermary House, London. She has worked on many private commissions for presentations, etc., as well as screen doors and windows in a number of Scottish churches and schools.

As the wife of the distinguished glass technologist, the late Professor W.E.S. Turner, she has 'lived' glass for most of her life and been a guide and inspiration for a continuing stream of young students at Edinburgh, often at the expense of time for her own creative work.

EXH: Primavera Gallery, London, 1957; Anson's, London, 1961; Smithsonian Institution, Washington, D.C. 'British Artist Craftsmen Exhibition', 1959–60; Corning, 1959, p.103.

LIT: Helen Monro-Turner, 'The Training of Students as Glass Artists', address reprinted in *Atti del III Congresso Internazionale del Vetro, Venezia* (Rome, 1954), pp.650–3; 'Glass Engraving', *The Studio*, October 1960; 'The designer: some problems', in *Studies in Glass History and Design*, papers read at the VIIIth International Congress on Glass, July 1968 (1970), pp.116–18.
Plate 193

Morales-Schildt, Mona Sweden
Comes from a family of artists. Her father was a composer and conductor and her mother a singer and teacher of singing.

She started at the School of Industrial Art in Stockholm and won scholarships to study porcelain in England and Germany. She also went to a painting school in Paris before starting at Gustavsbergs in 1936 as an assistant to Wilhelm Kage. From 1939 she worked for a year or two in Finland for Arabia Porcelain. She then returned to Stockholm and managed the new Gustavsbergs shop until 1941. After her marriage to the author Goran Schildt, she worked 1945–57 for Nordiska Kompaniet, the Stockholm department store, where she was responsible for all decorative art exhibits. In 1958 she joined Kosta Glass and has made her name with a very wide range of glass designs. Internationally, however, she is best known as the designer of the brightly coloured and faceted bibelots of the 'Ventana' type (1963) – a range extending into vases and plates with 'depth' obtained by 'cutting through' a range of warm colours.

COLL: Nationalmuseum, Stockholm; Corning Museum, New York; Kunstgewerbemuseum, Hamburg, etc.

EXH: The 'Ventana' range well known at George Jensen Inc., New York, September 1963 (catalogue); Rosenthal Studio Houses in Rome and Stuttgart; Svensk Form, Stockholm, etc.

LIT: *Kosta Glass*, 1963; factory literature.
Plates 80, 84, 87, 219, 249

Murray, Keith b.1893 New Zealand
A successful architect with but limited time for glass designing. He did, however, produce a very successful range of glass for Stevens & Williams of Brierley Hill, Staffordshire, from 1932–9. He also designed silver and a few pottery models. He was among the very few glass designers in England in the 1930s, allocating some three months in the year to the task. His work reflected a functional approach with simple engraved decoration.

LIT: 'The Design of Table Glass', article by the artist, *Design for Today*, June 1933; Polak, 1962, pp.59–61.
Plate 69

Myers, Joel Philip b.1934 U.S.A.
Was educated at Parsons School of Design (1951–4); studied ceramic design in Copenhagen (1957–8) and continued this at Alfred University, New York State College of Ceramics (1960–3), where he gained his Master's degree. In 1963 he was appointed Director of Design for Blenko Glass at Milton, West Virginia, but left them in September 1970 to become Associate Professor of Art at Illinois State University. The honours, purchase awards, exhibition participation and representation of his work in collections would fill over three pages of terse listing here. Sufficient to say that Joel Myers is one of the most significant designers working in America today.

EXH: Craftsmen, U.S.A. '66 (merit award); Toledo, 1966,
and 1968 (merit and purchase awards); Dallas,
1967; Museum of Contemporary Crafts, New York,
1968; Zurich, 1972.
LIT: *Craft Horizons*, March/April 1964; March/April 1967;
October 1972; *Decorative Art in Modern Interiors*
(Studio Vista, London, 1966–9); *The Crafts of the
Modern World* (World Crafts Council, 1968).
Plates 322, 324

Nash, A. Douglas 1885–1940   U.S.A.
One of America's most talented designers during the 1930s.
He purchased the Corona, Long Island, factory from Louis
Comfort Tiffany in 1928 and made his own glass there until
1931. When this ceased Nash joined the Libbey Glass
Company at Toledo and produced many successful lines, some
of them adapting original Tiffany patterns.
COLL: Toledo Museum of Art (Inv. 68.59).
Plate 70

Navarre, Henri b.1885   France
Was best known as a sculptor but he also engraved medals and
glass. He exhibited regularly in the French national salons
from about 1927. His work was often massive and stained
with coloured pigments and powdered metal oxides. Some of
these powdered colours were put on the surface of the 'marver'
on which the glassmaker rolled the molten glass. The swirling
colour bands 'arabesqued' the surface of the glass.
LIT: *Art et Décoration*, 1924, p.157; 1932, pp.41–50;
G. Janneau, *Modern Glass* (The Studio, London, 1931),
pp.12–13; Polak, 1962, p.43.

Németh, Magda Vadeszi b.1941   Hungary
Studied under Julia Báthory at the Secondary School for Fine
and Applied Art, Budapest. Designed for Ajkai Üveggyár at
Akjai since 1960.
Plate 98

Northwood, John I (1836–1902); *and* **John II** (1870–1960)
England
John Northwood I joined the glass-manufacturing firm of
W.H., B. and J. Richardson at Wordsley to learn among other
things the craft of painting and enamelling on glass. By about
1860 he had set up in business on his own and become an
important experimenter and pioneer of new techniques. His

Elgin Vase (plate 2), completed in 1873, equipped him to
tackle a reproduction of the Portland Vase in glass (1878) and
the Pegasus Vase (1882: Smithsonian Institution).
    The example set by John Northwood I encouraged his son
and other relatives to continue the carving of cameo glass.
Throughout the late nineteenth century either John Northwood I or his son was actively associated with Stevens &
Williams, guiding its artistic and technical progress.
LIT: Geoffrey Beard, *Nineteenth Century Cameo Glass*
(Ceramic Book Co., Newport, 1956); John
Northwood II, *John Northwood I, His Contribution to
the Stourbridge Glass Industry* (Stourbridge, privately
printed 1958).

Novák, Břetislav b.1913   Czechoslovakia
Trained 1933–6 at the Glassmaking Trade School, Železný
Brod; 1935–46, worked as a glass-cutter. Since 1945 he has
taught glass-cutting at Železný Brod and is a superb craftsman
in hand-sculptured cut-finished glass. He collaborates with
J. Schovánek in the technique of deep-etching glass sheets.
LIT: *Czechoslovak Glass Review*, special 'Art in Glass' issue,
1969, p.28.

Nurminen, Kerttu b.1943   Finland
Joined the Arabia Glass team in 1972 after training at the
Institute of Industrial Arts in Helsinki.
Plate 152

Nylund, Gunnar b.1904   Sweden
Studied architecture and worked as a ceramist at Saxbo and
in Copenhagen for Bing and Grondahl. Has also worked with
Rorstrands Porslin in Sweden. Since 1953, with Rune Strand
and Asta Suomberg, he has designed glass for Strömbergshyttan.

Nyman, Gunnel 1909–48   Finland
Pupil of Arttu Brummer (q.v.). Studied at the Central School of
Industrial Design, Helsinki, graduating in 1932. Her first glass
was designed for Riihimäki Glassworks in the early 'thirties,
but she only concentrated on this area after winning a
competition held for the 1937 Paris World Fair. She also
worked with other Finnish glassworks – Karhula, Iittala and
Nuutäjarvi – and achieved her peak at the Stockholm Fair of
1946. She used simple cutting as decoration and often

'designed' her glass as it spun hot on the blowing-iron.
COLL: Nationalmuseum, Stockholm.
LIT: *Designed in Finland* (Finnish Foreign Trade Association, 1968), pp.50–2; Beard, 1968, p.44.
Plate 73

Öhrström, Edvin b.1906   Sweden
Took up sculpture in the early 1930s. In 1936 he began work for two months each year as a designer with Orrefors. Here, with Gate, Hald, Palmqvist and others, he helped in the great revival of engraved glass. But Ohrström was determined to be a sculptor in glass, and concentrated on this after leaving Orrefors in 1957. He has pushed the medium to its limits: his 20-foot-tall glass fountain was installed in 1961 in the new Vasa House in Stockholm. His glass sculpture which forms one whole wall in the Town Hall at Vasteras pales before the great steel and glass fountain-sculpture 37.5 m. high erected in Sergel Square in Stockholm. (Plates 342–3.)
COLL: Most Scandinavian museums; Metropolitan Museum, New York; Paris, Musée des Arts Décoratifs, etc.
EXH: Malmö Museum, Sweden, 9–31 March 1968 (useful catalogue listing commissions, etc.).
LIT: *Kontur*, Swedish Design Annual, No.12, 1964.
Plates 65, 232, 311, 327, 341, 342

Okkolin, Aimo b.1917   Finland
A designer with Riihimäen Lasi Oy, Finland. He started with them as a cutter and engraver in 1937. The designs 'Water-lily' and 'Serpentin' are characterised by large faceted surfaces in cut crystal. The 'Hellea' collection is splendidly clean-cut and functional in appearance. The design 'Pack Ice' was designed and cut in clear lead crystal by the artist.
Plate 226

Oliva, Ladislav b.1933   Czechoslovakia
Trained 1948–51 at the Glassmaking Trade School, Kamenický Šenov; 1951–7, School of Applied Art, Prague; 1957–64, Nový Bor; 1964, Bohemia Glassworks, Poděbrady.
   In 1958 this talented young artist used the sand-blasting technique to produce a superb set of bowls and vases in lead glass which were awarded several international prizes. By the middle of 1964 he was working with a group of creative artists determined to tackle problems in a new field of Bohemian glass – hand-moulded lead crystal. His colleagues included Václav Hořaček (q.v.) and Václav Cígler (q.v.). A square-shaped

vase and jardinière made at Poděbrady were among the winning entries for the 1966 Czechoslovak Contest for the year's outstanding products (from a total of 705 applications). Since then Oliva has become one of Czechoslovakia's premier designers and his work is seen in all major exhibitions.
LIT: *Czechoslovak Glass Review* No.2, 1967; No.8, 1967; special 'Art in Glass' issue, 1969, p.8.
Plates 278, 285

Ollers, Edvin 1888–1959   Sweden
Studied at the School of Decorative Art in Stockholm 1905–9 and at Valand in Gothenburg, 1909–10. Belonged to the group of painters called 'Optimists' and exhibited widely with them. Subsequently designed for a long line of glassworks: Kosta, 1917–18 (and again 1931–2); Reijmyre, 1918–19; Elme, 1926–30; Limmared, 1929–40; Alsterfors 1930–4; Afors, 1934–40; and Ekenäs, 1946–7. It was however at Kosta, along with Gate and Hald, that Ollers created some of his most important glass; that in greyish glass with bubbles is very beautiful. He also designed ceramics for Uppsala-Ekeby, book-bindings, pewter and silver.
COLL: Nationalmuseum, Stockholm; Kosta, factory collection.
EXH: Nationalmuseum, Stockholm; February/March 1960.
LIT: Catalogue as above, written by Dag Widman; *Form*, 1960, pp.197–201; *Kosta Glass* (factory issued), 1963 edn.
Plate 45

Orr, Charles   Scotland
Succeeded Domnhall O'Broin as designer at the very successful Scottish firm, Caithness Glass of Wick. Manufacturing soda-lime glass for all normal use, Caithness and its designers have always paid serious attention to appearance and function of their glass.

Ortlieb, Nora b.1904   Germany
Studied engraving at the Kunstgewerbeschule, Stuttgart. Was assistant to Wilhelm von Eiff (q.v.) from 1933 to 1943 and started her own workshop at Stuttgart in 1943. Is the author of a biography of von Eiff, 1950.
EXH: Corning, 1959, p.163, Nos.130–1.
Plate 184

Orvola, Heikki b.1943   Finland
Joined the Arabia design team in 1968 after training at the

Institute of Industrial Arts in Helsinki. Designs for both utility and art glass, the latter being decorated with bright basic-colour spirals, marbled pastel shades, or in filigree techniques. *Plate 115*

Palmqvist, Sven b.1906   Sweden
After the Technical College, the Academy of Fine Arts, Stockholm, and then training under Paul Connet in Paris, he came to Orrefors and, like his colleague, Nils Landberg (q.v.), joined the firm's engraving school. He first appeared at the glassworks in 1928 and has recently retired. An intense man, teeming with ideas, his work was proof of the value to a glass-designer of a technical, constructive bent. He worked for years on extending the technical possibilities of glass-making, and his greatest contributions were in the field of coloured glass. He developed the Graal (Grail) technique into the styles known as 'Ravenna' (heavy, mosaic-like in bold glowing colours), and 'Kraka', with networks of contrasting colours between the layers of glass. His 'Fuga' bowls were ingeniously fashioned by centrifugal force – the blob of hot glass being spun to its shape in a revolving mould. He was awarded a Grand Prix at the Milan Triennale of 1957.
Plates 164, 338, 339

Peace, David b.1915   England
Educated Mill Hill and Sheffield University. Architect and town-planner. Self-taught glass-engraver exploring with considerable skill a life-long interest in lettering, heraldry and three-dimensional design. Has studied, written about and been inspired by seventeenth-century Dutch diamond-point calligrapher/engravers, and the perfection of the lettering of Eric Gill. Strives to achieve a close affinity in his work between the engraved design and the form of the glass. Master of the Art Workers' Guild, 1973.
COLL: Numerous private commissions; Victoria & Albert Museum, London; Corning Museum, New York; Royal Scottish Museum, Edinburgh; Manchester, Birmingham and Norwich Museums; Cambridge University, Kettle's Yard collection.
EXH: Royal Festival Hall, London (six engravers), 1961; Victoria & Albert Museum, London, 'Contemporary Calligraphy', 1965; Pilkington Glass Museum, 'Artists in Glass', 1969; Smithsonian Institution, Washington, D.C., 'British Designer Craftsmen', 1969–71; Victoria & Albert Museum, London, 'The Craftsman's Art',

1973. Seven one-man shows, 1956–74, including All Hallows Art Centre, London; the Minories, Colchester; Cambridge, Kettle's Yard; and University of York.
LIT: C.M. Heddle, *A manual of etching and engraving* (Tiranti, London, 1961), pls.24–6, 33–4; Laurence Whistler, 'Some Engraved Glasses by David Peace', *The Connoisseur*, July 1968, pp.175–7; David Peace, *Engraved glass, lettering and heraldry* (1968; 2nd edn. 1973); – 'A Calligrapher's approach to glass-engraving' in *Studies in Glass History and Design*, papers read at VIIIth International Congress on Glass, July 1968 (1970), pp.91–3; 'The Glass Engravers', *House and Garden*, May 1973, pp.96–7.
Plates 172, 177 ,181, 202, 203, 206

Percy, Arthur b.1886   Sweden
Studied in Stockholm and Paris. Joined Gullaskruf Glass in southern Sweden as a designer in 1951. Also a painter and a designer of ceramics and textiles.
EXH: Corning, 1959, Nos.240–1.
LIT: Polak, 1962, p.71, pl.75b.

Persson, Sigurd b.1914   Sweden
Studied gold- and silver-smithing in Germany and obtained his Master's certificate at the Stockholm Konstfackskolan in 1943. The son of a silversmith, he opened his own successful workshop. He has designed for Älghults Glass since 1966.
LIT: Graham Hughes, *Modern Jewelry* (Studio Vista, London, 1967), pp.97–8.

Persson-Melin, Signe b.1925   Sweden
Employed by Boda since 1967, Signe Persson-Melin has designed several successful table-ranges. Her 'Square Range' is particularly versatile, useful for all kinds of food preparation, preserving and serving. She is also known as a ceramist and received the Lunning Prize in 1958. Trained in Stockholm and Copenhagen.

Pianon, Alessandro b.1931   Italy
Has designed for Vetreria Vistosi at Murano since 1956, specialising in lamps and glass for series production.

Plátek, Miroslav b.1922   Czechoslovakia
Younger brother of Václav Plátek (*see below*). Trained 1936–9

at the Glassmaking Trade School at Železný Brod; 1939–46 at the School of Applied Art, Prague. In 1950 joined Železný Brod Glassworks as designer and engraver. Specialises in cut and engraved glass.
Plate 82

Plátek, Václav b.1917   Czechoslovakia
Trained 1932–5 at the Glassmaking Trade School at Železný Brod; 1935–40 at the School of Industrial Art, Prague, 1954–7. Now lectures at the School of Applied Art, Prague.

Poli, Flavio b.1900   Italy
Has worked as decorator, ceramist and glass designer. In glass he has worked for several Italian firms including Seguso Vetri d'Arte and Conterie E. Cristallerie and is one of Italy's leading glass designers, with an assured technique.
EXH: Corning, 1959, Nos.182–7.
Plate 77

Pollard, Donald b.1924   U.S.A.
Born in New York, Donald Pollard studied architecture and design at the famous Rhode Island School of Design in Providence. After working in silver, architectural theatre design and as a free-lance industrial designer, he joined Steuben Glass as a designer in 1950. His work is now well represented in public and private collections and is regularly exhibited.
Plates 166, 218

Pravec, Josef b.1925   Czechoslovakia
Trained 1945–8 at the Glassmaking Trade School, Nový Bor; 1949–55, the School of Applied Art, Prague. In 1951 he was appointed designer at the Bohemia Glassworks, Poděbrady. Specialises in cut and engraved glass.
EXH: Montreal, Expo '67.
LIT: *Czechoslovak Glass Review*, No.1, 1967, p.13.

Queensberry, Marquess of b.1929   England
Professor of Ceramics and Glass, Royal College of Art, London until 1974. Design consultant to Webb Corbett Glass and originator of several designs. He has also designed ceramics for W.R. Midwinter of Stoke-on-Trent.
Plate 159

Quénvit   France
This signature appears on enamelled French glass of the

1920s, which is similar in style to that created by Marcel Goupy and Delvaux (rue Royale, Paris).
LIT: Hilschenz, 1973, No.301.

Råman, Ingegerd b.1943   Sweden
Trained at the Stockholm Konstfackskolan. With Johansfors Glass since 1968.

Rath family *fl.*1876–1945   Austria
In 1918 Ludwig Lobmeyr's nephew, Stephen Rath, (1876–1951) founded a branch establishment of Lobmeyr of Vienna (q.v.) at Steinschönau where glass was made to his design and standard of quality. Hans Harold Rath (*b.*1904) studied at the School of Applied Arts in Munich and joined Lobmeyr in 1924, becoming chief designer in 1938. From 1920 to 1937 Stephen Rath's daughter, Marianne (*b.*1904), designed for the Steinschönau branch in particular, and Wilhelm von Eiff (q.v.) also worked with Rath for a short time in 1921. A successful collaboration was made for a short time, 1921–4, by Stephen Rath with the Czech glass designer, Jaroslav Horecj (q.v.).

Rickard, Stephen b.1920   England
Worked primarily as a sculptor until 1953 and since then has concentrated particularly on glass engraving. He works mostly on a commission basis, heraldic themes appealing particularly. Fellow of the Society of Designer Craftsmen.
LIT: G.M. Heddle, *A manual on etching and engraving glass* (Tiranti, London, 1961), pls.71–2; *Pottery Gazette*, April 1962, p.516; Beard, 1968, p.109.

Riedel, Claus Joseph b.1925   Austria
Born in North Bohemia where his family had glass factories (established since 1856), Riedel studied inorganic chemistry. He worked in major technical posts with various glass companies and founded the Tiroler Glashütte at Kufstein in Austria in 1957. In 1969 Professor Riedel built another glass factory at Schneegattern in Austria which is said to have the most modern construction and production methods in Europe. His work is remarkably 'clean' in line and the 'Exquisit' glasses are aptly named.
EXH: World Exhibition, Brussels, 1958 (Grand Prix); Corning, 1959, No.5 ('Exquisit' one of three objects selected as best by Edgar Kaufmann Jr. from the 1800 or so on display); Milan Triennale, 1960 (Medal);

Austrian National Prize, 1962; International design award for 'Manhattan' line, 1966; 'Premio Internazionale' at Vicenza for 'Olympia' vases, 1969.
Plate 107

Rosselli, Alberto b.1921   Italy
Graduated in architecture in 1950, and now Professor for Industrial Design at the Faculty of Architecture of Milan. He is an important product designer (furniture, machinery) and designs glass for Salviati of Venice and ceramics for Ceramiche di Laveno.

Roubíček, René b.1922   Czechoslovakia
1940–4, School of Industrial Art, Prague; 1945–52, Professor at Glassmaking Trade School, Kamenický Šenov; plastic artist at Nový Bor and then chief plastic artist at Bor (Exbor Studios). Roubíček is among the best known in international terms of all Czech glass-designers. His chandeliers (e.g. Czech Embassy, London), his spatial compositions and cut-finished sculptures, mostly made in the Exbor Studios at Nový Bor, have earned for him a considerable reputation. Many of his fine creations (some made in collaboration with glassmaker J. Rozinek) are in all major Czech glass exhibitions. His wife, Miluše Roubíčkova (b.1922), is also a glass designer.
EXH: Brussels, Expo '58; Corning, 1959, No.39; all major Biennales and subsequent Expos; Victoria & Albert Museum, London, February 1965, Nos.207–9.
LIT: *Czechoslovak Glass Review*, March/April 1959, pp.2–7; special 'Art in Glass' number, 1969, pp.16–18.
Plates 229, 254, 292

Rousseau, François Eugène 1827–91   France
Dealer in china and glassware, but much more than that. In 1867 he started to decorate drinking glass services after his own design. Later he had glass blown to his design at Appert's works at Batignolles. At the time of the 1878 Paris Exhibition he had overlay glass made in colours and allowed the glass mixture to run down the surface and solidify in drops. Here was the early spirit of Art Nouveau, realised for him by the Appert brothers. He revived the Venetian technique of *craquelé* glass and showed it at the 1884 exhibition as well as agate glass and imitation gems. In 1885 his business was taken over by Léveillé who continued to make glass in an Art Nouveau style, and in imitation of Japanese art.
COLL: Musée des Arts Décoratifs, Paris.

EXH: Paris, 1878, Paris, 1884.
LIT: Polak, 1962, pp.21–3; Hilschenz, 1973, p.342 (cites extensive bibliography).
Plate 9

Rudge, Lawson Ernest b.1936   England
Attended Stourbridge College of Art, and after his National Diploma in Design, went on to the Industrial Glass course at the Royal College of Art, 1959–62. Subsequently lectured in ceramics and glass in the sculpture department of Exeter College of Art.
Plate 315

Sabino, Maurius-Ernest fl.1910–30   France
Worked in Paris 1920–30 and exhibited at the 1925 Paris Exhibition. Could be said to be an imitator of Lalique (q.v.).
LIT: G. Janneau, *Modern Glass* (The Studio, London, 1931), pp.141–82.

Sala family fl.1870–1950   Spain
Spanish glass-makers who settled in Paris represented by Dominique, his son Jean (b.1895) and Bienvenu. Dominique was in Paris by 1910, Bienvenu was represented by three items of 1919 in the Paris 1966 Exhibition and Jean worked a studio workshop on the Left Bank for several years and became one of France's leading glass craftsmen.
COLL: Musée des Arts Décoratifs, Paris; Toledo Museum of Art (Inv. 51.352).
LIT: Paris, 1966, catalogue; Polak, 1962, p.43, pl.27a.

Sarasin, Betha b.1930 *and* **Teff** b.1931   Switzerland
Betha studied at the Art School at Basel, 1947–51. She has been a free-lance artist since 1961 and with her architect husband designs furniture, and glass for Salviati of Venice. They work in Venice and have a studio in Basel.
EXH: Venice Biennale XXXIV (gold medal); Mostra del Vetro di Murano, 1963 (prize); Expo '67 (gold medal).
Plates 135, 334

Sarpaneva, Timo b.1926   Finland
Graduated from the graphics department of the Institute of Industrial Arts in 1948. Employed by Karhula-Iittala Glassworks from 1950 where he designs on a free-lance basis, along with Tapio Wirkkala (q.v.). Sarpaneva's design versatility is almost unequalled and he has taught textile design and

cloth-printing, designed glass, cast-iron ware, textiles and packaging as part of his own studio's output.

He was awarded the Lunning Prize in 1956 and has taken a number of Grand Prix and Gold and Silver Medals at the Milan Triennale. Honorary Royal Designer of Royal Society of Arts, 1964; gold medal, Royal College of Art.

COLL: Most major museums, including Victoria & Albert Museum, London; Nationalmuseum, Stockholm; Gothenburg; München; Museum of Modern Art, New York, etc.

EXH: Bonnier's, New York, October 1967; Expo '67.

LIT: Kerttu Niilonen, *Finnish Glass* (Tammi, Helsinki, 1967), pp.65–76; Beard, 1968, pp.48–9; *Designed in Finland* (Finnish Foreign Trade Association, 1973), pp.42–5.

Plates 111, 145, 271, 299

Schlyter-Stiernstedt, Margaretha b.1927   Sweden
Trained at the Stockholm Konstfackskolan as a ceramist and worked extensively in London, Sèvres, Holland and Sweden. Has designed for Björkshults Glass since 1953.

Schulze, Paul b.1934   U.S.A.
Born in New York and educated at its university and the Parsons School of Design, Schulze was engaged by Steuben Glass as one of its designers in 1961. His work was shown in the two 1966 Steuben exhibitions, 'Studies in Crystal' and 'Islands in Crystal'.
Plate 224

Schoder, Marianne b.1918   Germany
Pupil and assistant of Wilhelm von Eiff (q.v.). Set up her own workshop in Stuttgart in 1938 and uses 'blanks' from several German glasshouses.

EXH: Corning, 1959, No.140.

Seager, Harry b.1931   England
Seager, one of the most talented of the English 'glass sculptors', trained at Farnham College of Arts, graduating in 1955. Since that date he has moved forward with a consistent number of exhibitions and commissions, as well as an active teaching programme. In 1974 he was Associate Professor at the University of Rhode Island and is presently Senior Lecturer in Fine Art at Stourbridge College of Art.

COLL: Leeds Art Gallery; Hirschorn Collection, and Hirschorn Museum and Sculpture Garden, Washington, D.C.;

Contemporary Art Society, London.

EXH: One-man and group shows at Gimpel Fils, London and New York, 1965–74; 10th Biennale, Middelheim, Belgium; Rotterdamse Kunsttring, Holland; Redfern Galleries, London; L'Uomo e l'Arte, Milan, etc.

Plates 312, 325

Selbing, John b.1908   Sweden
Started at Orrefors in 1927 as an assistant in the drafting department. Eventually his superb camera technique made him a master (surely the best) in the difficult art of glass photography and his lens became an important tool for his colleagues in visualising glass forms. In his well-equipped studios at Orrefors the complete history of each design was charted in imaginative photographs and transparencies, and a generous selection appear in this book. But John Selbing also designed glass, and some fine pieces of engraving are the result. He has also achieved, with simple clarity, light airy bubbles of glass which he regards as 'the most expressive form of glass'. The world of geometric form is in general his point of departure – and he explored the by-ways of design with humility and competence as befitted the pupil of Simon Gate and Edward Hald. He was awarded a State cultural scholarship in 1967, and retired from Orrefors in 1970.
Plate 165

Severin, Bent b.1925   Denmark
Graduated as architect from Royal Academy of Fine Arts in 1952. Designs stainless steel, ceramics and metal objects as well as interiors.

EXH: Corning, 1959, Nos.58–9.

Sigvard, Gosta b.1939   Sweden
Has designed for Lindshammar since 1965.

COLL: Nationalmuseum, Stockholm.

EXH: Växjö, Smålands Museum, June/September 1968.

Siiroinen, Erkkitapio b.1944   Finland
A designer with Riihimäen Lasi Oy, Finland, since 1968. Works with glass, metal, plastics and packing design.

Sinnemark, Rolf b.1941   Sweden
As one of the younger generation of Swedish designers, Sinnemark graduated from the School of Industrial Art in 1963 as a silversmith. He was awarded first prize in the Boda

Glassworks contest in 1963 and worked there for three months in 1964. He then visited America (1965–6) and worked as a sculptor and silversmith. In 1967 he joined the Kosta group – at Kosta for glass designing and at nearby Boda for wood and iron.

EXH: Denver (sculptures), 1966; glass in Malmö, 1969; glass in Jönköping, 1970.

Plates 113, 298, 313

Sipos, Judit Kekesi b.1937   Hungary
Studied under Julia Báthory at Secondary School for Fine and Applied Art, Budapest. Has designed for Paradi Üveggyár at Parádsavár since 1960.
Plate 106

Sjögren, Christer b.1926   Sweden
Studied at the Stockholm Konstfackskolan, 1947–51, and worked as a sculptor thereafter. Much of his work for Linds-hammar Glass has a sculptural quality but he has designed much table-glass; some of it, like 'Sextett', with stacking ability.

EXH: Växjö, Smålands Museum, 1965, 'Seven Designers'.
LIT: *Form*, no.9, 1965, pp.614–15.

Skawonius, Sven Erik b.1908   Sweden
The Technical School and the School of Arts in Stockholm gave Skawonius his start. He turned firstly to theatre design, but also did duty as art director of the ceramic firm Uppsala-Ekeby. He followed this with a period of teaching glass design in Stockholm, 1945–62. In summary (if that is possible with so varied a talent): painter, interior decorator, designer of posters, book-bindings, silver, textiles, wallpapers, ceramics and also glass, for Kosta, for two periods, 1933–5 and 1944–50.
Plates 68, 78

Slang, Mrs Gerd Boesen b.1925   Norway
Trained at the Oslo State School and was engaged by A/S Christiania Glasmagasin in 1948 where she specialised in designing decor for sand-blowing and engraving glass and crystal. After a period of free-lance work (1952–62) she was engaged in 1963 by Hadeland Glassworks.

EXH: Forum, Oslo, autumn 1967.

Smith, David b.1921   England

Trained at Webb Corbett's Tutbury factory and acted in various capacities, 1963–66. Transferred to the parent factory at Stourbridge and has originated most designs since that date, latterly in liaison with the head designer of Royal Doulton (of which group Webb Corbett is now part). Smith is also a competent engraver and cutter.
Plate 213

Smrčková, Ludvika b.1903   Czechoslovakia
Trained 1921–7 at the School of Applied Art, Prague; from 1928–48 she was a teacher at various pedagogical institutes and secondary schools. In the years 1948–52 she co-operated with Inwald Glassworks; from 1952 to 1958 she acted as designer at the Central Plastic Art Centre of Glass Industry in Prague. In 1966 she became a Professor and Meritorious Artist and was invited to design a collection of vases for the reception rooms of Prague Castle. Many of her ideas are realised at the EXBOR Studios and she has also designed for Moser (e.g. Cut Bowl, No.1990), and continues an active career after her first showing at the 1925 Paris Exhibition.

Solven, Pauline b.1943   England
Trained at Stourbridge College of Art, 1961–5, and the Royal College of Art, 1965–8. Then she spent 1968 in Sweden at Åsa Brandt's glass studio at Torshälla. She returned to England in 1969 for the exciting start of the Glasshouse, London. This centre, offering production facilities and glass for sale, is closely connected with the Crafts Centre and one of its directors is the distinguished glass designer, Sam Herman (q.v.). Pauline was appointed the first studio-manager, but has now become a free-lance glass artist at the Glasshouse. She started her own studio in 1974 near Newent in west Gloucester-shire.

COLL: Corning Museum, New York; Museum of South Australia; Malmö Museum, Sweden; Greater London Council collections.
EXH: Glass Manufacturers' Federation, 1964; Corning Museum, New York (Art Schools exhibition), 1968; Form Design Centre, Malmö, Sweden, 1969; British Pavilion, Expo '70, Osaka, Japan; Heal's, London, July 1970; Oxford Gallery, Oxford, 1971; Victoria & Albert Museum, London, 1973; Ulster Museum, Belfast, 1973; Galerie 'L', Hamburg, 1974; Design Centre, London, 1974.

Colour plate 110

Sovánka, István 1858–1945   Hungary
Sculptor and glass artist; Master of acid-etching workshop at glassworks of Zayngróc and Ujantalvölgy in northern Hungary. Pupil at school for wood-carvers, 1875–80. Studied under György Zala. Produced glass in Gallé style and overlay glass with etching and wheel-engraving techniques.
COLL: Museum of Applied Arts, Budapest.
EXH: Milan, 1906 (gold medal); Budapest, 1959, cat., fig.4; Budapest, 1961, cat., fig.25.
LIT: G. Pazaurek, *Moderne Gläser* (Leipzig n.d., 1901), p.119; J. Koós, 'Hungarian Art Nouveau Glass' in *Studies in Glass History and Design*, papers read at the VIIIth International Congress on Glass, July 1968 (1970), pp.55–61.

Stennett-Wilson, R.S. b.1923   England
Associated with J. Wuidart & Co. Ltd., glass importers, and with the Royal College of Art. Founded King's Lynn Glass in 1968 (subsequently acquired by Wedgwood's and renamed Wedgwood Glass). Author of *The Beauty of Modern Glass* (London, 1958). Designer of modern production of Wedgwood Glass.
EXH: Corning, 1959, No.63.
LIT: Polak, 1962, pp.78, 80, 81.
Plates 130, 138

Stevens, Irene M.   England
Designer for Webb Corbett of Stourbridge until her appointment as Head of the Department of Glass at the Foley College of Art, Stourbridge. By her leadership and example this School has become one of the most important in the training of young glass designers working for a Diploma (subsequently Degree) in Art and Design.

Still, Nanny – *see* **McKinney, Nanny Still**

Strömberg, Edvard 1872–1946   Sweden
Started at Kosta in 1891 and led the firm, with the help of director Alex Hummel, to triumphs at the Stockholm Exhibition of 1897. From that time Swedish glass became known to an international public. In 1905 he acquired, with Hummel, the Sandviks Glassworks at Hovmantorp and ran this from 1906 to 1917. He came back to Kosta for a short while and then moved in 1918 to the post of administrative manager at Orrefors. His first years there were likewise spent in preparing

for the great 1925 Paris Exhibition at which Orrefors (and good Swedish glass) became even better known. In 1928 he moved to Eda and, with his wife, he started to design the lines which were created at Strömbergshyttan, from 1933.
   Despite a busy practical life, Strömberg had a strong interest in the history and traditions of Swedish glassmaking and wrote a number of important papers on various aspects of it. These survive in the extensive archives of the Smålands Glass Museum at Växjö.
LIT: Edward Hald, 'Edvard Strömberg, in memoriam', *Form*, 1947, 1, p.3.

Strömberg, Gerda 1879–1960   Sweden
Wife of Edvard Strömberg (*see above*). She designed glass at the first family firm at Eda and afterwards at Strömbergshyttan. These were usually handblown and simply designed in soft grey-blue or brown-grey glass with no additional decoration.[1]
LIT: Elisa Steenberg, *Modern Swedish Glass* (Lindqvists, Sweden, 1949).

Šuhájek, Jiří b.1943   Czechoslovakia
After the usual thorough Czech training at the Kamenický Šenov Trade School of Glassmaking, Šuhájek worked for the Moser Glass Company for two years as a designer. Then he spent five years working under Professor Libenský (q.v.) at the College of Applied Art in Prague, rounding off with two years in England, 1968–70, at the Royal College of Art.
LIT: *Czechoslovak Glass Review*, No.7, 1966, pp.197, 199.
Plate 242

Sutcliffe, Rod b.1946   England
Trained at Rochdale and Hammersmith Colleges of Art and the Royal College of Art, 1970. Interested in glass technology and the use of industrial glass in a sculptural context.

Thesmar, André Fernand 1843–1912   France
Trained as a painter and showed landscapes at the Salon of 1875. Interested in the art of enamelling, he gave up painting to devote himself to making glass objects decorated with beautifully modelled reliefs of plants and flowers.
LIT: Elka Schrijver, *Glass and Crystal*, II (Merlin Press, London, 1964), p.30.

Thomassen, Gerard b.1926   Holland
Received his glass education at the Leerdam Glass School and

worked for the factory as a designer until he took up a position elsewhere in Holland in 1967.

EXH: Centre for Industrial Design, Amsterdam (permanent exhibit); 'Gulden Vorm' award 1965; 'Gouden Noot' award for glass package designs, 1966.

COLL: National Glass Museum, Leerdam, Holland; Smithsonian Institution, Washington, D.C.

Thompson, George b.1913   U.S.A.
The Class Medal for 1936 at the Massachusetts Institute of Technology was awarded to George Thompson when he graduated in architecture; he also won the Boston Society of Architects' Prize. In this year he joined Steuben Glass as a designer and for over thirty years has designed unique pieces for various important royal and public collections. His work has been shown at important exhibitions in Paris (1937, 1951) and in every major Steuben show.

Thomson, Alan b.1935   England
He commenced art-glassblowing in 1971 and has been a member of the technical staff in the Department of Chemistry at Lancaster University since 1964. He works almost entirely with boro-silicate glass, fashioned by lamp-work, as opposed to the offhand techniques of most young artists. His work, and that of colleagues of the Society of Scientific Glassblowers (of which he is Librarian), reveals an increasing awareness of the aesthetic aspects of utilitarian objects.
Plate 314

Thrower, Frank b.1932   England
Designer for Dartington Glass in Devon, founded in 1967. Duke of Edinburgh Design Award, 1972.
EXH: Design Centre, London, 1967; Heal's, London, 1967–8; Bath, Summer Festival, 1970.
Plate 103

Thuret, André b.1898   France
One of the few artists who attempted to carry on the important early twentieth-century traditions in French glass. He has experimented with introducing metallic oxides into his bubbled-glass individual pieces.
LIT: Polak, 1962, p.77, pl.84a.

Tiffany, Louis Comfort 1848–1933   U.S.A.
As a designer and maker of bronze, silver and jewels, and of glass of revered and fantastic colour and shape, Tiffany's name is synonymous with the experimental verve of the late nineteenth century. He studied painting in Paris and carried through a great variety of commissions. Of Tiffany glass (which can seldom be dated, but for which many patents exist), it can be stated that there were few equals though many competitors. The iridescent 'favrile' glass – the result of exposing hot glass to fumes from metallic oxides – brought Tiffany great success. His new glassworks at Corona, Long Island, was opened in about 1893 with Arthur Nash (from Thomas Webb's in England) in charge. Nash's two sons, Douglas (q.v.) and Leslie, also joined the firm, which employed hundreds of workers to help purvey Tiffany products to an eager market.

COLL: Most national museums; special collection at Accrington, Lancs., home-town of Joseph Briggs, manager for Tiffany Glass, c.1902.

EXH: Museum of Contemporary Crafts, 'Louis Comfort Tiffany', 1958.

LIT: Valentine van Tassel, *Antiques Magazine* (New York), July/August 1952; Larry Freeman, *Iridescent Glass* (New York, 1956); Robert Koch, *Louis Comfort Tiffany, Rebel in Glass* (Crown Publishers, New York, 1964); Ray and Lee Grover, *Art Glass Nouveau* (1967); Mario Amaya, *Tiffany Glass* (London, Studio Vista, 1969); Hilschenz, 1973.

Colour plate 1 and plates 12, 14

Tockstein, Jindřich b.1914   Czechoslovakia
Trained 1929–34 at the Glassmaking Trade School, Železný Brod. From 1934–6 he was at the School of Applied Arts, Prague, and studied under Professor J. Drahoňovský (q.v.) and from 1945–50 at the Academy of Fine Arts, Prague. He is now a designer and glass-engraver at Železný Brod. His taut linear engravings have an ethereal quality.
EXH: Heal's, London, February 1970.

Toikka, Oiva b.1931   Finland
Born on 29 May, 1931 in Viipuri, which was then a part of Finland. Studied at the Institute of Industrial Art in Helsinki. Was employed by Oy Wärtsilä Ab Arabia from 1956 to 1959 as a ceramist. Was for four years an elementary school teacher in Lapland, but in 1963 returned to Wärtsilä, this time to Nuutäjarvi Glass. Was awarded the Lunning Prize in 1970 and a scholarship of the State of Finland in the same year. Oiva Toikka designs both household glass and *objets d'art*. His creations often

have masculine and straight lines, but he also finds new and surprising solutions. Examples of his production are the 'Kastehelmi' (Dewdrop) plate, a combination of romance and modern design; the elegant Flora and Fauna glass lines; and restrained or free, fanciful glass sculptures in which are enclosed geometric and narrative motifs. To decorate these he often uses gold or platinum particles fused in glass; otherwise, he prefers clear glass, and if he uses colours, they are mostly dark purple and rose. In 1973 he was appointed Art Director of Arabia Glass.

EXH: Has exhibited in Finland in 1958 (ceramics); with Kaj Franck in 1963 (glass) and 1966; in Stockholm, in 1966; and in 1967 with Bertil Vallien (q.v.); Helsinki, 1969; Heal's, London, 1969.

LIT: Factory literature such as Arabia's *Ceramics and Glass*, especially No.1, 1966, and centenary issue, 1973.

Colour plate 7 and plates 276, 306, 344

Toikka, Inkeri b.1931   Finland
Wife of Oiva (*above*). Trained at the Institute of Industrial Arts, Helsinki, 1951. Joined Arabia Glass in 1970.
Plate 144

Toso, Giusto b.1939; *and* **Renato** b.1940   Italy
These two brothers are both graduates of the University Institute of Architecture at Vicenza. As part of the family firm of Fratelli Toso of Murano their work has been exhibited widely from 1960, including the Venice Biennales, Milan Triennales and Expo '67, Montreal. Their father, Ermanno Toso, also does some designing and exhibited work at the Corning Museum, New York (1959, No.174).
Plates 301, 328

Tynell, Helena b.1918   Finland
Studied at the Institute of Industrial Arts, Helsinki, graduating in 1943. Since 1945 one of Riihimäki's leading designers who has done much to advance the cause of well-designed glass for everyday home use. From the simple cut-crystal bowl 'Twist' of 1943, she has constantly strived to utilise the flowing shapes created in hot glass and retain them for functional use when annealed and cold. She often makes prototypes in wood in order to be able to demonstrate to the mould-makers and blowers her ideas. She won the Finnish Association of Industrial Designers' Prize in 1968.

LIT: Kerttu Niilonen, *Finnish Glass* (Tammi, Helsinki, 1967),

pp.89–97; 'Moebel', *Interior Design*, 12, 1967, pp.82–3.
Plates 274, 295

Tysoe, Peter b.1935   England
Educated at Oxford Technical School, Oxford School of Art and Goldsmiths' College, University of London. Started full-time professional practice as producer of decorative murals, screens, sculpture and utilitarian products in 1966. In 1967 won first prize in an open competition held by the Worshipful Company of Glaziers for the design and production of a glass architectural feature to commemorate the VIIIth International Congress on Glass held in London, July 1968. This object in glass and resin is now mounted in the head office of the National Westminster Bank. Tysoe travelled on a Churchill Fellowship Award in Scandinavia in 1970 to study production and design of glass. Fellow of the Society of Designer-Craftsmen. Works also in metal and acrylics.

COLL: various, most cited and illustrated in article noted below.

LIT: P. Tysoe, 'Murals, screens and sculpture in glass, metals and resins' in *Studies in Glass History and Design*, papers read at the VIIIth International Glass Congress, July 1968 (1970), pp.106–8.

Valkema, Sybren b.1916   Holland
Sybren Valkema was born at The Hague and received his formal education there at the School of Design. Taught aesthetics at the Leerdam Glass School and designed for the Royal Leerdam Glassworks some drinking services, flower-vases, 'Serica' and 'Unica' pieces.

Since 1950 Valkema – at first as deputy, now as assistant-principal – has joined the Rietveld Academy of Art at Amsterdam where he founded a glass department in 1969. He also teaches designing (textiles) and the art of composition. He has been a member of the design team in the experimental department of the 'Porceleyne Fles', Delft (Holland).

COLL: Municipal Museum, Amsterdam; Museum Boymans-Van Beuningen, Rotterdam.

LIT: *Craft Horizons*, October 1972, p.16.
Plate 252

Vallien, Bertil b.1938   Sweden
Educated 1956–61 at the Konstfackskolan, Stockholm. He then visited the U.S.A. on a scholarship and won top honours as a ceramist in the Young America contest against extensive competition. He became known almost overnight and his

whole ceramic production sold out at once. He was also awarded first prize in the bi-annual exhibition at the Everson Museum of Art in New York. In 1963 he returned to Sweden, eager to try a new interest in the design of glass, and was attracted to the Åfors-Boda glassworks (now part of the Kosta group). He quickly proved his competence and has remained one of Sweden's most innovative glass designers. He has travelled extensively, to Japan in 1974.

EXH: Bonniers, New York, May 1966 (225 exhibits); Stockholm, February 1967 (with Oiva Toikka, q.v.); Expo '67; Pilkington Glass Museum, September 1969, Nos.16–17; Bonniers, New York, autumn 1973; Heal's, London, April 1974.

LIT: Dido Smith, 'Bertil Vallien . . .', *Craft Horizons*, September/October 1967, pp.7–13.

Colour plate 13 and plates 132, 239, 240, 245, 263, 275, 287

Vallien, Ulrica b.1938   Sweden
Wife of Bertil (*above*). Trained at the Konstfackskolan as a ceramist. Has worked for Boda Glass on a free-lance basis from 1971 onwards. Much of her glass is enamel-painted and fired in a ceramic kiln.

EXH: Bonnier's, New York, autumn 1973; Heal's, London, April 1974.

Plates 233, 321

Venini, Paolo 1895–1959   Italy
'One of the finest glass designers of the present century' might provide the appropriate epitaph for Venini who, as owner and chief designer of the firm he established at Murano (after his considerable success at the Paris 1925 Exhibition), combined traditional craftsmanship with superior design. Influenced by the strong Functionalist movements, his work was a reflection of form determined solely by function.

A descendant of a glass-blower's family, Venini first studied law at Milan University and established a practice in the town. His dismay at the paucity of good design in glass led him to abandon his career at the Bar and devote himself to glass-making. In 1921 he became a joint partner with Giacomo Cappelin at Murano and two years later took over sole control. Venini always engaged foremost designers and from 1923 to his death they earned many international prizes for their output. In particular, the designs of Gio Ponti, Napoleone Martinuzzi, and the Swedish designer Tyra Lundgren, helped along by Venini's own skills and flair, put them well ahead in

almost every Milan Triennale. Their effects of colour and texture with revivals of old techniques such as the lacy Venetian *latticino* did much to encourage other manufacturers in Murano towards better design.

Plates 79, 126, 156, 248, 251

Verboeket, Max b.1922   Holland
A painter, graphic designer and worker in pottery and stained glass. He has done several successful designs for Maastricht Glass, particularly in mould-blown forms.

Vida, Zsuzsa b.1944   Hungary
Pupil, and later assistant, of Julia Báthory at the Secondary School for Fine and Applied Art, Budapest. Studied at the High School for Applied Art, Prague, 1963–9. Does some designing for Ajkai Üveggyar at Ajka.

Vistosi, Gino, Luciano and **Oreste**   Italy
These three brother–directors of Vetreria Vistosi of Murano collaborate in every stage of design and production of, in particular, lamp fittings and the series production of table glass.

Wagenfeld, Wilhelm b.1900   Germany
After finishing at school, Wagenfeld became an apprentice in the design office of a Bremen silverware manufacturer, and at the same time went to the School of Arts and Crafts. This was followed by some two years at the Drawing Academy of Hanau. After a further year at Bremen he joined the Bauhaus at Weimar. At this famous school he worked mainly in the metal workshops under Moholy-Nagy and took apprentice's examinations as a silversmith.

In 1925 he was an assistant in the metal workshop at the Weimar Academy of Architecture. In 1929 he became a lecturer and head of the metal workshop, and began a practical association with industry. His first industrial commission was in domestic metalware and lamps. In 1930 free-lance activities took over and his advancement of the glass crafts in Thüringer Wald introduced him more thoroughly to this material. From 1931 to 1935 he taught in various posts at the Berlin Academy of Art. His first porcelain service was produced in 1934, and a year later Wagenfeld gave up teaching and assumed the artistic direction of the Vereinigten Lausitzer Glasswerke. Here he improved current utilitarian production and introduced a 'quality sector'. From 1935 to 1939 he produced new glass designs for Jenaer Glass and a porcelain service for Rosenthal titled 'Daphne'.

After military service he was appointed in 1946 to the Werkakademie at Dresden. In 1947 he moved to Berlin on being appointed head of the department of styling, and later professor, at the Higher School there. In 1954 he set up his own 'Wagenfeld Workshop' in Stuttgart for experimental and practical work and is a distinguished international designer.

LIT: *Wilhelm Wagenfeld*, exhibition catalogue issued by Landesgewerbeamt, Baden-Württemberg Museum, Stuttgart, May 1965 (references cited).

Wainwright, Kenneth b.1923   England

The eleventh member of a glass-making family, Wainwright started as an apprentice under his father at John Walsh Ltd., of Birmingham, in 1937 and continued there until 1951. For the next four years he worked at Stourbridge Glass Co., then moved to an assistant lectureship at Stourbridge College of Art, and in September 1965 took up a lectureship in the glass department of Edinburgh College of Art.

EXH: Various, including 1969/70 tour of British craftsmen's work in America. Made set of glasses presented to H.M. Queen Elizabeth II on 1957 visit to Stourbridge.

Walker, Colin b.1946   England

Manchester College of Art; Royal College of Art, 1969; interested in glass-ceramic sculpture especially in conjunction with natural materials (soil, water, plants, etc.).

Plate 237

Wallander, Alfred 1862–1914   Sweden

Wallander studied first at the Academy of Arts in Stockholm, then spent several years in Paris. He decided to change to the field of industrial art and became in 1896 art director of the Rorstrands China Company. He also designed silver and furniture; in glass, he was active at Kosta from 1905–10.

COLL: Kosta, factory collection.

Walter, Almaric 1859–1942   France

Worked for the Daum brothers at Nancy and in 1919 set up his own workshops. Some of his work is in pâte-de-verre and was done in collaboration with the painter and sculptor, Henri Bergé.

COLL: Kunstmuseum, Düsseldorf.

LIT: J.L. Vallières, *Le Verre* (April 1925), pp.76–82; Ray and Lee Grover, *Art Glass Nouveau* (1967), pl.361;

Martin Battersby, *The Decorative Twenties* (London, Studio Vista, 1969); Hilschenz, 1973, p.356.

Walwing, Folke b.1907   Sweden

Born at Maleras, Walwing joined the engraving school at Orrefors and studied under their great designers Simon Gate and Edward Hald. He rejoined Maleras Glass doing some engraving and all the designing of (particularly) pressed glass. He has been recently assisted by designers Annette Swiberg-Krahner and Hannelore Dreutler.

EXH: Nationalmuseum, Stockholm, 'Svenskt glas', 1954.

Wärff, Ann b.1937; **Goran Wärff** b.1933   Sweden

Ann Wärff was born in Germany at Lübeck and trained in Hamburg, Ulm and Zurich. She moved to Sweden on her marriage and worked with her husband, Göran, at Pukebergs Glass (1959–64). In 1964 they moved to Kosta, where they worked on a vast number of glass designs and realised many exciting pieces. They were joint Lunning Prize winners in 1969. They both now design free-lance for Kosta and Göran Wärff has recently spent time touring in Australia.

LIT: *Dansk Kunsthandverk*, 1967–8, 1, pp.19–23; Beard, 1968.

Colour plate 5 and plates 150, 151

Waugh, Sidney 1904–63   U.S.A.

Sidney Waugh, one of the great names of American glass history, was educated at the School of Architecture of the Massachusetts Institute of Technology, and at the École des Beaux Arts in Paris, as the pupil and assistant of Henri Bouchard. From these last years, 1928–9, came bronze and silver medals at the Salon du Printemps in Paris and the Prix de Rome in 1928. Represented in at least twenty-five major collections, including the leading museums in New York, Chicago, Leningrad, London, Toledo, four royal collections, the White House, and that of Pope Pius XII, Sidney Waugh's work for Steuben Glass was characterised by superb engraving and was included in every major Steuben exhibition from 1935. Membership of important Academies, honorary and military awards graced Waugh's career. Chief Associate Designer for Steuben Glass for thirty years, 1933–63.

LIT: Steuben Glass, Public Relations Information, June 1965; Waugh's two books *The Art of Glassmaking* (Dodds, Mead & Co., 1939); and *The Making of Fine Glass* (Dodds, Mead & Co., 1947).

Wayne, James b.1942   U.S.A.
Educated at San José State College, California. Has had considerable success with merit and purchase awards in several American exhibitions including those at Wichita, 1966; Miami, 1966; Craftsmen, U.S.A. '66; Toledo and Dallas. A glance at the current exhibitions listed in *Craft Horizons* will usually reveal his name. He feels form is of the utmost importance.
EXH: Dallas, 'New American Glass', May/June 1967.

Webster, Jane   England
Born in Tanganyika in the mid-1930s, Jane Webster went to school in England, then to Portsmouth College of Art where sculpture was her main subject. She decided to study glass-engraving and transferred to Stourbridge College of Art, gaining first-class honours in Glass Design and Decoration. From Stourbridge she went on to the Royal College of Art with the Alexandra, Princess of Wales Scholarship. Graduated Des. R.C.A. Since then she has practised as a free-lance engraver and is a Fellow of the Society of Designer-Craftsmen.

Jane Webster is a superb copper-wheel engraver who exploits the transparent nature of blown glass to the full, inter-relating the pattern on one side with that on the other.

Since about 1969 her interest in blown glass has waned and she has been working with great success on optical, plate and crown glass combined with other materials, such as bronze and marble. Some of her pieces are also designed to exploit a wider range of techniques – deep sand-blast, brilliant cutting, diamond-point or pepper sand-blast with diamond-point textures to give contrast.
COLL: Many commissioned pieces, including Victor Ludorum Trophy for Horse of the Year Show; Pye Colour Television Award; windows in Westminster Bank, Chesterfield; Pilkington News Trophy, etc.
LIT: G.M. Heddle, *A manual on etching and engraving glass* (Tiranti, London, 1961), pls.11–13; Beard, 1968.
Plates 123, 174, 175, 179, 180, 217, 218

Welch, Robert b.1929   England
Born in Hereford, he studied silversmithing at the Birmingham College of Art and the Royal College of Art. Opened his own workshop and shop at Chipping Campden in 1955. Royal Designer to Industry, 1965. Has designed the 'Serica' range of glass goblets, made in full lead crystal by the Bridge Crystal Glass Co., which are on sale only in his shop.

LIT: Graham Hughes, *Modern Silver* (Studio Vista, London, 1967); *Mobilia*, August 1967.

Wennerberg, Gunnar Gunnarsson 1863–1914   Sweden
After studying art in Paris, Wennerberg painted mostly still-life and portraits. He first became involved in the decorative arts from 1892 to 1908, as art director for Gustavsbergs China, and in these years (and particularly 1898–1901) he was active at Kosta Glass. His style, similar to that of the French artist, Emile Gallé, was given a personal touch and may be studied in several designs in the Kosta factory archives. He exhibited at Paris, 1900.
COLL: Kosta, factory collection.
Plate 30

Whistler, Laurence b.1912   England
Educated at Stowe School and Balliol College, Oxford, Laurence Whistler has established two careers: that of a distinguished writer, architectural historian and poet, and as a leading exponent of diamond-point engraving. The revival of this craft in England he shared with W.J. Wilson (q.v.), teaching himself entirely. His original intent was simply to write a sonnet on the window of a friend's house, and this led to further work on windows and on goblets. As well as engraving many individual pieces of glass he has since provided engraved windows in churches and other large-scale glass at Sherborne Abbey (reredos); Moreton, Dorset; Eastbury, Berks. (a memorial window to the poet Edward Thomas and his wife). He was awarded the O.B.E. in 1955 and the C.B.E. in 1974.
COLL: Victoria & Albert Museum, London; Fitzwilliam Museum, Cambridge; Bristol and Brighton Art Galleries; Royal Scottish Museum, Edinburgh; Buscot Park, Faringdon (National Trust); Corning Museum, New York.
EXH: Royal Festival Hall, London, 1963; Agnew's, London, April/May 1969; Kettle's Yard, Cambridge, November 1971; Marble Hall, Twickenham, January/April 1973; Corning Museum, New York, June/October 1974.
LIT: *The Engraved Glass of Laurence Whistler* (Cupid Press, London, 1952); *Engraved Glass, 1952–8* (Hart-Davis, London, 1959); *Pictures on Glass* (Cupid Press, London, 1972); *The Image on the Glass* (John Murray, London, 1975); G.M. Heddle, *A manual on etching and engraving*

glass (Tiranti, London, 1961); catalogues of exhibitions at Agnew's and Marble Hill (above); 'Engraved Pictures on Glass', in *Studies in Glass History and Design*, papers read at the VIIIth International Congress on Glass, July 1968 (1970), pp.94–6.
Plates 188, 194–5, 198–9, 200

Whistler, Simon b.1940   England
Son of Laurence and the late Jill Whistler (*née* Furse), whose marriage was commemorated in Laurence Whistler's poignant book, *The Initials in the Heart*, 1964. Educated at Stowe and the Royal Academy of Music. He began to engrave in 1954, learning from his father (*see above*). He now lives in London and divides his time between playing the viola in chamber orchestras and quartets, and engraving.

In 1963 exhibited with his father and four other engravers at the Royal Festival Hall, London, and in 1969 showed three glasses in an exhibition of his father's work at Agnew's of Bond Street, London. In 1974 he also exhibited at the Corning Glass Museum, New York.
Plates 169, 171, 196, 197

Wier, Don b.1903   U.S.A.
Don Wier's retirement from Steuben Glass in 1969 brought a quarter of a century's service to a close, latterly as Director of Graphic Design. Born at Orchard Lake, Michigan, he was educated at the University of Michigan, the Chicago Academy of Fine Arts, and the Grand Central School of Art in New York. It was at the Grand Central School that as well as winning the Medal for Decorative Design (1929) he was to act as an instructor until 1935. Between these years and 1950/1, when he was awarded the Institute of Graphic Arts Certificates of Excellence in two consecutive years, Wier had joined Steuben as a designer. Like that of his contemporary the late Sidney Waugh (q.v.), his work was commissioned by many important collectors and collections. It is a truism of unique Steuben pieces that they are usually found in the collections of royal families and heads of state. This is true of at least six Wier pieces which, as usual, are superbly engraved.
LIT: 'Poetry in Crystal' (Steuben Glass, 1963); 'Islands in Crystal' (Steuben Glass, 1966).

Wiinblad, Bjørn b.1919   Denmark
This versatile designer was born in Copenhagen and studied at the Royal Academy of Art. As painter, illustrator and ceramist

he has designed sets for the Royal Ballet Theatre in Copenhagen and beautifully finished ceramics, cutlery and glass for the Rosenthal Studio Line. His cheerful blue and white ceramic figures grace the Danish Design exhibition 'Den Permanente'.
LIT: Beard, 1968, p.151; *Portrait of an Idea: Rosenthal Studio Line* (Rosenthal AG, Germany, 1974).
Colour plate 9 and plates 157, 158

Williamson, Hardie b.1907   England
Williamson has been most successful in creating ranges suitable for fully-automated production. The 'Five Star' range of stem-ware, produced by Ravenhead Glass, has been particularly successful. He retired from that company in 1972 and their designs are now initiated by John Clappison, *b.*1937.

Willson, Robert   U.S.A.
On faculty of Art Department of University of Miami, Florida, 1952. Taught ceramics, enamelling and design. Corning Museum of Glass Research Fellowship, 1956; worked in Venice with Ermanno Toso (q.v.) at Fratelli Toso. Important as a glass-maker who has pioneered methods for producing layered molten glass, incorporating gold leaf in glass, impressing prunts and tooling on glass surfaces.
EXH: Harmon Gallery, Naples, Florida, February 1966 (first American exhibit of glass sculptures done at Murano, 1964); Venice, Museo Correr (selection toured U.S.A.), 1968.
LIT: Giovanni Mariacher, 'Drawings in search of glass by Robert Willson'; ibid., 'The Glass Sculptures of Robert Willson' (Museo Correr, Venice, 1968); Paul N. Perrot, 'Robert Willson: Sculptor in Glass – An Appreciation', *Art Journal*, fall 1969, Vol. XXIX, No.1, pp.46–7.

Wilson, William J. b.1914   England
Has spent his distinguished career with the firm of James Powell & Sons, now Whitefriars Glass. He joined them in 1928, became managing director in 1950, and retired in 1973. He played an important part (along with the work of Laurence Whistler) in the revival of the art of diamond-point engraving in 1935. Has contributed much to the training of students.
LIT: W.J. Wilson, 'The Role of the Designer', Society of Glass Technology, *Journal*, XLII, 1958, p.55; G.M. Heddle, *A manual on etching and engraving glass* (Tiranti, London, 1961), pls.1–3; Beard, 1968, p.108.

Wirkkala, Tapio b.1915   Finland
Glass designer, industrial designer, graphic artist and Finland's leading contemporary designer. It would be possible to describe the achievements of Wirkkala's career by citing all the prizes and honours bestowed on him, but this would be no real assessment of the skill and detachment he is able to bring to all he does. Educated at the Institute of Industrial Arts in Helsinki, he graduated from its sculpture department in 1936. He became glass designer for Karhula-Iittala Glassworks in 1947, was Artistic Director at the Institute of Industrial Arts 1951–4, and Head of Design Department of A. Ahlström Oy 1956–65. Now, as a free-lance, he continues his designs for Iittala and for a wide range of international contacts, notably the Rosenthal 'Studio Line'. Wirkkala has designed a number of Finnish exhibitions and Pavilions abroad, particularly those for the Milan Triennales.
EXH: Milan Triennale, 1951, 1954; Finnish exhibit at Brussels World Fair, 1958. He was awarded the Lunning Prize in 1951 and now has Triennale gold and silver medals, and seven Grand Prix; Corning, 1959, Nos.87–93.
LIT: Beard, 1968; *Portrait of an Idea: Rosenthal Studio-Line* (Rosenthal AG, 1974).
Colour plate 8 and plates 147, 162, 221

Witt, Anton Peter b.1900   Czechoslovakia
Trained in Dresden as a graphic artist then turned in 1922 to glass-engraving. His work was done on vases of a pure functional line and was characterised by great spontaneity.
LIT: *Studio*, 95, 1928, pp.178–180.

Woodall, George 1850–1925   England
One of the most successful of the English school of cameo-glass carvers, Woodall led a successful team at Thomas Webb & Sons of Stourbridge and worked extensively on a free-lance basis. His fine eighteen-inch plaques are miracles of technique, if a little cloying in design sentiments.
COLL: Stourbridge & Brierley Hill municipal collections; Corning Museum, New York.
LIT: Geoffrey Beard, *Nineteenth Century Cameo Glass*, 1956 (gives catalogue of figure vases and plaques).
Plates 33, 55

Wünsch, Karel b.1932   Czechoslovakia
Trained 1946–50 at the Glassmaking Trade School, Nový Bor, 1953–9 at the School of Applied Art in Prague. From 1959 he has been a plastic artist at the Bor Glassworks. His engraved, cut and painted glass has been well exhibited in recent years, particularly at Expo '67 in Montreal. The technique of cut-finished hand-sculptured glass has found new application in Wünsch's cased-cut vases and plates made in the Exbor Studios.

Žahour, Vladimir b.1925   Czechoslovakia
Trained 1939–43 at the Glassmaking Trade School, Železný Brod, and 1944–50 at the School of Applied Art in Prague. In 1954 he became a plastic artist at the Bohemia Glassworks in Poděbrady. His cut lead-crystal designs for this factory are outstanding and with his colleagues Ladislav Oliva (q.v.), Josef Svarc and Josef Pravac (q.v.), something new is always being produced.
EXH: Expo '70, Osaka.
LIT: *Czechoslovak Glass Review*, No.8, 1966; 'Art in Glass' special issue, 1969, pp. 8–13.
Plates 85, 88, 267

Zwart, Piet b.1885   Holland
Worked in H.P. Berlage's office: part of the yellow furnace-proof breakfast-set he then designed is in the National Glass Museum at Leerdam. Was one of the founders of new typography in the Netherlands in the 1920–30 period, a skilled photographer and a profound philosopher about industrial art and its modes of realisation. The drinking set he designed in 1967 is based on the relation of the Golden Section and on his statement that 'designing and the use of material are not a question of individual inclination but responsible factors in the community'.
EXH: Haags Gemeentemuseum, The Hague, March–July 1973.
LIT: *Studio International*, April 1973, pp.176–80.

Bibliography

An excellent annual Bibliography of books and articles about glass is published in the *Journal of Glass Studies* issued from Vol.1, 1959 by The Corning Museum of Glass, New York. This present Bibliography concentrates on books dealing in part with glass of the late 19th and 20th centuries, or which give a good general survey of the glass of a particular country.

GENERAL

Battersby, Martin *The Decorative Twenties*, London, Studio Vista, 1969.

Beard, Geoffrey, *Nineteenth Century Cameo Glass*, Newport, Ceramic Book Company, 1956.

Modern Glass, London, Studio Vista: New York, E.P. Dutton, 1968.

Corning Museum, New York, *Guide to the Collections*, 1955.

Dillon, Edward, *Glass*, London, Methuen, 1907.

Duncan, H.S., *Bibliography of Glass (to 1940)*, Sheffield, *Society of Glass Technology*, 1960.

Glass 1959, Corning Museum, New York, exhibition catalogue, 1959.

Grover, Ray *and* Lee, *Art Glass Nouveau*, 1967.

Carved and Decorated European Art Glass, 1970.

Both published at Vermont, Chas. E. Tuttle & Co.

Haynes, E.B., *Glass through the Ages*, Harmondsworth, England, Penguin Books, 1948. (frequently reprinted).

Honey, W.B., *Glass*, London, A. & C. Black, 1946.

Janneau, G., *Modern Glass*, London, The Studio, 1931.

Kampfer, Fritz *and* **Beyer**, K.G., *Glass: A World History*, London, Studio Vista, 1966.

McGrath, Raymond *and* **Frost**, A.C., *Glass in Architecture and Decoration*, London, Architectural Press, 2nd edn., 1961.

Pazaurek, G.E., *Moderne Gläser*, Leipzig, Seeman, 1901.

Kunstgläser der Gegenwart . . . Leipzig, Klinkhardt & Bierman, 1925.

Polak, Ada, *Modern Glass*, London, Faber & Faber, 1962.

Revi, Albert C., *Nineteenth Century Glass: Its Genesis and Development*, New York, Thos. Nelson & Sons, 1967.

Schrijver, Elka, *Glass and Crystal: from 1850 to the present day*, London, The Merlin Press, 1964.

Thorpe, W.A., *English Glass*, London, A. & C. Black, 3rd edn., 1961.

Toledo Museum of Art, *Art in Glass; a guide to the glass collections*, Toledo, 1969.

Vávra, Jaroslav R., *5000 Years of Glassmaking*, Prague, Artia, 1955.

Wills, Geoffrey, *Country Life Pocket Book of Glass*, London, Country Life, 1966.

*See also articles by H.E. van Gelder and Hugh Wakefield in the 1929 and 1957 editions of *Encyclopedia Britannica* respectively.

COUNTRIES

America

Amaya, Mario, *Tiffany Glass*, London, Studio Vista, 1967.

Freeman, Larry, *Iridescent Glass*, New York, Watkins, 1956.

Koch, Robert, *Louis Comfort Tiffany, Rebel in Glass*, New York, Crown Publishers, 1964.

Lee, Ruth W., *Early American Pressed Glass*, Northboro, Mass., 1946.

Lindsey, Bessie M., *American Historical Glass*, Vermont, Chas. E. Tuttle & Co., 1967.

McKearin, Helen *and* George, *Two Hundred Years of American Blown Glass*, New York, Doubleday & Co., 1950.

The Story of American Historical Flasks, Corning Museum, 1953.

American Glass, New York, Crown Publishers, 1941, 6th printing, 1966.

Plaut, James S., *Steuben Glass*, New York, H. Bittner & Co., 1951.

Revi, Albert C., *American Pressed Glass*, New York, Thos. Nelson & Sons, 1964.

Van Tassel, Valentine, *American Glass*, New York, Gramercy Publishing Co., 1967.

Austria

Schmidt, R., *100 Jahre österreichische Glaskunst Lobmeyr: 1823–1923*, Vienna, 1925.

Belgium

Chambon, R., *Histoire de la verrerie en Belgique*, Brussels, Editions de la Librarie Encyclopedique, S.P.R.L., 1955 (contains an extensive bibliography).

Czechoslovakia

Bohemian Glass, London, Victoria & Albert Museum, 1965.

Modern Bohemian Glass, Prague, Artia, 1963.

Peštová, Z., *Bohemian Engraved Glass*, London, Paul Hamlyn: Prague, Artia, 1968.

Denmark

Boesen, G., *Gemle Glas*, Copenhagen, Thaning & Apel Forlag, 1950.
140 Years of Danish Glass exhibition, organised in Denmark and circulated in the U.S.A., by the Smithsonian Institution, 1968–70.

England

Angus-Butterworth, L.M., *British Table and Ornamental Glass*, London, Leonard Hill, 1956.
Beard, Geoffrey, *Nineteenth Century Cameo Glass*, Newport, Ceramic Book Co., 1956.
Elville, E.M., *English and Irish Cut Glass*, London, Country Life, 1954.
Guttery, D R., *From Broad Glass to Cut Crystal*, London, Leonard Hill, 1956 (an account of the Stourbridge glass industry).
Powell, Harry J., *Glass-making in England*, Cambridge, University Press, 1923.
Turner, W.E.S., 'The British Glass Industry', *Journal of the Society of Glass Technology*, Sheffield, Vol. VI, 1922.
Wakefield, Hugh, *Nineteenth Century British Glass*, London, Faber & Faber, 1961.

Finland

Niilonen, Kerttu, *Finnish Glass*, Helsinki, Tammi, 1966.

France

Amic, Yolande, *L'opaline française au XIXe siècle*, Paris, 1952.
Barrelet, James, *La Verrerie En France De L'Epoque Gallo-Romaine A Nos Jours*, Paris, Librarie Larousse, 1955.
Blount, B. and H., *French Cameo Glass*, Iowa, 1968.
Imbert, R. and Amic, Yolande, *French Crystal Paperweights*, Paris, 1948.
Janneau, G., *Le verre et l'art de Marinot*, Paris, 1925.
Rosenthal, Léon, *La verrerie française depuis cinquante ans*, Paris and Brussels, 1927.

Germany

Bernt, Walther, *Altes Glas*, Munich: Prestel Verlag, 1952.
Hilschenz, Helga (ed). Katalogue des Kunstmuseums Düsseldorf, *Glas*, 'Jugendstil und 20er Jahre', 1973 (one of the most comprehensive of recent publications with extensive literature citations and 460 illustrations).
Internationales Jugendstilglas, Munich, Stück Villa, 1969.
Schabe, Günter, *Deutsches Glas*, Leipzig, Koehler & Amelang, 1969.
Schmidt, R., *Das Glas*, Berlin, De Gruyter, 2nd edn., 1922.

Holland

Gelder, H.E., van, *Glas en Ceramiek*, Utrecht, 1955.
Gemeentemuseum, The Hague, *Catalogus van noord-en zuidnederlands Glas*, 1962.
A useful illustrated catalogue (with a bibliography), especially for examples in diamond-point engraving.

Hungary

Borsos, Béla, *Glassmaking in Old Hungary*, Budapest, Corvina Press, 1963.
Koos, J., 'Hungarian art nouveau glass', article, pp.55–61 in *Studies in Glass History and Design*: papers read at the VIIIth International Congress on Glass, London, 1968. (Distributed by Society of Glass Technology, Sheffield.)

Italy

Gasparetto, A., *Il vetro di Murano*, Venice, Neri Pozza Editore, 1958.
Mariacher, G., *Italian Blown Glass*, London, Thames & Hudson, 1961.
Le Verre, Milan, Electa Editrice, 1959.
Three Centuries of Venetian Glass, exhibition, Corning Museum of Glass, 1958.
Vetri di Murano, exhibition, Palazzo della Gran Guardia, Verona, 1960.

Norway

Berntsen, Arnstein, *En samling Norsk Glass*, Oslo, Gyldendal Norsk Forlag, 1962.

Polak, Ada, *Gammelt Norsk Glas*, Oslo, Gyldendal Norsk Forlag, 1953.

Russia

Bezborodov, M.A., *Steklodenia v drevnei Rusi* (Glass-making in ancient Russia) Minsk, 1956.
Shelkonikov, B.A., 'Russian Glass in the second half of the 19th Century', *Journal of Glass Studies*, 9, 1967, pp.122–128.

Spain

Frothingham, A.W., *Hispanic Glass*, New York, Hispanic Society of America, 1941.
Spanish Glass, London, Faber & Faber, 1964.

Sweden

Anderbjörk, Jan Erik, *and* **Nisbeth**, Åke, *Gammalt glas*, Västerås, ICA-Förlaget, 1968.
Anderbjörk, Jan Erik, *Svensk Glaslitteratur*, Växjö, C. Davidsons Boktryckeri, 1950 (an excellent bibliography).
Hald, Arthur, *Simon Gate–Edward Hald*, Stockholm, 1948.
Hernmarck, C., *Graverade glas i Nationalmusei samlingar*, Stockholm, 1946.
Kosta Glasbruk, 1742–1942, Jubileumsskrift, Stockholm, 1942.
Nationalmuseum, Stockholm, exhibition catalogue, *Svenskt Glas*, 1954.
Nordström, Olof, *Svensk Glasindustri, 1550–1960*, Lund, Gleerupska Universitets-Bokhandeln, 1962.
Paulsson, G. ed: *Modernt Svenskt Glas*, Stockholm, 1943. Issued as a volume of essays by various writers on Edward Hald's 60th birthday.
Steenberg, Elisa, *Modern Swedish Glass*, Stockholm, Lindqvists, 1949.
Svenskt Glas, Forum, 1964.
Wettergren, E., *Orrefors glasbruk*, Paris, 1937.
*The serious enquirer on Swedish glass will need to examine the excellent collection of books and articles at the Glass Museum at Växjö.

MANUFACTURE

Burton, John, *Glass, Handblown, Sculptured, Coloured: Philosophy and Method*, London, Pitman, 1969.

Hammesfahr, J.E. *and* Strong, C.L., *Creative Glass Blowing*, London and San Francisco, W.H. Freeman, 1968.
Heddle, G.M., *A Manual on Etching and Engraving Glass*, London, Tiranti, 1961.
Labino, Dominick, *Visual Art in Glass*, Ohio, 1968.
Tooley, F.V., *Handbook of Glass Manufacture*, New York, Glass Publishing Co., 1960.
Waugh, Sidney, *The Art of Glass Making*, New York, Dodds Mead & Co., 1938.

JOURNALS AND MAGAZINES

Journal of Glass Studies, annual, 1959–   (The Corning Museum of Glass, New York).
Arts Vitraria, annual, 1966–   (Museum of Glass and Costume Jewellery, Jablonec, Czechoslovakia).
Ceramics Monthly (America).
Ceramics and Glass (Helsinki, house journal of Arabia and Notsjö Glass).
Craft Horizons (America).
Czechoslovak Glass Review, monthly.
Die Schaulade (Germany).
Form (monthly: Sweden).
Glaswelt (Germany).
Pottery Gazette and Glass Trade Review (England).
Szlloi Ceramika (Poland).
Vetro e Silicati (Italy).

Glossary

Annealing   Helps to temper the glass by a process of controlling the heat and gradually cooling the glass. It prevents strain and stress. Imperfect annealing in the past means such stresses are often still present in, say, Georgian glass.

Batch   The mix of chemicals and ingredients used in the glass-making operation. There are many formulae but basically lead crystal is composed of sand, red lead, potassium carbonate, saltpetre and arsenic or manganese de-colourisers. The lead crystal usually contains at least 30 per cent of red lead. A soda-lime mix is composed of sand, soda-ash and lime. The boro-silicate formulae are for heat-resistant purposes and are composed of sand and boric acid.

Blanks   Glass which is formed but not decorated.

Blown Glass   Glass formed by blowing with the mouth into a tube of steel – the 'blowing-iron'. The glass is free-formed or free-blown when formed entirely by this method. It can also be mould (q v.) blown.

Burning-off   The removal of surplus glass by melting it from (usually) the blowing-iron.

Cameo Glass   Composed of one or more layers, the upper layers being cut away to expose gradated parts of the pattern. Extensively employed in Roman times, and in the 19th century in France and England.

Chair   (a) The glass-blower's seat which has long projecting arms on which the blowing-iron is rolled forwards and backwards during making. (b) The collective noun for the glass-making team.

Crizzle   The fine surface cracks on glass, which frequently appear on Venetian and antique glass. May be introduced by controlled methods as a form of decoration.

Cullet   Broken glass, suitable to be remelted; must be of the same chemical make-up.

Cutting   Scoring the glass surface by cutting it with power-driven metal, stone and composition wheels. The blank is held above the revolving wheel and lowered on to it. The wheel is revolving away from the operator. Various grades of wheel are used for roughing and then smoothing. The piece is finally acid-dipped and then washed to rid it of grease, fingermarks etc.

Diamond-point Engraving   Decorating cold glass with a hand-held diamond pencil or tool. Some engravers use tungsten-carbide tools.

Enamel   Opaque white or coloured vitreous coatings which are used to decorate glass. They are fused on to the surface at a lower temperature than in normal working for shape.

Engraving   Decorating cold glass by bringing it in contact with the edge of revolving copper wheels of varying size. The wheels are mounted on spindles in a lathe (plate 184) and 'fed' with a flux of emery powder suspended in light oil. The object is brought to the 'back' of the wheel (unlike the process of cutting) and a complete set of wheels will range from four inches over some fifty gradations to a pin-head size – hence 'wheel engraving'.

Etching   There are several forms of etching but for the most part they involve hydrofluoric acid action under controlled conditions on certain unprotected areas of the glass. Pattern stencils are used, and acid resist paint is applied to the areas which are not to be etched.

Flint Glass   A term in frequent use in the 19th century implying that calcined flints were included in the batch, and also denoting colourless glass.

Friggers   Small novelty glass objects made by apprentices to be carried in the glassmakers' processions.

Gaffer   The head of the team or 'chair' of glassmakers.

Glory-hole   A small furnace where reheating of the glass to maintain its workability can be done.

Intaglio   A stage between wheel engraving and cutting. A similar lathe is used but the spindles carry small cutting stones which give a shallow cut. Intricate patterns were done by this method, particularly in the late 19th century.

Lehr   The tunnel, usually gas-fired, through which glass is carried on a mesh conveyor-belt. The heat is gradated through its length and allows the glass to cool slowly, or 'anneal'.

Marver   An iron slab, akin to a large anvil, on which molten glass can be rolled to give it a shape before blowing.

Metal   Usually denotes hot molten glass.

Moil   Waste-glass on a blowing-iron, or in the process of cracking-off.

Mould   A receptacle, usually metal or wood, in two equal halves in which glass is shaped by blowing or pressing. In mould-blowing the two halves of the mould are opened by a foot action, or by the help of a member of the 'chair'. The 'line' left by the mould can frequently be seen on cheap machine-moulded glass.

Off-hand   Free-formed glass made throughout by hand.

Oxides   Colour is added to the metal by including small amounts of metallic oxides in the batch. Those in frequent use are:
Purple *Nickel or Manganese*
Red (Ruby) *Copper, Selenium or Gold*
Brown *Manganese or Iron*
Green *Copper, Chromium or Iron*
Blue *Cobalt or Copper*
Amber *Selenium*
The metal is 'decolourised' before the definite oxide colours are introduced, by adding arsenic salt or manganese oxide. This gives a clear metal to receive the colour.

Pot   The crucible of fire-clay in which the batch is melted. A furnace usually has 8, 10 or 12 pots built into its circumference, and these are pot-changed in rotation – to maintain a good clean metal. The average life of a pot is about eight weeks.

Pressed Glass   The glass shape is produced by forcing molten glass into a mould by the action of a gob or plunger. Hand-pressing is done frequently in Scandinavia and implies transferring the pattern from a flat disc to the glass, in a manner akin to impressing a mark in sealing-wax with a fob.

Prunt   A moulded glass seal or mark pressed on the hot glass surface by an end-patterned 'prunty iron'.

Punty (Pontil)   The iron rod used in holding glass objects during making. When the rod is cracked from the glass it leaves a punty or pontil mark which is now ground away, but appears frequently on antique glass.

Sandblasting   Directing a jet of abrasive on to the glass surface by compressed air. Done in a closed cabin with efficient air-extraction of the abrasive powder. The operator directs the work with his hands and arms inserted in specially made gloves and sleeves, and views it all through a window sight.

Stippling   A form of diamond or steel-point engraving in which the glass surface is punctured by a series of tiny dots.

Index

Italic figures refer to illustration numbers

Aalto, Alvar   32, 46, 216
Abels, Gustaf   25
Acid-etching   31
Afors Glass, Sweden   209
Agate glass   18
Aladin, Tamara   216, *137*
Alberius, Olle   216
America, art glass   20, 38
Ander, Gunnar   216
Appert brothers, Clichy   17, 18
Arabia Glass   209
Argy-Rousseau, G.   216
Ariel Glass, Orrefors   *25, 65*
Art Nouveau   18, 21
Artek   32
Artel Group   21
Aselius-Lidbeck, C.   216
Asti, Sergio   216
Atkins, Lloyd   216
Awashima, M.   45, 216, *108, 139*

Baccarat Glass   28, 209
Bäckström, Monica   216, *114, 134, 328*
Bang, Jacob E.   29, 36, 216; Michael   216
Bar-Tal, Ariel   217
Báthory, Julia   40, *217*
Baxter, Geoffrey   217, *271*
Bergh, Ellis   28, 29, 217, *67, 76*
Bergqvist, Knut   25
Berlage, H.P.   25
Berndt, Viktor   218
Beyer, Johann   45
Bing, Samuel   21
Birmingham, College of Art   40
Blomberg, Kjell   218
Boda Glass, Sweden   209
Bohemia Glass, Poděbrady   209
Bohnert, Gertrude   218
Boissier, Phyllis   218
Borgström, Bo   218

Borgström, Carl-Einar   218
Boro-silicate Glass   34, 37
Boylen, Michael   218
Boysen, Bill   218, *237*
Brandt, Åsa   218
Branzell, Sten   218
Brocard, Philippe-Joseph   18, 218, *7*
Brörby, Severin   37, 219
Brummer, Arttu   29, 34, 219
Brychta, Jaroslav   219, *304*
—— Jaroslava   219, *338*
Burian, Ivan   219
Burkert, Frank   37
Burton, John   220

Cabla, Bohumil   220
Cameo Glass   19, 20
Cappellin, Giacomo   28, 220, *157*
Carder, Frederick   28, 220
Cerny, Jan   220
Chevalier, George   28, 220
Clarke, Dillon   220
Clutha Glass   21
Cochius P.M.   25, 26
Cook, John   220, *232, 245*
Copier, Andriès Dirk   26, 32, 35, 40, 46, 221, *75, 129,*
   250, 264
Corning Glass   30; Museum at   34, 37, 40
Couper, James & Sons   21
Craquelé Glass   18
Cros, Henri   19, 221, *29*
Cummings, Keith   221
Cyrén, Gunnar   39, 221, *125*
Czechoslovakia, glass of   21, 35, 41, 45
—— trade schools   25, 31, 40

Daden, Frederick   221
Dahlskog, Ewald   28, 221, *49*
Dammouse, Albert-Louis   19, 222, *31*
Darlington Glass   43
Daum, family of   19, 24, 28, 210, 222, *Col. Pl. 3, 19,*
   226, 303
De Bazel, K.P.C.   23, 25, 26

De Stijl Group   25
Decorchement, F-E.   222, *42*
Delvenne, René   222
Denman, J.R.   31
Denmark, glass of   35, 36
Dennis Vase (Northwood)   19, 20
Design, glass, 30, 33, 34, 39–41, 43, 45
Design Industries Association   24
Despret, Georges   19, 223
Deutscher Werkbund   30
Drahonovsky, Josef   223
Dreiser, Peter   223, *169, 180*
Dresser, Dr. Christopher   21
Drobnik, Antonin   223
Durand, Victor   223

Eckhardt, Edris   223, *266, 296*
Edenfalk, Bengt   37, 224
Edinburgh, College of Art   40
Eiff, Wilhelm von   224
Eisch, Erwin   224, *257*
Elliott, George   224
Elmhirst, Shiela   224, *187, 191, 192, 201*
England, glass in, (1953)   34
Englund, Eva   225
Ericcson, Henry   28, 29, 225
Erixson, Sven   215
Etching   31
Exhibitions
    Amsterdam, 1947   35
    Antwerp, 1869   23
    Barcelona, 1929   28
    Brussels, 1958   35
    Chicago, 1893   20, 23
    Dallas, 1967   38
    Gothenburg, 1923   25
    London, 1851   41
    London, 1915   24
    London, 1931   29
    London, 1935   32
    London, 1937   32
    Moscow, 1872   23
    New York, 1939   32
    New York, 1959   36

    Paris, 1867   21
    Paris, 1878   17, 19, 23
    Paris, 1884   18
    Paris, 1889   19, 27
    Paris, 1900   21, 22
    Paris, 1925   24, 25, 26, 28, 31
    Paris, 1937   29
    Philadelphia, 1876   23
    Prague, 1891   21
    Prague, 1952   35
    St. Louis, 1904   21, 31
    St. Petersburg, 1870   23
    Stockholm, 1917   24
    Stockholm, 1930   29, 31, 32, 35
    Vienna, 1873   23

Fagerlund, Carl   225
Fanta, Josef   21
Fedden, Bryant   225, *206*
Filan, Wayne   225
Filip, Milos   225
Finland, glass, in 1920s   28–29; labelling of   44; packaging of   46; Society of Decorative Artists   29, 33; success at Milan Triennales   33
Fogelberg, Sven   34
Franck, Kaj   37, 39, 225, *Col. Pl. 6, 265*
Fratelli Toso   45
Fritsche, William   20
Fritz, Robert C.   226
Fuga Glass (Orrefors)   35
Functionalist movement   211

Gacs, György   226
Gallé, Emile   18, 19, 226, *5, 20, 23–28*
Gaspari, Luciano   226
Gate, Simon   24, 25, 29, 34, 226, *62, 63*
Gates, J. Monteith   30
Gehlin, Hugo   227
Gentili, Giorgio   227
Gordon, Ernest   227
Goupy, Marcel   227, *46*
'Graalglass' (Orrefors)   25, 34
Graffart, Charles   227

Gruppe '21   44
Gunderson, Jon   227
Gunther, Alfred   227

Habermeier, Konrad   227
Hadelands Glass, Norway   36
Hald, Edward   24, 25, 29, 33, 34, 227, *61, 64*
Hammond, David   34, 228, *90, 117*
Heal, Sir Ambrose   24, 30
Heaton, Maurice   228, *246*
Hellsten, Lars   228, *116, 300*
Hennix, E. and M.   228
Herman, Samuel J.   38, 40, 228, *241, 242, 319*
Hill, Tom   32
Hilton, Eric   229, *284*
Hlava, Pavel   229, *176, 230, 262*
Hobbs, Brockunier & Co.   18
Hodgetts, Joseph   19
Höglund, Erik   37, 229, *110, 132, 147, 163, 276, 308,*
      329, 330
Holmegaard Glass, Denmark   36, 211
Holmgren, Christer   229, *115*
Holmgren-Exner, C.   229
Hongell, Goran   32, 229, *74*
Hopper, David   229
Horacek, Paclav   229
Horejc, Jaroslav   229, *47, 48*
Houston, James   230, *168*
Houtart, Eugène   22
Hradec Králové, glass school   25

Iittala Glass, Finland   22, 32, 44, 46, 210, *44*
Ingrand, Max   230
Israel, glass of   45

Jahn, Roland   231, *256*
Janneau, Guillaume   27
Japan, decorative influence of   18, 20; Design
      Centre of   45
Jelinek, V.   231
Jenaer Glass, Germany   210
Jobling, James A., & Co.   37, 210

Johannsen, Jan   231; Willy   36, 231
Jutrem, Arne Jon   37, 231

Kallenberg, Fritz   231
Kaplicky, Jan   35
Karmenický Šenov, glass school   25
Kastrup Glass, Denmark   36, 211
Kedelv, Paul   231
Klinger, Miroslav   231
Knight, Dame Laura   32
Knoll, Isabel Giampietro   231, *105*
Kny, F.E.   20, *3*
Koepping, Karl   18, 232, *Col. Pl. 2*
Koppel, H.   232
Kosta Glass, Sweden   19, 24, 25, 211; archives at   22, 24
Kotera, Jan   21
Kotik, Jan   232

Labino, Dominick   38, 40, 232, *Col. Pl. 11, 239, 259, 312,*
      313
Lahque, Marc   232, *148, 153*
Lalique, René Jules   24, 27, 28, 232, *43, 50–53*
Lallerstedt, Lars   233
Landberg, Nils   233, *101, 121*
Latham, Richard   176
Leafgreen, Harvey   38
Lebeau, Chris   26, 233
Le Corbusier   27, 28
Lecjaks, Maria   233
Leerdam Glass, Holland   23, 25, 32, 35, 40, 211
Legras, August V.F.   233
Lenoy   45, 46
Léveillé, Ernest Baptiste   18, 233, *8, 10*
Libbey Glass Co., America   21, 31, *71*
Libensky, Stanislav   35, 233, *338*
Lindberg, Stig   40
Lindstrand, Vicke   29, 34, 234, *66, 102, 214, 291*
Linssen J.F.   234
Lipa, Oldrich   234
Lipofsky, Marvin   38, 40, 234, *109, 236, 320*
Liskova, Vera   37, 234, *305*
Littleton, Harvey K.   38, 40, 234, *Col. Pl. 12, 258, 314,*
      316

Lobmeyr, J. & L.   19, 211; Louis   21
Loffelhardt, H.   235, *124, 155*
London, Royal College of Art   38
Luce, Jean   28, 235
Lundin, Ingeborg   38, 235, *119, 149, 178, 221*
Lundgren, Tyra   235
Lunning Prize   34, 39
Lütken, Per   36, 235, *100, 260*
Luxton, John   236

Marble Glass   18
Marinot, Maurice   23, 24, 28, 236, *Col. Pl. 4, 57–60*
Marsh, Honoria D.   237, *209, 210*
Martens, Dino   37, 237, *127, 128*
Matura, Adolf   237, *179, 273*
McCutchen, Earl   236
McKinney, Nanny Still   236, *97, 120, 131*
Meadows, William   237, *211, 286*
Meydam, Floris   237, *91, 93, 253*
Milan, Triennales at   29, 32
Model, Hanns   237, *224*
Monro, Helen   238, *188*
Montalto, Maude-Roxby   237
Morales-Schildt, Mona   238, *81, 84, 87, 219, 249*
Moulds   39, 43, 47
Mount Washington Glass Co., America   20
Mourey, Gabriel   21, 24
Moyano de Muniz, L.   37
Murray, Keith   30, 32, 238, *70*
Myers, Joel Philip   238, *323, 324*

Nancy, Daum family at   19; Gallé glass at   19
Nash, Arthur J.   21; A. Douglas   21, 28, 31, 239, *71*;
         Leslie   21
Nash, Paul   32
Navarre, Henri   239
Nemeth, M.V.   239
New England Glass Co., America   20
New York, Museum of Modern Art   32; World Fair
         (1939)   32
Northwood, John I.   19, 20, 239, *2*; John II.   20, 239
Norway, glass of   35, 36
Novak, B.   239

Novy Bor, Czechoslovakia   210
Nurminen, Kerttu   239
Nuutajarvi Glass, Finland   29, 38, 209
Nylund, Gunnar   239
Nyman, Gunnel   29, 239, *69*

O'Fallon, J.M.   19
Ohrström, Edvin   25, 240, *65, 232, 311, 327, 341, 342*
Okkolin, Aimo   240, *223*
Oliva, Ladislav   45, 240, *267, 285*
Ollers, Edvin   24, 25, 240
Ornamo   29, 33
Orr, Charles   240
Orrefors Glass, Sweden   24, 25, 29, 34, 38, 39, 212, 65,
         221
Ortlieb, Nora   240, *184*
Orvola, Heikki   240, *112*

Palmqvist, Sven   34, 35, 241, *164, 339, 340*
Pantin, Cristallerie de   214
Paris, Cup (1925)   25; Exhibitions at, *see* Exhibitions;
         Musée des Arts Décoratifs   19
Pâte de verre   19, 22
Paulsson, Gregor   24, 32
Peace, David   241, *172, 177, 181, 182, 202, 203, 205*
Peacock glass (Tiffany)   21, 31, *Col. Pl. 1*
Pellat, Apsley   18
Percy, Arthur   241
Persson, Sigurd   241
Persson-Melin, Signe   241
Phoenix Glass, England   34
Pianon, A.   241
Pitchford, T.F.   34
Plátek, M.   241, *82*; V.   242
Poli, Flavio   242, *77*
Pollard, Donald   242, *166, 217*
Powell, Barnaby   32; Harry J.   21
Prague, Exhibition (1891)   21; School of Industrial
         Art   25
Pravec, J.   242
Pressed glass   32, 39, *273, 274*
Proctor, Dod   32

Queensbury, Marquess of   40, 242, *154*
Quénvit, France   242

Raman, I.   242
Rath, Stephan   21, 25, 28, 242
Ravenhead Glass, England   39
'Ravenna' Glass (Orrefors)   35
Ravilious, Eric   32
Reilly, Sir Paul   34
Rickard, Stephen   242
Riedel, Claus J.   37, 42, 214, 242, *107*
Riihimäen Lasi Oy, Finland   28, 29, 212
Rosenthal, Germany, 'Studio Line'   41, 42
Rosselli, Alberto   243
Roubicek, René   40, 243, *229, 254, 293*
Rousseau, François-Eugène   17, 18, 243, *9*
Royal College of Art, London   38
Rudge, L.E.   243, *318*
Russell, Sir Gordon   30

Sabino, M-E.   243
St. Louis, Cristalleries de, France   213
Sala family, France   28, 343
Salviati & Co., Italy   213
Sand-blasting   31
Sandvik Glass, Sweden   25
Sarasin, Betha and Teff   243, *138, 337*
Sarpaneva, Timo   46, 213, *111, 145, 272, 299*
Scent bottles (Lalique)   27
Schoder, M.   244
Schulze, Paul   244, *225*
Schyler-Stiernstedt, M.   244
Seager, Harry   244, *315, 325*
Selbing, John   244, *165*
Severin, Bent   244
Sèvres, Cristallerie de, France   213
Shirley, Frederick   20
Sigvard, G.   244
Siiroinen, E.   244
Silveria Glass (Stevens & Williams)   20, *21*
Sinnemark, Rolf   244, *113, 298, 309*
Sipos, J.K.   244, *106*
Sjogren, C.   244

Skawonius, S.E.   245, *68, 78*
Slang, Mrs. G.B.   245
Smith, David   245, *213*
Smrckova, L.   245
Soda glass   21, 28
Solven, Pauline   245, *Col. Pl. 10*
Sovánka, I.   246
Stennett-Wilson, R.S.   246, *130, 135*
Steuben Glass, America   28, 30, 31, 38, 213
Stevens, Irene M.   40, 246
Stevens & Williams, England   19, 32, *21*
Still, Nanny *see* McKinney, Nanny Still
Stockholm, Konstjackskolan   40
Stourbridge, College of Art   40
Strömberg, Edward   32, 246; Gerda   32, 246
Strömbergshyttan   32
Stuart & Sons, England   32, 214
Stumpf, Touvier, Violette et Cie, France   214
Suhájck, Jiri   246, 243
Sweden, early cut glass   21, 29; Society for Industrial
    Design   23

Thesmar, Fernand   18, 246
Thomassen, G.   246
Thompson, George   247
Thomson, Alan   247, *306*
Thrower, Frank   247, *103*
Thuret, André   247
Tiffany, Louis Comfort   18–21, 247, *Col. Pl. 1, 13, 14*
Tiroler Glasshütte, Austria   214
Toikka, Oiva   39, 247, *Col. Pl. 7, 277, 310, 344*
Toledo, Museum of Art   31, 37, 38; Glass Nationals at   38
Toso, G. and R.   248, *301, 326*
Turner, Mrs. W.E.S., *see* Monro, Helen
Tynell, Helena   248, *279, 295*
Tysoe, Peter   249

Unica Glass (Leerdam)   26, 32

Val Saint-Lambert, Belgium   214
Valkema, Sybren   248, *252*

Vallien, Bertil   248, *Col. Pl. 13, 136, 238, 240, 263, 275, 287*
—— Ulrica   249, *233, 321*
Venini, Paolo   28, 32, 37, *79, 126, 157,* 248, 251
Verboeket, Max   249
Vida, Z.   249
Vistosi, G., L., and O.   249
Voysey, C.F.A.   23

Wagenfeld, Wilhelm   249
Wagner, O.E.   28
Wainwright, Kenneth   250
Walker, Colin   250, *235*
Wallander, Alfred   250
Walter, Almaric   250
Walton, George   21, 23, *11, 12*
Warff, Ann *and* Goran   250, *Col. Pl. 5, 150, 151*
Waterford Glass, Ireland   215
Waugh, Sidney   30, 250
Wayne, James   38, 250
Webb Corbett, England   215
Webb, Philip   21, *1*
Webb, Thomas & Sons, England   19, 20, 30, 34, 46
Webster, Jane   251, *123, 174, 175, 177, 183, 218*
Welch, Robert   251

Wennerberg, G.G.   19, 251, *30*
Whistler, Laurence   34, 251, *193–198;*
—— Simon   252, *170, 171, 199, 200*
Whitefriars Glass, England   21, 30, 32, *32, 34, 36*
Wier, Don   252
Wiinblad, Bjørn   42, 252, *Col. Pl. 9, 158, 159*
Williams-Thomas, H.S.   30
Williamson, Hardie   39, 252
Willson, Robert   252
Wilson, William J.   252
Wirkkala, Tapio   33, 34, 42, 46, 252, *Col. Pl. 8, 146, 162, 222*
Wisconsin, University of   38
Witt, A.P.   253
Wittman, Otto   38
Woodall, George   19, 20, 22, 253, *33, 55;*
——, Thomas   19
Wünsch, K.   253

Zahour, V.   253, *85, 88, 268*
Železný Brod, Czechoslovakia, Glass Trade School at   25, 31, 215
Zwart Piet   253
Zwiesel   214